IMAGINING ETHIOPIA

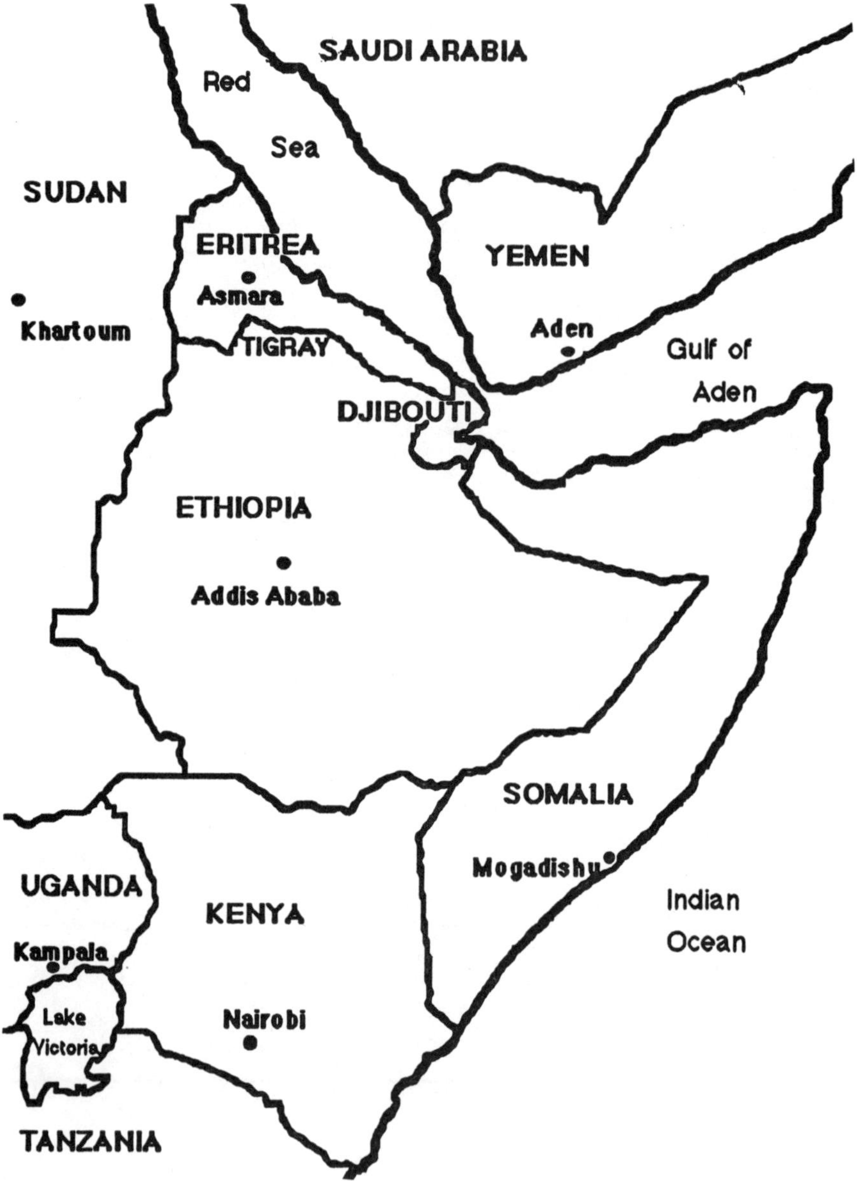

THE HORN OF AFRICA

IMAGINING ETHIOPIA

Struggles for History and Identity in the Horn of Africa

JOHN SORENSON

Rutgers University Press
New Brunswick, New Jersey

Library of Congress Cataloging-in-Publication Data

Sorenson, John, 1952–
Imagining Ethiopia : struggles for history and identity in the
Horn of Africa / John Sorenson.
p. cm.
Includes bibliographical references and index.
ISBN 0-8135-1972-1 (cloth) 0-8135-1973-X (pbk.)
1. Ethiopia—Politics and government—1889–1974—Public opinion.
2. Ethiopia—Politics and government—1974–1991—Public opinion.
3. Ethiopia—Foreign public opinion. 4. Famines—Ethiopia—
History—20th century. 5. Famines in mass media—Ethiopia—
History—20th century. I. Title
DT387.S67 1993
963′.05—dc20 92-35967
CIP

British Cataloging-in-Publication information available

Manufactured in the United States of America

For Atsuko

CONTENTS

ABBREVIATIONS

EDU: Ethiopian Democratic Union
ELF: Eritrean Liberation Front
ENATAD: Ethiopian National Alliance to Advance Democracy
EPDA: Ethiopian People's Democratic Alliance
EPLF: Eritrean People's Liberation Front
EPRDF: Ethiopian People's Revolutionary Democratic Front
EPRP: Ethiopian People's Revolutionary Party
ERA: Eritrean Relief Association
FAO: Food and Agricultural Organization
MEISON: All-Ethiopian Socialist Movement
MERIP: Middle East Research and Information Project
NGO: nongovernmental organization
OAU: Organization of African Unity
OLF: Oromo Liberation Front
REST: Relief Society of Tigray
RRC: Relief and Rehabilitation Committee
TPLF: Tigrayan People's Liberation Front

PREFACE

This study grew out of my involvement with the Eritrean Relief Association in Canada (ERAC), which from 1979 has been working to provide humanitarian assistance to the people of rural Eritrea who have suffered under the double burden of war and famine. As part of an international network of such organizations, ERAC delivered assistance to the areas held by the Eritrean People's Liberation Front, which has since formed a provisional government. Throughout my involvement with ERAC, I have been impressed with the concern and commitment of its members. Regardless of one's views on any of the conflicting nationalisms in the Horn of Africa, I think that the critical humanitarian role played by the Eritrean Relief Association cannot be denied. As this book deals with products of the imagination, I think it is appropriate to acknowledge the dedicated efforts of those who have imagined a brighter future for the people of Eritrea, one which is free from hunger, poverty, and the violence of warfare. I hope that vision of the future can be supported and shared by all the people of the region.

I am grateful to those who have read versions of the manuscript and offered useful advice: Araia Desta, Malcolm Blincow, Ian Jarvie, Jordan Gebre-Medhin, Roy Pateman, Patricia Stamp, and the anonymous reviewer at Rutgers University Press. I also thank Norm Buchignani, Noam Chomsky, and Teun A. van Dijk, for encouraging me to carry on with this work, and Stephen Arnold, who influenced the ideas that shape this book. Much of the information in the book is based upon discussions and interviews with Eritrean, Ethiopian, and Oromo refugees and immigrants, and I thank all those individuals, although not all of them will agree with my interpretations. I am also grateful to the Social Sciences and Humanities Research Council of Canada for two grants that allowed me to continue the research for this book.

In different form, sections of this book have appeared in the following journals: *Dialectical Anthropology*, *Discourse and Society*, and the *Journal of Modern African Studies*. I thank the editors and the respective publishers of these journals, Kluwer Academic Publishers, Sage Publications, and Cambridge University Press, for permission to reprint this material here.

My greatest thanks go to Atsuko Matsuoka, who not only made useful suggestions about the manuscript but has been a constant source of inspiration, encouragement, and support.

INTRODUCTION: IMAGES OF DISASTER

On October 23, 1984, BBC television broadcast a news report that depicted shocking scenes of famine in Ethiopia. Quickly adopted by international media, these horrifying images startled viewers around the world. The BBC report sparked a rush of journalists to the area, and mass starvation in the Horn of Africa became one of the major news stories of the decade. This terrifying spectacle provoked a massive international relief operation and inspired events such as the Live Aid charity concert. Virtually overnight, it seemed that a new image of Ethiopia had been created.

That image was one of absolute deprivation and helplessness. Ethiopia appeared as a nightmarish zone of human suffering, a distillation of Third World horrors. The horrors were not imaginary; it was impossible not to be shocked into silence as television cameras explored the ghastly contours of famine. Whether concentrated in the close-up photographs of emaciated children with huge, staring eyes and wizened skin or dispersed across landscapes of misery, the impact was staggering. For many who reported on the famine, or tried to explain it later in books and articles, these scarcely believable scenes conjured up visions of the end of the world and apocalyptic terror. Ethiopia became the emblem of disaster, a symbol of the nightmarish collapse of all order.

These images of starving Ethiopians seemed to appear from out of nowhere, giving an impression that tragedy had struck suddenly and without warning. Yet relief agencies had pleaded for media coverage as famine approached. In 1983, while attempting to alert Canadian media to the impending disaster, the Eritrean Relief Association in Canada was told by one newsroom editor that "the Third World isn't news and starving Africans in particular aren't news." It was only when a crisis had been reached and when the most sensational scenes of suffering were available for the cameras that famine became a news item.

Accompanying this sensationalism was the construction of a moral parable concerning famine. This parable ignored the historical context of famine in the region and attributed widespread starvation to the policies of the Marxist-Leninist government of Ethiopia while also indicating the general culpability of Africans for creating their own problems. Famine was depicted in the terms of an older colonial discourse that had survived into the renewed Cold War narratives of the 1980s and was interpreted as one result of an act of betrayal by Ethiopians of the West's civilizing mission. The media emphasized the charitable impulses and relief efforts of the West, concentrating on individual acts of genuine generosity and concern as well as on the mammoth celebrity spectacles such as Live Aid.

While these spectacles of starvation and suffering provided certain novel images, explanations of famine incorporated an already existing set of representations of Ethiopia. These representations offer a peculiar set of contradictions, for Ethiopia has both served as a symbol of Africa and been perceived as an atypical African nation more akin to European states. While discourse on famine in the Horn was permeated with images from a more general conception of Africa as a zone of primitive chaos, Ethiopia has been seen as a unique African country with a real history.

Furthermore, while discourse surrounding famine in the Horn was determined by these more general representations, which must be examined in their political context, the history of the region ensured that depictions and explanations of famine were shaped by concerns about the nature of the Ethiopian state under its Marxist government. While Ethiopia has been represented as one of the most enduring states, solidly rooted in antiquity, local challenges have been mounted to both its history and future existence. In Western discourse on the nature of the Ethiopian state, certain voices were given prominence while others were ignored and silenced. Scholarship has been focused on the culture of the highland Amhara people who have been presented as the unifying genius of Ethiopia, bringing together disparate ethnic groups within a common identity.

That identity was challenged from various perspectives. One of the most significant was that of the nationalist movement in Eritrea, the former Italian colony on the Red Sea coast which had been fighting for independence from Ethiopia since 1961. The Eritrean nationalist struggle, Africa's longest war and one of the most prolonged conflicts of the century, received little attention in the Western mass media until the late 1980s, and there was little analysis of connections between the war and famine. Similarly, both the history and the nationalist aspirations of the Oromo people, the largest ethnic group in Ethiopia, have been almost entirely ignored. Other challenges were raised by groups such as the Tigrayan People's Liberation Front (TPLF), which was based in the northern highland province of Tigray and which sought a reordering of the state but did not reject Ethiopian identity. The fact that the Amhara and the Tigrayans formed the core of highland Abyssinian culture and supplied the rulers of the Ethiopian state has encouraged many Oromo nationalists to regard the Amhara and the Tigrayans as mere rivals for power in the expression of Abyssinian chauvinism. The complex nature of these struggles in the Horn gave Western discourse its peculiar character.

This book is about the creation of images, the construction of histories, and the formation of identities in the Horn of Africa, focusing on Eritrea and Ethiopia. Ethiopia, in a famous phrase, has been seen as "a museum of peoples," but it is also a warehouse of images, a repository for obsessions and projections of various identities both from within the region and from without. I will analyze various representations of the Horn, discussing not only the depiction of famine and its causes but also investigating other ways of imagining Ethiopia, including the clashing local versions of regional history and opposed nationalist struggles, as well as external explanations of conflict in the Horn, and I will suggest how these representations formed part of a broader discourse on the Third World in general. While this involves a study of imagery and rhetoric, it should not be assumed that these are purely textual matters. Instead, these conflicts over images, histories, and identities are struggles for power and efforts to create and define reality. As Pierre Bourdieu (1991:221) points out,

> One can understand the particular form of struggle over classifications that is constituted by the struggle over the definition of "regional" or "ethnic" identity only if one transcends the opposition that science, in order to break away from the preconceptions of spontaneous sociology, must first establish between representation and reality, and only if one includes in reality the representations of reality, or, more precisely, the struggle over representations, in the sense of mental images, but also of social demonstrations whose aim it is to manipulate mental images (and even in the sense of delegations responsible for organizing the demonstrations that are necessary to modify mental representations).

The struggle over representation, especially but not only in terms of ethnic identities, is a struggle to enforce meaning, a vision of the world, and it is these imposed meanings themselves that create the realities of which they speak through the construction of consensus about the nature and the existence of groups. Struggles for identity may be conducted on the battlefield but also appeal for recognition from institutional authorities, and these struggles may draw other powers, as well as specialists from fields such as anthropology and history who compete to impose their vision of truth, sometimes for shared motives and sometimes in the pursuit of goals dissimilar to those of local protagonists. Consideration of the social context of such expressions of authority may reveal the situational interests of these experts. Acts of representation and classification are thus located at the nexus of power and knowledge. What Bourdieu calls "the act of social magic which consists in trying to bring into existence the thing named" (223) succeeds through the exercise of authority, which determines and legitimizes. To question representations, then, is to question the powers that generate them.

Chapter one outlines a theoretical approach that can assist in an examination of representations of Ethiopia and Eritrea. I have sought to address these representations as part of a unified system of statements that will allow us to perceive the creation of Ethiopia as an object of knowledge, to examine the recurrence of certain terms and themes, and to understand the relations between knowledge and power. Important here is the idea of discourse, derived from the work of Michel Foucault and as taken up by Edward Said in his investigation of Western writing on the Middle East. In contrast to other works that address an Africanist discourse, I do not adopt a deconstructionist approach but instead employ a more straightforward form of political reading and ideology critique as a form of interpretive analysis. In this respect, I have found it useful to apply an analysis that directly addresses the role of mass media and intellectuals in techniques of ideological control. Through the use of such an analysis, I argue that statements about famine and war in the Horn of Africa form part of a broader discourse that constructs certain characterizations of the Third World in general. Support for this type of analysis comes from the work of Noam Chomsky and Edward S. Herman.

Thus, the book is not merely a study of Western representations of Africa; instead, I hope to show how these representations are linked to the local invention and construction of certain images, histories, and identities. By examining the contested nature of regional histories, the competing constructions of the past, and the conflicting forms of identity that are championed by Eritrean, Ethiopian, and

Oromo nationalists, I suggest a more complex model of discourse that avoids the flaws of a unidirectional approach and that does not present the Horn of Africa as simply an undifferentiated "Other." By considering the clash of various subaltern histories and identities and examining how certain local histories and identities mesh with the goals of global powers, I hope to avoid presenting Third World agents as simply passive and to give more weight to the operation of these subaltern narratives.

Chapter two examines some of the early images of Ethiopia, as well as the figure of Haile Selassie, the last emperor of Ethiopia. I argue that these images have consistently served political functions, either by legitimizing the power of certain groups or offering consoling and inspiring symbols for those who have suffered under racist and colonial oppression. Paradoxically, Ethiopia became a symbol of the glories of the African past, of African identity, and of African liberation at the same time its ruling elites rejected such an African identity. Doubling this paradox, this same symbol of African liberty and identity is regarded by many of those living within the boundaries of the Ethiopian state as the condition of their own oppression and the negation of their own identities. Thus, these images from the past have served to give peculiar resonance to contemporary discourse on the Horn and to reinforce support for or opposition to various forms of competing national identities.

The Horn of Africa is the site for a clash of nationalist struggles that offer competing narratives of the past and of contemporary forms of identity, imagining Ethiopia in sharply contrasting ways. Whereas Greater Ethiopian nationalism has created for itself a genealogy that stretches into the biblical past and suggests a virtually primordial and essential identity shared by all those who live within the current boundaries of the Ethiopian state regardless of their particular ethnic affiliation, other forms of national identity exist in opposition to this and insist that this Greater Ethiopian identity is in reality an expression of Amhara chauvinism. Eritrean identity takes a less essentialist form based on historical transformations created by Italian colonialism and on the experience of the nationalist struggle itself, while Oromo nationalism is premised on ethnicity. All of these forms of identity involve different understandings and interpretations of the past. Whereas Greater Ethiopian nationalism has regarded these dissident forms of identity as illegitimate secessionist movements bent on ripping apart an ancient state, Eritrean and Oromo nationalists have argued that their own histories have been stolen from them and suppressed. These conflicting versions of the past and visions of the future are considered in chapter three, which is informed by contemporary debates within anthropology about the invention of tradition, the construction of identity, and the nature of history.

Famine's irruption into discourse is taken up in chapters four and five, which discuss mass media coverage of starvation in the Horn of Africa along with various efforts to explain famine. I argue that, as with the struggles over different forms of national identity in the region, these explanations of famine also offer different versions of the past, particularly in terms of the colonial impact on the Horn but also in terms of more recent policies of various Ethiopian governments. Through an ellipsis of the historical context, famine was presented as the direct result of the policies of a Marxist-Leninist regime and was inserted into a narrative of anticommunism. Racism also contributed to the discursive construction of famine, as Africans in general were presented as incompetent and the efforts of indigenous relief agencies were overlooked.

Discourse on famine in Ethiopia served as a vehicle to delegitimize both the Marxist government and its enemies. In chapter six, I evaluate reports on Eritrea. While the Ethiopian regime was identified as part of the evil empire of communism, none of its opponents in the region were considered suitable for direct U.S. support as proxy warriors in the so-called low-intensity conflicts sponsored elsewhere. To achieve its own interests, the U.S. had consistently supported the idea of Ethiopia's "territorial integrity" and opposed Eritrean nationalism. Despite its aversion to the Marxist regime in Ethiopia, the U.S. maintained this policy and its belief that the Soviet Union's influence on Ethiopia would be temporary. This required the production of a discourse that delegitimized Eritrean nationalism, by emphasizing its recent character and attributing it to the work of foreign agents.

The political circumstances of the Horn generated two different narrative structures, which I examine in chapter seven. The first of these narratives suggested that the alliance between Ethiopia and the Soviet Union would not be maintained and previous international relations could be restored. The texts that form this narrative essentially confirm the local version of history that defines a united Greater Ethiopia. The second narrative tendency presented famine in Ethiopia as an apocalyptic sign of impending disaster for the West. Within this construction, the Third World in general and Africa in particular are viewed as zones of chaos, corruption, and contagion. Within this narrative a moral parable is suggested that presents the West as a generous and charitable benefactor to the Third World. Whereas some of the media reports examined in chapter four had suggested that African incompetence was to blame for starvation, this second narrative constructs a darker scenario in which Western charity is betrayed by venal Africans and their liberal or socialist collaborators in the West. This idea of betrayal is incorporated into a broader narrative of global confrontation between good and evil forces, a narrative not restricted to the realm of textuality but that actually formed the basis for intervention by a number of right-wing and Christian fundamentalist groups. Some of the institutional links of this discourse are indicated in this chapter.

Summary remarks are made in the concluding section, which indicates the character of recent changes in the Horn. While the cessation of conflict in Eritrea indicates some positive change and hope for the future, events elsewhere in the region are less promising. In addition to the general impoverishment and instability brought by decades of war, the future course of Oromo nationalism and the possibilities of continued ethnic conflict are very much open questions and ones that should be answered through negotiations rather than through greater bloodshed. Outside Eritrea and Ethiopia, conditions appear even worse. While Sudan seems to have entered into a more or less permanent state of emergency, Somalia has virtually disintegrated. Efforts to resolve conflicts in the region will require a clear understanding of the mythologizing of national identities and histories, while efforts to implement truly effective development in the region cannot be based on fantasies. If this book assists with these efforts, it will have accomplished its task.

1

DISCOURSE AND THE OTHER

A Crisis of Representation

To question the creation of certain images of Ethiopia is to engage with what contemporary critical theory terms a crisis of representation. In the most abstract sense, this concerns the relations between power and knowledge, a rupture between signifier and signified, an inability of words to adequately describe their objects, and the "return of the repressed." Central to these debates is the matter of what has been termed "the Other." This term was created to indicate the non-European world in general, although more recently it has also been used in discourses of class, gender, and race; however, the original referent remains, as employed, for example, in David Maybury-Lewis's 1992 television series, "Millennium." A key aspect of this crisis concerns the description of other cultures in the social sciences, literature, and mass media. In anthropology, the crisis is conceived as one of ethnographic authority and has led to a fundamental rethinking of the discipline. The debates carry over in popular culture in discussions of multiculturalism and political correctness.

A key work that inspired this sense of crisis is Edward Said's *Orientalism*. Defining the term as "a Western style for dominating, restructuring, and having authority over the Orient," Said argues that European writers constructed an imaginary Orient that embodied their obsessions, and he critiques scholarly discourse on the Middle East as being thoroughly implicated in the process of imperialism (1979:3). Orientalism manifests itself not only in description but also in a vast system of colonial administrations and bureaucracy, exploration societies, research institutes, academic networks, military intelligence units, anthropological foundations, and other institutions. Within this system, all details of the Orient are described through the expression of authority (both intellectual and political) and used to administer and exploit the colonial world. In related works, Said examined representations of the Middle East in media and political discourse, arguing that distorted images served Western power.

Said's work provoked enormous controversy. Many academics, defending their profession, furiously denounced *Orientalism* as mere polemic. Some, noting Said's Palestinian origins, attacked his work as a case of racism-in-reverse. Others credited Said with creating "an object of analysis called 'colonial discourse' [which] has proved one of the most fruitful and significant areas of research in recent years" (Young 1990:173). This overlooks previous works that addressed similar issues (e.g., Berkhofer 1978; Curtin 1964; Daniel 1958, 1966, 1975; Keen 1971; Kiernan 1969; Pearce 1953). *Orientalism* did spawn renewed interest in analysis of Western representations of colonized peoples, but much of this has concentrated on textual rather than political aspects of discourse. The study of colonial discourse has been taken up by deconstructionists such as Homni Bhaba, Christopher Miller, and Gayatri Spivak, who base their work on that of Jacques Derrida. In general, deconstruction is limited by a deliberately obscurantist vocabulary masking banal conclusions, failure to consider historical context, and a tendency to rediscover the same idea in every text. Ostensibly radical, it has been criticized as an apolitical retreat into "textuality." As Said himself has remarked, there is a striking absence of discussion of the political context of discourse, particularly concerning imperialism, in these theoretical discussions.

Nevertheless, there are insights to be gained from this body of critical theory. Stripped of its obscurantist vocabulary, it can offer useful ways of analyzing the images that surround us. Application of some of these theoretical insights concerning discourse to representations of famine and war in the Horn of Africa can clarify how "Ethiopia" functioned as part of dominant ideological formations during the 1980s and how such images continue to shape conceptions and policies toward Africa at the present time. However, this book is more than a study of an image of Ethiopia created by the West; instead, I analyze local struggles over the meaning of "Ethiopia" and the challenges to a unified Ethiopian identity by those who identify themselves in different terms, such as Eritreans or Oromos, and examine the interpenetration of local and external discourses to determine the manner in which this image of Ethiopia has been created, maintained, and challenged at the intersection of various discourses. At the local level, the ruling Amhara elites of Ethiopia invented and perpetuated a mythical history that legitimated their own power. Eritrean and Oromo nationalists, in the Horn itself and in sizeable refugee communities abroad, challenged this image and argued for different readings of history. On the global level, both the U.S. and the Soviet Union chose to support the Amhara version of Ethiopian history in order to extend their own influence. The clash of these discourses questions not only the nature of Ethiopian history and the future existence of an Ethiopian state but some fundamental features of African identity. Because the image of Ethiopia has exerted such a powerful influence on the construction of other identities, any discussion of possible modifications to the Ethiopian state prompts intense reaction.

Conceptual Tools

In order to construct an analytical framework in which to consider the representation of Ethiopia, some conceptual tools are necessary. I have adopted the idea of discourse, from the work of Michel Foucault, to examine various statements about Ethiopia and Eritrea. The concept of discourse allows us to look beyond the ordinary boundaries of individual texts and to propose different continuities. Discourse refers to dispersed groups of statements, which form coherent unities, and involves a common object, style of reference, conceptual unity, persistent themes, ordered systems, connected transformations, and regularities. I have used the term in a loose sense to indicate a tradition in which individual authors produce their works, while analyzing the political context and institutional affiliations of those writers and stressing the basic relationship of power and knowledge, as Said has done in his consideration of writing on the Orient.

While Foucault's ideas are provocative as a point of departure, they cannot be taken up without qualification. The concept of discourse is a useful one, but Foucault's work is often vague, provides no coherent methodological system, contains a number of unsupportable assumptions, particularly regarding notions of power, and ignores the colonial context. Deconstructionist approaches also share these flaws, and when examining representations of Ethiopia it is important to recognize that certain regularities exist and are part of a system of statements on Africa and the Third World in general without assuming that discourse is detached from all other types of relations or that it determines them. Whereas Foucault himself originally believed that discursive practices function autonomously and order all other nondiscursive practices, he left the nature of this ordering vaguely expressed and later abandoned concentration on discourse to examine relations between discourse and institutions.

In order to avoid the flaws of the deconstructionist approach and some of Foucault's vagueness, I have supplemented the idea of discourse with an analysis that is more firmly grounded in concrete historical conditions and examines the roles and interests of those who produce these discourses, such as nationalist intellectuals, mass media, and representatives of the state. Rather than adopting a postmodern focus on the surface of images, I argue that it is necessary to examine representations of Ethiopia in the framework of an ideology critique that attends to the political character of various narrative constructions. For example, certain depictions of regional history serve to legitimize the interests of particular groups. Similarly, depictions of famine in the Horn reinforce power relationships by emphasizing certain explanations and ignoring others. Placing media images in such a context can clarify the manner in which they support certain interests. Rather than being seen as directed solely by internal textual determinants, statements about the Horn of Africa can be considered as products of historically concrete conditions. Here it is useful to employ the propaganda model of mass media suggested by Edward S. Herman and Noam Chomsky (1988). This model rejects ideas of "oppositional" media and argues that media serve the mutual interests of state and corporate power by framing news in a manner that supports established privilege and limits debate. Thus the media are ideological institutions, performing functions of thought control in democratic societies and restricting challenge to superficial and individual cases rather than addressing basic structures of power.

Intersecting Discourses

To analyze Western discourse on the Horn of Africa it is necessary to recognize three other discourses that have shaped it: racism, anticommunism, and Christian mythology. Each is a distinct ordered system, with a specific history, but many terms and concepts are transferred and shared. Racist thought has an extensive genealogy incorporating specific cycles of meaning, such as Apartheid, Manifest Destiny, Recapitulationism, Social Darwinism, the Vietnam Syndrome, the White Man's Burden, and the Yellow Peril. It is unsurprising that racism colors certain statements about war and famine in Africa. However, racist thought takes on a peculiar elaboration in relation to Ethiopia, which often has been compared with medieval Europe rather than with other African states. Various texts categorize Ethiopians in an intermediate position between whites and blacks. Of course, racism and racial classifications are not uniquely Western preoccupations; in Ethiopia, the Amhara ruling elite sometimes have classified themselves as white but always as superior to the darker-skinned people of the south. Just as Europeans felt themselves preordained to bring civilization to savages, so did the Amhara feel themselves possessed of a civilizing mission as they expanded their empire into areas occupied by other ethnic groups such as the Oromo (Baxter 1983; Triulzi 1983).

The mythology of anticommunism has its own history although it incorporates earlier ideas about the "lower orders" and the "undeserving poor." Two major aspects of anticommunism were characterization of the Soviet Union as an empire of absolute evil and belief that it wished to impose its ideology on the world. Other characteristics included a tendency to overlook any advances in communist regimes and the conditions under which they were made, selectivity in condemning communist abuses but ignoring those committed by right-wing regimes, and attribution of Third World revolutions to the machinations of the Soviet Union (Miliband and Liebman 1984).

Some suggest that the U.S. administration actually welcomed aggressive action by the Soviet Union in order to build a domestic consensus for its policies (Wolfe 1984). Such techniques are standard in hegemonic discourse; identification of and mobilization against external enemies is an effective means of creating loyalty, uniformity, and mystical attachment to the state (Bourne 1977). Thus, Cold War rhetoric and anticommunist hostility targeted the U.S. public, not only the Soviet Union. Although this is often disparaged as conspiracy theory or an overly instrumentalist view of the state, state officials and corporate executives are often frank in their assessments of the operation of power and admissions of the need to engineer domestic consensus (Chomsky 1982, 1986, 1988).

In the Horn, anticommunist rhetoric characterized U.S. involvement, providing justification for establishment of a strategic communications station at Kagnew, near the Eritrean capital city of Asmara. Anticommunism also provided the rationale for decades of financial and military support to Emperor Haile Selassie, who exploited Cold War sentiments for his own objectives and built one of the largest armies in Africa. Following the Emperor's deposition by a military coup in 1974, and the subsequent alliance of the Derg (as the new regime was known in Amharic) with the Soviet Union, anticommunism took a new twist. Ronald Reagan attacked the Derg as part of the Evil Empire, and the media directly linked famine to communism. However, this discourse took a unique form due to the absence of an ideologically acceptable ally opposed to the Derg and a persistent belief, eventually justified, in the superficiality of Soviet influence.

Anticommunism has had a specific trajectory but in many respects it is compatible with racist thought; since both are political mythologies the imagery is readily transferred. For example, racial segregation frequently has been defended by anticommunist rhetoric (Dower 1986:348 n40). Similarly, war in Vietnam, typically portrayed as a battle against communism, was easily depicted in terms of racist struggle, exemplified in Lyndon Johnson's determination not to allow the U.S. to be "easy prey to any yellow dwarf with a pocket-knife" (quoted in Chomsky 1986:67). The same system of signification allowed the former U.S. Ambassador to Ethiopia, David Korn (1986: 36), to warn of the devious character of governments "of an oriental . . . bent" when referring to Soviet-allied Somalia.

Racist and anticommunist discourses readily incorporate elements of Christian mythology. These elements merged to create a demonic image not just of Ethiopia but of the Third World in general. For example, in Guatemala, Rios Montt, a convert to the California-based Christian evangelical sect Gospel Outreach, came to power in a 1982 army coup and launched a slaughter of the native population; a pastor of the Gospel Outreach–associated Verbo Church justified the attacks: "The Army doesn't massacre the Indians. It massacres demons, and the Indians are demon-possessed; they are communists. We hold Brother Efrain Rios Montt like King David of the Old Testament. He is the king of the New Testament" (in Diamond 1990:166).

Christian mythology has long shaped discourse on Ethiopia. Traditionally, the Amhara viewed themselves as inhabiting a Christian island surrounded by hostile Islam, and this idea of Ethiopia as a Christian outpost was strong in the West. Christianity was one aspect of the civilizing mission which the Amhara saw as their imperial duty. In contemporary discourse, in order to delegitimize Eritrean nationalism, Ethiopian rulers resurrected the image of a Christian land threatened by surrounding Muslim states. With the objective of maintaining its own power in the region, the West incorporated this theme into discursive representations of regional conflict and portrayed the Eritrean independence movement as Arab-inspired.

Christian mythology also influenced discourse on famine in Ethiopia, principally in writing on relief and development efforts. Development essentially signifies a process of replication, by which the Third World will duplicate the historical and economic trajectory of the industrialized West. Foreign aid is presented as a means by which the Third World is to achieve this transition to modernity. Typically, the West was depicted not only as a charitable and generous benefactor to Ethiopia and other undeveloped areas but also as a model for their future. The notion of charity has its own genealogy. In American Puritan discourse it glorifies the giver and indicates one's status among the Elect, who are nonetheless despised and persecuted for their good works; similar themes influenced U.S. foreign policy (Augelli and Murphy 1988). While the West was portrayed as a model for the developing world, Ethiopia functioned as an inverted mirror image, bearing warnings for the West. Racism and anticommunism merged with Christian mythology to connect Ethiopian famine with apocalyptic visions. The discourse of militant fundamentalism interpreted famine as the sign of an approaching final battle between good and evil, prophesied in the Bible, and personified by the U.S. and the Soviet Union.

"Ethiopia" and Discourse on the Third World

The concept of discourse allows Ethiopia to be seen as a created image, a discursive construction. In this construction, mythologies created by the Amhara elite to maintain their power over other peoples in the region were incorporated within a broader Western discourse that emerged at a point where U.S. hegemony appeared to be under threat. This process had been underway for two decades and was exemplified by the rise of new economic powers such as Japan, a series of Third World revolutions (including Ethiopia), and the strain on U.S. resources resulting from its assault on various Asian countries throughout the 1960s and 1970s. The situation crystallized in the Vietnam syndrome, a national malaise supposedly characterized by reluctance to intervene militarily. Watergate, the fall of Third World allies, and defeat in Vietnam were incorporated into a moral fable of betrayal by untrustworthy allies, the media, and subversive elements. Events in the Horn, particularly the instructive 1977 realignment in which the U.S. and the Soviet Union switched spheres of influence in Ethiopia and Somalia, contributed to the development of a renewed Cold War and a neoconservative ideology based on a sense of a world divided into good and evil powers (Halliday 1983). The reaction to the sense of weakness engendered by this hegemonic decline was a reassertion of a will to power that expressed itself in a doctrine of global military confrontation, state terror, and nuclear escalation; this became the unquestioned foundation of U.S. foreign policy for both political parties, the mass media, and the educated public in the 1980s (Petras 1987:223). The Reagan administration saw its mission as restoration of U.S. hegemony through Cold War revival, increased Third World intervention, and direct support for right-wing regimes and regional enforcers such as South Africa and Israel. Statements on famine and war in the Horn of Africa must be understood in this historical context. Adopting a headline from *Newsweek*, we may identify these statements as a discourse called "An African Nightmare." That nightmare was part of the reassertion of Western dominance during the renewed Cold War atmosphere and incorporated elements of the classic works of imperialist thought.

By the 1990s, the narrative had shifted to assertions of U.S. victory over the Evil Empire in the Cold War. With the collapse of the Soviet Union, the U.S. was secure in its military pre-eminence but no longer dominant economically. Accompanying the decline of the Soviet Union, several Third World villains, such as Muammar Qadaffi, Manuel Noriega, and Saddam Hussein, made temporary appearances as satanic adversaries threatening world peace. In the context of the "New World Order," depictions of the Third World will undergo a number of transformations as external threats become necessary to mobilize domestic populations (Chomsky 1991). To understand these, it will be useful to consider some of the discursive constructions of the Third World during the last decade. The case of Ethiopia is interesting both in its own specific contours and in the way in which it has influenced current images of Africa.

The Dual Image of Africa

Before discussing the image of Ethiopia, it is useful to note how discourse on Africa has been studied so far. Christopher Miller's *Blank Darkness* (1985) suggests that an Africanist discourse exists which is comparable to, but fundamentally different from, Orientalism. He argues that this discourse is created by a basic ambiguity and contradiction between ideas of blackness and whiteness; Miller claims that the instability of these terms defines the character of Africanist discourse, which is characterized by primary themes of loss of identity, self, and authority. He maintains that, unlike Orientalism, this discourse has no object because Africa is only a blank space, unknowable, and lacking identity. This emphasis on abstract textuality virtually ignores the historical context of Africanist discourse. Furthermore, Orientalist discourse also contains contradictory images, rendering the differences less striking. In general, Miller's deconstructionist jargon and failure to consider historical and political context detract from the work's usefulness.

A more historically grounded study of Africanist discourse is William Schneider's *An Empire for the Masses* (1982). Schneider also detects two images of Africa but grounds them in history and politics rather than in a vague textuality. One image, the "Africa of Exploitation," emphasized abundant resources useful to both Europeans and Africans; proponents of economic liberalism and social imperialism claimed that mutually beneficial trade was prevented only by natural barriers. Riches, geography, and infrastructural development were emphasized and Africans were portrayed as a market of consumers eager to trade raw materials for manufactured goods. Another image, the "Africa of Conquest," developed later to explain African resistance to the supposed benefits of European colonialism. Mention of resistance was deliberately suppressed until it could no longer be overlooked: a need for order and security led to the emergence of themes of savagery. Barbarism and bizarre religious practices became more prominent themes, although the press still distinguished between groups and claimed that the African masses favored European imperialism and were only prevented from cooperating by their leaders. Similar imagery is evoked in contemporary discourse on Ethiopia. For example, there is a dual conception of Ethiopia as a symbol of modernizing, progressive Africa and as a zone of savagery. Rather than concentrating only on their textual character, it is necessary to see these images in historical context.

Orientalist and Africanist Discourses

To what extent can we distinguish between Orientalist and Africanist discourses? Arguing for the specificity of Orientalism, Said suggests a unique and persistent virulence of attitude within Orientalism as a discipline, in media, and in popular discourse. He claims that ethnocentrism and religious antipathy have solidified in Orientalist discourse while studies of other Third World areas have "changed in fairly massive ways" (1988:35). As noted, Miller (1985) proposes a unique Africanist discourse, distinguished by its themes of loss and instability. However, a study of discourse concerning the Horn does not support these claims. Instead, this discourse dredges up images of savagery and helplessness from classical works of colonialism (both fictional and nonfictional), exemplified by Conrad's *Heart of Darkness* (1902) and Lugard's *The Dual Mandate* (1923); it remains thoroughly permeated with many of the same ethnocentric biases which Said detects in Orientalism.

Discourse on Africa is haunted by ideas of danger, contagion, and the threat to identity. The colonial image of Africa as the disease-infested "White Man's Grave" has been followed by theories that locate Africa as the source of AIDS. Not only is Africa seen as a zone of physical danger, it is also presented as a zone of ontological danger, a region of instability of meaning where order is threatened, and in which even racial "essence" can be reversed or subverted. This instability of racial identity has a particularly interesting elaboration in relation to ideas of Ethiopia, taken as a symbol of African identity but also viewed as a mirror image of the West. As elaborated below, the very nature of Ethiopian identity, of the Ethiopian self, has been bitterly contested both on the battlefields and in discourse, with competing versions of past and future. Racial factors also influenced African perceptions of this conflict, as Eritreans charged that their national liberation struggle was ignored because they were subject to black, rather than white, colonialism.

Themes of loss of identity, self, and authority characterize Africanist discourse. Yet this disintegration is not confined to the literary works Miller studies, and explanations other than textual ones are possible. For example, in *French Colonialism In Tropical Africa, 1900–1945*, Suret-Canale (1971) suggests that this reflects the attractions of colonialism for certain psychological types, largely undesirables, such as alcoholics, drug addicts, and criminals. Furthermore, there are numerous parallels in other discourses, for example in that perennial fear of colonialists everywhere: "going native," losing one's moorings in class and race and sinking even lower than the debauched locals. A prime example occurs in T. E. Lawrence's remarks on "Yahoo life" in *Seven Pillars of Wisdom* (1962:27–30), a key Orientalist work.

Thus, Orientalist and Africanist discourses cannot be divided neatly into completely distinct categories. In the case of Ethiopia, factors such as the country's historical significance as a Christian state surrounded by Muslims, the Amhara elite's assertion of ancient links to Israel (exemplified in the legend of Solomon and Sheba, discussed below), more contemporary political and military ties between Ethiopia and Israel, and Arab support for Eritrean independence all create correspondences with Orientalist discourse. At the same time, factors such as the specific elaborations of racist theories about Africa, the circumstances of the 1935 Italian invasion, conflicting nationalist histories, and the character of superpower intervention in the Horn ensure that discourse on Ethiopia has a unique character and a specific imagery, and that it cannot be subsumed under Said's model of Orientalism.

Analyzing Discourse on Ethiopia

An analysis of discourse on Ethiopia and Eritrea cannot remain at the level of a unidirectional approach that suggests "Ethiopia" is entirely the creation of Western obsessions and projected fantasies. Instead it is necessary to consider both the clash of local images, histories, and identities and the manner in which these have been supported or negated by external interests. *Orientalism* has been criticized for taking an approach to the non-European world that conceptualizes it as inert and ignores the contribution to discourse made by indigenous ruling classes (Mani and Frankenberg 1985). Said's later work addresses those issues but, as a cautionary note, the point is relevant. A related criticism is that Said "acknowledges no political or cultural divisions among the subject peoples he is allegedly defending" (Marcus and Fischer 1986:1).

By incorporating such criticisms into an examination of discourse on Ethiopia, I hope to avoid a unidirectional model and to suggest a more complex view of discourse on the Third World. Colonial expansion throughout the world was not an entirely uniform process; instead there is a range of variation in interactions, with differential impact depending upon the time of contact. The West has dominated and exploited its Third World colonies, but Third World ruling classes exert their own power and perpetuate their own ideological truths. Despite their subordinate positions, these local ruling classes cannot simply be regarded theoretically as inert or as passive. Instead, within certain limits, there is a collusion of interests between local-level elites and external forces. Rather than examining hegemonic and subaltern discourses as totally discrete entities, it is necessary to see that they are not formed in isolation but interact with one another. Furthermore, subaltern discourses may contain their own internal oppositions and strive to impose their own hegemonic versions of history and identity (O'Brien and Roseberry 1991).

In the Horn of Africa, discourses of Third World ruling elites have been adopted by external powers for their own ends. This can be seen most clearly in relation to Eritrea, where Eritrean nationalist history was suppressed by the hegemonic mythology of the Amhara elites. During the pre-federation period, both superpowers acknowledged the validity of Eritrean claims for independence but dismissed them in order to extend their own influence in Ethiopia. The hegemonic mythology created by Ethiopian elites was accepted by numerous scholars, perpetuated in the mass media, and adopted by both superpowers to further their strategic interests as well as by other African governments who feared that Eritrean independence might legitimize nationalist or secessionist struggles elsewhere. Thus, struggles for control of representation of history and identity were carried out at various levels and particular versions of these struggles were authorized and legitimized by different types of authorities. The struggles were rendered particularly complex because, in the past, Ethiopia functioned as a symbol of African antiquity, civilization, and liberty. Consequently, in addition to an established scholarly tradition of Ethiopian studies, there has been considerable emotional investment in and support for the image of a unified Greater Ethiopia within other subaltern discourses, including those of Africans and African-Americans. Defenders of the Ethiopian revolution also rejected the claims of Eritrean nationalists on the basis of an identification with the political character they ascribed to the regime.

"Ethiopia" can be understood as a historical fiction based on and maintained by power, just as Said discusses "the Orient" as an imaginary construction. Indeed, Holcomb and Sisai (1990) argue that Ethiopia was created as a dependent colonial state that could serve the interests of European powers. This has been a controversial intervention and, indeed, a threatening one to those who identify with Ethiopia as a long-unified state. In discussing Ethiopia as a created image, however, it is important to recognize that it was not simply an invention of Western power; the image of Ethiopia was constructed on the basis of an already-existing discourse of domination, that of the Amhara elite. This discourse proposed a particular version of history in which the boundaries of the contemporary state were projected backwards into a distant historical period. The image of Ethiopia contained within this discourse is one of African grandeur, liberty, modernization, and stability. It was the version of Ethiopian history accepted by the United Nations, other African states, and both superpowers. External powers, including both the United States and the Soviet Union, used this discourse to extend their own influence over the region.

Contrasting with this image of historical unity, progress, and grandeur is the Ethiopia of impoverishment, famine, and disaster. Rather than considering these images as having been generated from tension between basic tropes of Africanist discourse, it is more fruitful to examine how they were rooted in particular historical circumstances and deployed in order to serve specific political objectives.

2

HISTORY OF AN IMAGE

Early Images of Ethiopia

Discourse on Ethiopia is premised on a racial distinction that is taken to constitute a fundamental difference but has always been ambiguous. Examining the etymology of the word Ethiopia, Miller (1985) suggests that it is the earliest Western name for all of Africa. It signifies "burntface," reflecting assumptions that the skin color of the inhabitants resulted from exposure to African sunlight. Miller believes this indicates the unique character of Africanist discourse: "the collapsing together of black and white—of their inability to remain as meaningful opposites—and of the frustrations of meanings attached to them" (30). As has been long recognized, efforts to define races have no scientific precision or validity, so that these frustrations of meaning are not entirely peculiar to Africanist discourse. Furthermore, "Ethiopia" was applied not only to Africa but also to Arabia and India. Thus, Miller's claims for an ambiguity unique to Africanist discourse seem somewhat overstated.

Nevertheless, this ambiguity is significant in discourse on Ethiopia. The correspondence between territory and terminology is unclear. While many insist that "Ethiopia" is one of the world's oldest states, others argue that it is a recent creation. Anthropologist Donald Levine (1974) suggests that by the fourth or fifth century "Ethiopia" came to be associated with the region that now bears the name. However, Levine refers to ancient Axum, and the borders of that kingdom and contemporary Ethiopia are not coterminous. Holcomb and Sisai (1990) use "Ethiopia" to refer to the mid-nineteenth century expansion of territory by the northern highland regions previously known as "Abyssinia."

The fact that the term described widely different regions at various historical periods undermines claims made by Ethiopian nationalists for continuity between the contemporary state and the Ethiopia of biblical and classical references. As several other images have figured in the mythology created by the ruling elites of Ethiopia and in contemporary political debates, it is useful to consider some of them and the uses they have served.

The image of Ethiopia in ancient Greek, Roman, and Christian works is examined in a study by Frank M. Snowdon, Jr. (1970), as part of an effort to trace the genealogy of racist thought. In *The Odyssey*, Ethiopia is presented as a distant land, and the idea of remote Ethiopia situated at the very ends of the earth became a standard theme of early Greek works. In various texts, Ethiopia refers to different locations, from Cameroon to India, but increasingly, the term came to describe the Nubian civilization of Meroe in northern Sudan. The blackness of their skin appears to have been the distinguishing mark of these particular Ethiopians, although various types were identified on the basis of other remarkable characteristics, such as their amazing height or swiftness; the cave-dwelling Ethiopians of the south were said to speak a language resembling the squeaking of bats. Just as Ethiopia's location varied, so too the identities and physical characteristics of Ethiopians were reported in different terms.

One quality consistently ascribed to Ethiopia was piety. In *The Odyssey*, the gods delight in visiting Ethiopia, where they are honored by elaborate festivals. The Ethiopians were seen as the first people who were taught to honor the gods and to make sacrifices. Just as the Ethiopians loved the gods, so were they divinely favored and remained free from subjugation. Many works called them the "beloved of the gods." Such positive assessments lead Frank Snowdon to conclude that Ethiopians were highly esteemed in antiquity and that doctrines of white supremacy did not exist at that time. It was only later, following the growth of Christian imagery of spiritual qualities associated with black and white, that these doctrines developed and came to be applied to Ethiopians and other peoples of Africa. Snowdon's effort to reveal negative racial stereotypes as recent historical inventions exemplifies the tendency of discourse on the Ethiopian past to figure as intervention in contemporary political issues.

The remote nature of Ethiopia was identified not only in spatial terms but also in temporal ones (Levine 1974). Travelers in Ethiopia frequently described the experience of being transported backwards in time to medieval or biblical periods. Similar references characterize contemporary discourse on Ethiopia. Yet once again, this is not unique to Africanist or Ethiopianist discourse. Similar themes appear in Orientalist texts. For example, the works of Charles Doughty, T. E. Lawrence, and Wilfrid Blunt on their travels in Arabia frequently mix allusions to both biblical and medieval periods. Ideas of distance and piety that characterized views of Ethiopia in antiquity merged later in medieval conceptions of the country as a remote Christian outpost pressured by surrounding Muslim forces. In this century, the Ethiopian government played upon these long-established images to delegitimize Eritrean nationalism, characterizing it as an Arab-inspired effort to shatter an ancient Christian state.

Solomon and Sheba

Just as ancient images of Ethiopia were employed in studies opposing racist discourse, so did these images figure in efforts to demonstrate the richness of the African past. Until recently, it was assumed that Africa was unchanging and that its history began only with European contact. Images from antiquity served to reinforce Ethiopia as a signifier of the greatness of Africa's past. One such image concerned the legendary visit by the Queen of Sheba to King Solomon in Jerusalem. The legend was well-known in the West from biblical references, art, literature, and music (see Hansberry 1974:33–59). Different suggestions were made concerning the actual location of Sheba's realm. The *Kibra Negast*, the Amharic "national epic" dated from the fourteenth century but possibly based on earlier copies, claims that the Queen of Sheba was actually Queen Makeda (said to have reigned 1005–955 BC in the coastal Assab region); Menelik I, son of Solomon and Makeda, visited his father in Jerusalem, was anointed with the holy oil of kingship, and returned to Abyssinia with the Ark of the Covenant. Transportation of the Ark shifted the status of the chosen people from the Hebrews to the Ethiopians. Jones and Monroe (1969:16) identify this "entirely apocryphal" legend as a means by which the ruling elite invented an ancient and divine genealogy to legitimize their rule. The legend has been used in this manner up to recent times: Article Two of the 1955 Constitution of Ethiopia recognized a direct line of descent from Solomon and Sheba to Haile Selassie; the Emperor's divinity was acknowledged in Article Four.

These mythological assertions of continuity served to project the power of the modern Ethiopian state into the distant past. In contemporary discourse, the Solomon and Sheba legend and the associated myth of a continuously existing Ethiopian state acted as ideological signifiers on two hegemonic levels. On the level of local power, they endorsed the legitimacy of the Amhara elite by emphasizing the antiquity and sacred authority of their rule. On the global level, they were used to endorse or condemn political alliances. Emperor Haile Selassie's alliance with the West was portrayed as a process of evolutionist "modernization" respectful of antiquity. In contrast, the Soviet Union's alliance with the Derg was presented as aberrant and intrusive, a fundamental transgression of Ethiopian national character, and a disruption of sacred history.

Prester John

The legend of Prester John arose in the twelfth century when Europe was threatened by Islam and the Mongols: it was said that a Christian king somewhere in the East had won victories over these enemies and sought an alliance with the kings of Europe. The legend revived national and religious confidence in Europe despite the fact that Prester John's kingdom could not actually be found. Various locations were suggested; by the fourteenth century, however, it was widely believed to be in Abyssinia. Numerous expeditions were sent to the region to establish alliances with Prester John.

As with the Solomon and Sheba legend, the image of Prester John signifies antiquity and legitimacy but it also permits the operation of the rhetorical processes of projection and reflection that have been constant in discourse on Ethiopia. Hansberry (1974:110–150) and Jones and Monroe (1969:59–63) describe the legend's history; Miller (1985:59) expresses its essence: "The desire for Prester John is the desire for an Other who is a perfect reflection or fulfillment of yourself, a prince who at the farthest reaches of the earth will make you whole and allow you to encircle your enemy, these 'Saracen miscreants.'"

"Ethiopia" was the locus of this desire not only for Europeans, who found in Prester John and, later, in the imperial regime, a reflection of their own desire for state order sanctified by antiquity and endowed with absolute authority, but also for Africans who regarded "Ethiopia" as a symbol of their own mythologized past. The figure of Prester John contributed to the development of an image of Ethiopia as a magnificent kingdom and a desirable ally; this image characterized the reign of more recent rulers, such as Emperor Menelik at the end of the nineteenth century, as well as that of Haile Selassie (Levine 1974:7–9). Western journalists and government officials constructed an "Ethiopia" eager to modernize and emulate the U.S. while taking its proper place as a faithful ally in the international hegemonic order. Even Mengistu Haile Mariam, Ethiopia's military ruler from 1977 to 1991, was originally seen as a responsible leader who would maintain ties with the West.

An Ancient Kingdom, A Unified State

Famine in the 1980s was not the first instance in which Ethiopia captured international headlines. Italy's 1935 invasion focused the world's attention on Ethiopia. During that period Ethiopia was a potent signifier, particularly for other African nations and for African-Americans. Probably Ethiopia meant little to African-Americans until the Italians invaded and its fate became an international concern (Asante 1977; Magubane 1987). Opposition to the invasion sparked the growth of African nationalism, and leaders such as Marcus Garvey, W.E.B. Du Bois, and Edward Blyden stressed Ethiopia's antiquity to promote pan-Africanism. Asante (1977:9) suggests that the imposed inferior status of blacks throughout Africa "evoked a psychological complex which fastened strongly upon the compensating idea of an independent African kingdom." The battle of Adwa, where the Ethiopian emperor Menelik had defeated Italian troops in 1896, became a key image in this reflex against imperialism and racism, and because Ethiopia was not directly colonized during the Scramble for Africa, it became symbolic of black greatness, pride, and liberty. Thus Ethiopia once again served as a signifier for all of Africa, although now invested with new meanings. Biblical and Classical Greek references to "Ethiopia" apparently confirmed the continuing existence of an ancient African kingdom, although these ancient "Ethiopias" were in various locations and did not correspond with the contemporary state of the same name.

The term "Ethiopia" effected an ideological condensation, a collapsing together of present and past employed to counteract racist claims regarding civilization and barbarism. To consolidate their own power, Ethiopian rulers asserted the antiquity and divine authority of their lineage, claims accepted elsewhere in Africa at face value. For example, in the 1930s, the Gold Coast *African Morning Post* ran a series of articles stressing the glories of Ethiopian achievements; however, there was a confusion of ancient Ethiopia with the contemporary state: "The Ethiopia to which the *African Morning Post* devoted its series was the classical Ethiopia which was Nubia on the upper Nile, and not the medieval or modern Ethiopia which is traceable to the ancient kingdom of Axum. Ethiopia of the 1930s was therefore quite distinct historically from the classical Ethiopia widely referred to in the New Testament. Thus, the Ethiopians of the twentieth century have no direct historical claims to the glories of ancient Ethiopia" (Asante 1977:58).

Asante himself appears to confuse the contemporary state with a mythical past by accepting the connection to Axum. This connection was challenged by a counter-discourse of Eritrean nationalism. For example, Okbazghi (1991:27) states: "There are no material records that show that Axum extended southward to what is today the habitat of the Amharas in northern Ethiopia. Contrary to the Ethiopian claim, the limited available evidence shows that the history of Axum, more than anything else, is the history of southern Eritrea and northern Tigrai. Furthermore, there is no historical indication of any kind that the Amharas were part of the Axumite empire."

Nevertheless, the image of Ethiopia as an ancient African empire figured largely in protests against the Italian invasion. The Black press "overflowed" with articles on Ethiopia and the invasion became a "fundamental issue in black life in 1935–36"; in this context, Haile Selassie was elevated to the status of a Christlike or messiah figure, a position he still maintains in the Rastafarian cult today (Scott 1978: 169). Organizations were formed to support Ethiopia, such as the International Council of the Friends of Ethiopia, the Nationalist Negro Movement, the Provisional Committee for the Defense of Ethiopia, the American League Against War and Fascism, the League of Struggles for Negro Rights, and many others. Enthusiasm continued despite the fact that Haile Selassie, while in exile, snubbed Garvey, leading the latter to denounce him as the "snobbish Lion of Judah . . . ruler of a country where black men are chained and flogged" (quoted in Scott 1978:170).

Scholarly interest was also encouraged by the Italian invasion. The Ethiopian Research Council, directed by William Leo Hansberry, was formed to stimulate opposition to the invasion and promote academic study of Ethiopian history. In the context of virulent racism in North America, Hansberry struggled to institute university courses on African history and to encourage pride in the African past. For scholars such as Hansberry, Ethiopia provided an effective image to counter negative views of Africa and African-Americans. As did Snowdon,

Hansberry turned to Ethiopian studies to demonstrate that racism was a product of slavery.

African-American discourse on Ethiopia also invoked a myth of a Promised Land that fueled the Back to Africa Movement. Two trends dominated this movement: an assimilationist tendency that sought a "genuine African experience" and a liberationist tendency that sought to usher in the millennium by ousting colonial rule (Shack 1974). The leading exponent of the latter tendency was the Reverend Henry McNeil Turner of the African Methodist Episcopal Church, but such sentiments also functioned in the "Ethiopianism" of secession from white nonconformist churches in South Africa during the 1920s, where the term also indicated a sense of African nationalism (Shepperson 1953). The image of Ethiopia as a Christian kingdom surrounded by Muslims or pagans was also important in generating interest and support among African-Americans (Shack 1974). Groups such as Garvey's Back to Africa Universal Negro Improvement Association and the Ethiopian World Federation Incorporated not only advocated defense of Ethiopia but encouraged emigration.

More recently, Ethiopia again became a symbol of African liberation. As the headquarters of the Organization of African Unity (OAU) and supplier of aid to certain anti-apartheid groups in South Africa, Ethiopia acquired the reputation of a champion of African liberty and anti-imperialist struggle. Yet in the nineteenth century Ethiopia had expanded its territory through collusion with European colonial powers, and later, Haile Selassie aligned himself with European powers against African nations (Amare 1989:485).

Blacks and Whites

The paradoxical aspects of representation of Ethiopia as a symbol of African freedom and grandeur were multiplied by assertions of Ethiopian rulers such as Menelik and Haile Selassie that Ethiopians were neither Africans nor blacks. Rejecting such identities, Amhara elites instead stressed their links to ancient Israel, as described in the Solomon and Sheba legend. The Amhara used such links to claim superiority over other peoples in the region and to justify their conquests and civilizing mission.

Some Ethiopians do not consider themselves black, a fact that demonstrates the social construction of such supposedly fundamental biological categorizations. Not surprisingly, this has afforded amusement for some Western observers who take such classifications as commonsense realities. For example, *Time* (June 14, 1943) remarked upon the exotica of the Olympia Cabaret in Addis Ababa "where British officers and visiting Americans drink and dance with lush Ethiopian beauties who bridle when they are called 'Natives' [and] consider themselves white." Robinson (1985:53) notes that U.S. representatives in Ethiopia defended such "racial pretensions of Ethiopia's ruling class." Prejudice among Ethiopian elites has been frequently noted: Perham (1969:397) says that in Amharic the term *shankalla* (black) is a term of abuse and insult; Levine (1965:78) finds that the Amhara consider themselves superior to both whites and blacks; Spencer (1984:123–124) notes Ethiopian prejudices against those of dark complexion, irrespective of ethnic origin. An Ethiopian friend of the author once characterized his homeland as "the most racist country in the world," an exaggeration, surely, but one indicative of the unfortunate prevalence of such attitudes.

Considerable controversy flared over the appropriate racial classification of the Ethiopians. In the 1930s, the "dominant issue" in the West African press and in local political organizations became the "true racial identity" of Ethiopians; in Haiti the press concluded that Ethiopians, although black, were not Negroes, a paradox that resulted in a sudden decline of interest in their situation. Actually, the view that Ethiopians considered themselves whites appears to have been "first given prominence by an editorial in *West Africa*, a European-controlled weekly" with the aim of sowing disunity and discouraging any sense of solidarity (Asante 1977:54–55).

Although the ancient Greeks had named the Ethiopians with a term intended to signify difference, European discourse later emphasized similarities, such as Christianity and a state supposedly rooted in antiquity. The result was ambivalence about racial classification. This ambivalence was heightened by Ethiopian military prowess. Ethiopians were regarded as whites following the Italian defeat at Adwa because racist discourse excluded the possibility of black victory (Marcus 1975:3–4). Gibbon (1929, 5:175–177) also gave Ethiopians an intermediate position; he ascribes to them an "olive" complexion and says that "in their lonely situation, the Aethiopians had almost relapsed into the savage life," but he finds that their racial essence (he regards them as Arabs) had preserved them from the savagery of neighboring Nubians. Christianity is also an element, linked directly to race: "A metaphysical religion may appear too refined for the capacity of the negro race; yet a black or a parrot might be taught to repeat the words of the Chalcedonian or Monophysite creed."

Placing the "Aethiopians" above the "Nubians" was one thing, but the "pretensions" of the Amhara elite sometimes had to be deflated. For example, *Time* (June 1, 1962) refers to a growing recognition of newly independent African states by Ethiopia, which had scorned black Africans as *barya* (slaves) for centuries, and quotes a cabinet minister: "It's our heritage and duty to lead our recently enlightened brethren into the modern age." (It is noteworthy that this support from Ethiopia for African independence did not extend to Eritrea, which was annexed four months later.) As a U.S. ally, Ethiopia would be maintained and armed but *Time* made it clear that there should be no doubt about who would lead whom. After pointing out poverty, disease, corruption, and absolute rule in Ethiopia, *Time* supplies "one visiting Senegalese" who utters the required lines: "If this is the heritage of freedom, I say 'Bring back the colonialists.'" Invented or not, this Senegalese functions as a rhetorical device, namely, ventriloquism: the use of a local, or in this case, "an African," to enunciate and give validity to the author's views. It is a standard technique of contemporary hegemonic discourse.

Discussion continues about the proper racial classification of the Ethiopians. For example, Soviet Africanist Georgi Galperin places Ethiopians in an intermediate position between whites and blacks, asserting that they are closer to what he identifies as the "European race" (Jordan 1989:8,17n29). As in Africanist discourse generally, racial distinctions are manipulated to serve specific political objectives. Desire for closer political alliance, for example, leads to stress on European features, while efforts to vilify a particular regime are usually accompanied by references to African qualities.

These remarks indicate a trope whose essential features are in contradiction: an Ethiopia that does not exist—or a multiplicity of Ethiopias, blacks who are whites, the quintessential Africans who reject African identity. However, rather than seeking deconstructionist explanations for an Africanist discourse based on nullity, one can propose a historical context for these contradictions. The fact that racial distinctions are easily manipulated and reversed indicates the absurdity of any claims that they have an objective basis and locates these distinctions where they actually occur, in the operations of power. In recent discourse on Ethiopia, ideas of race show this direct connection with power: famine is presented as the result of essential African qualities of savagery and incompetence. These qualities are presented as dangerous threats to Western civilization (also conceived in racial terms—as white), which require a reassertion of power over the Third World generally. This theme of racial essentialism relates to the idea of the Third World as contagion and involves fear of erosion of racial identity through contact. Themes of racist and anticommunist discourse are interwoven and the famine that affected large regions of Africa is distilled into an Ethiopian famine, presided over by the nightmare figures of the Savage and the Communist who merge to produce pure negativity.

Haile Selassie

Many of these paradoxes and contradictions are concentrated within the figure of Haile Selassie, the last emperor of Ethiopia. Possibly the best-known African leader in the West, Haile Selassie was famous for his impassioned speech to the League of Nations following the Italian invasion. As Ullendorf (1973:184) puts it, "There could have been no more dramatic or moving scene in the history of the League." In 1936, Haile Selassie was *Time*'s "Man of the Year," but adulation was not limited to North America: John M. Melly wrote in *The Spectator* (July 19, 1935) that Haile Selassie was "the wisest and most enlightened man ever to hold the reins of government in that country." Although Melly found Ethiopia to be "still centuries behind European civilization," due to the emperor's modernizing efforts "order [was] emerging out of chaos." Juxtaposition of a modernizing emperor with a backward and savage nation was a frequent rhetorical technique. *Time* (April 7, 1941) recorded Haile Selassie's instructions that his troops not castrate captured Italian soldiers, which it averred was common practice. While pointing out that British forces actually controlled Ethiopia and that Haile Selassie's sovereignty was only "nominal," *Time* (May 17, 1943) stressed "his great personal sense of dignity, his enormous palace, and a measure of authority over the once rambunctious tribal chieftains of the interior." *Time* (June 14, 1943) characterized this rambunctiousness by reference to Ethiopia's "Unpainted Commandos" and the proposal of Ethiopia's Minister to London, Blatta Ayela Gabre, that "his spear-toting countrymen lead Commando raids into Italy. Said he 'Fascist blood would turn to water. The Ethiopians will never be satisfied until they can rip an Italian gullet.'" *Time* contrasted old Ethiopia ("brigands on the highways . . . wife-drawn plows . . . filth and squalor") with the Emperor's modernizing efforts, significant among which was his desire for closer ties with the U.S.

Haile Selassie was seen as a modernizer even by supporters of Italian colonialism. For example, the Italian Community of Toronto published a booklet by T. Mari entitled *What Do You Know About Ethiopia?* (1935), which mixes facts with a number of racist slurs. Pointing out that the boundaries of the Ethiopian state had been expanding since 1882, Mari stresses that a distinction must be made between the original state and its conquered territories. Mari emphasizes Ethiopian barbarities, including slavery and the *ghebbar* system (in which inhabitants were forced to support soldiers stationed in their area and became subservient to them). Mari finds significant differences (racial, social, political, religious, linguistic, historical) between Ethiopians and the inhabitants of the areas they conquered. There are obvious reasons for such an assertion, although they do not necessarily negate the existence of differences.

Mari's text is littered with racist condescensions as he attacks Ethiopians' "blind racial pride [over] . . . each tiny step towards some form of less barbarous life" (8–9). Yet even Mari notes Haile Selassie's attempt to transform Ethiopia into a modern state. Not surprisingly, however, Mari concludes that such efforts are doomed because of the general "barbarism and disorder" prevailing in the country; therefore, external (i.e., Italian) intervention is needed to truly civilize the population. The racist attitudes displayed in Mari's text were also those of the Fascist leadership in Italy, which developed an apartheid-type system in Eritrea.

These examples indicate the shape of the rhetorical construction: on one hand, the exotic appeal of the emperor, growing U.S. interests in the region, and Haile Selassie's willingness to accommodate them, with concomitant praise for him as a modernizer; on the other hand, the blatant racism of the period that allowed *Time* to portray other Ethiopians as pretentious but amusing savages and Mari to dismiss them as barbarians. In this respect, "the emperor" is part of a broader hegemonic discourse applied to Africa. The idea of kingship was a central component of imperial ideology in Africa, allowing for collaboration with indigenous elites to serve mutual interests of power (Ranger 1983). Ethiopia, and the Amhara imperial mythology, was celebrated as a paradigm of African kingship in general while immediate European interests could be served in the Horn by supporting traditional authority. The U.S. also found traditional authority to be in its own interests in the region after World War II. Haile Selassie's authority was not simply restored but increased as the U.S. pushed federation through the United Nations and handed the former Italian colony of Eritrea over to their ally. The emperor continued to emphasize his loyalty to the West during the Cold War period, appealing for and receiving substantial military aid from the U.S.

During the 1960s, Haile Selassie was one of the most important

U.S. allies in Africa, receiving millions of dollars of economic and military aid. Pentagon officials stated that "if the Emperor wanted it in solid gold Cadillacs . . . he could have it that way" (Halliday and Molyneux 1981:218). This was due not only to the Horn's strategic significance but also to Ethiopia's special relationship with both Africa and the Middle East, Haile Selassie's position as an ally of Israel, and Ethiopia's role as home of the OAU; Ethiopia supported U.S. policies, provided the Kagnew communications base in Eritrea, and sent troops to Korea.

Thus the figure of the emperor is the point of intersection for themes drawn from racism, Christian mythology, and anticommunism and allows permutation of their meanings within discourse on Ethiopia. Favorable reporting on the emperor continued to the time of his deposition. For example, *Time* (February 24, 1967) sympathetically portrayed the "Lonely Emperor['s]" efforts to balance absolute rule with modernization, and articles on the 1974 coup note his enduring dignity. This concentration on the emperor's personal dignity masked the catastrophic effects of his rule.

Many studies comment favorably on Haile Selassie. Ullendorf (1973), translator of his autobiography, also stresses the emperor's dignity. Holden (1973) recalls childhood memories of the noble Haile Selassie threatened by Italian invasion and employs them in a typical juxtaposition: although "one of the most benighted lands in Africa," Ethiopia breaks the relentless monotony of a continent where "it is often all too easy in the general sameness to mistake one people for another, the next place for the last"; in this undifferentiated backwardness, Ethiopia stands out and "smacks of authority as well as intrigue" (77). Foreshadowing the emperor's final appearance in *Time*, Holden attributes this to the "lonely dignity" of Haile Selassie, who emerges from the chaos of ghastly poverty as the center that holds Ethiopia together.

Marcus (1987:x) finds Haile Selassie "a uniquely gifted political genius" and records other expressions of admiration for the emperor's dignity and regal bearing. For Marcus (1975:4), these qualities made Ethiopia a model for other African states, particularly those seeking traditional forms of authority. The attractions included "[an] increasingly centralized government . . . [and] monarchical non-party state; in which the sovereign has increasingly dominated every facet of national existence. All allegiance is owed to him and to the apparatus of royal power. Only by accommodation to the official culture of the state can the individual hope to succeed."

This model of authority is the ideal of hegemonic discourse, provided that the ideological affiliation of "the sovereign" is acceptable. Kapuscinski (1983) is unique in his portrayal of the Ethiopian court as a paranoid and sycophantic universe whirling around the enigmatic emperor; it is surely an allegory, although Marcus (1987:182n2) condemns it as "misguided and absurd."

The benevolent character of Haile Selassie's rule is also suggested by Jackson and Rosberg (1982), who schematize *Personal Rule in Black Africa* as a distinctive system with specific characteristics and processes (such as coups, plots, corruption, factionalism, and purges). They suggest that African politics is a power game that contrasts with a Western model of institutionalized order of roles and organizational rationality. Jackson and Rosberg identify four primary types of African rulers: princely, autocratic, prophetic, and tyrannical. They minimize violent aspects of Haile Selassie's rule and place him in the most benign category: as the Prince, Haile Selassie incorporates all power within his person, acting as a modernizer. In contrast, the Derg embodies tyranny, although Jackson and Rosberg think the regime is best described even in its excesses as "revolutionary" because it claimed to act in the service of a "higher moral authority" (241). The value of this classification is dubious; violence is simply relativized and "higher moral authority" remains unexamined.

In general, the violent and repressive aspects of Haile Selassie's rule have been overlooked. "The emperor" has haunted discourse on Ethiopia, serving as an image of antiquity and of legitimate authority that could be juxtaposed with the Soviet-allied regime of Mengistu (e.g., Harris 1987:173; Henze 1986a:7; Hoben 1985:17; Thomas 1987:53). Regardless of the undeniable barbarism of the Derg, construction of "the emperor" as the sign of legitimate authority is achieved through falsification and through a rhetorical technique that may be termed construction of absence (referring to deliberate omission of significant and readily available information for ideological purposes). For example, writing in the *New Republic*, anthropologist Allan Hoben (1985) lauds Haile Selassie as a champion of modernization but fails to note that the emperor ignored widespread famine in which thousands starved to death and that his policies established the conditions for the future recurrence of famine. Similarly, Paul Henze (1986b) also praises a U.S. ally: "In comparison with developments in most of Africa in the intervening years, Haile Selassie's record in Eritrea up to 1974 is hardly one of extraordinary duplicity or savagery."

By constructing significant absences, Henze ignores violations of international law, leading up to and including annexation of Eritrea, violent suppression of the 1958 general strike, imprisonment of thousands of civilians suspected of sympathizing with the Eritrean Liberation Front, the burning of villages and the massacre of their inhabitants (such as 600 people executed in 1970 in retaliation for the ambush of an Ethiopian general, or the bombing of Keren, which caused 500 civilian casualties and 30,000 refugees), and the fact that "in the towns arbitrary arrests, detention for long periods and the use of torture became increasingly common" (Firebrace and Holland 1985:21).

Henze is speaking in relative terms, and perhaps in comparison with the estimated 100,000 people who starved to death in Ethiopia under Haile Selassie during the famine of the 1970s, the above-mentioned acts of savagery in Eritrea cannot be considered "extraordinary"; certainly Mengistu's brutality eventually surpassed that of Haile Selassie both in Ethiopia and in Eritrea.

The violence of African politics is also an important aspect of the work of Peter Schwab, academic advisor to the Hoover Institution at Stanford University. Like most biographers of Haile Selassie, Schwab (1979:21, 148) praises the emperor, seeing him as the "conscience of humanity" in his 1936 League of Nations speech and as the Great Man of Ethiopian history. However, Schwab is unusual in that he later offered a similar uncritical assessment of Mengistu Haile Mariam, championing him as "the spearhead of the revolution. Whatever happens in the future, he has carved an original niche into the historical tradition of socialism. He has been the engine of the revolution and deserves to be given much of the credit for its success" (1985:118).

The cost of this attempt to carve a niche into whichever "historical tradition of socialism" Schwab has in mind is uncertain, depending upon how accountable one might hold Mengistu for the power struggle and purges of the Red Terror in 1977–78 (between 3,000 and 10,000 killed), for continuing the war in Eritrea (62,000 Ethiopian troops killed), or for worsening the effects of drought and creating famine in the Horn (1 million dead) (Ottaway 1982:136; Luckham and Dawit 1984, 1:19; Smith 1987:37n31). These figures are dated to the approximate time of Schwab's tribute, but the death toll rose much higher, including casualities among various opposition forces and civilians, before Mengistu eventually fled to Zimbabwe in 1991.

Schwab's enthusiasm for revolutionary violence has been noted by reviewers (Alem 1986; Fenton 1985). Through references to Mao and Fanon, he seems to celebrate violence not merely as a necessary process but as a redemptive and spiritually liberating act. He excuses the Derg's use of violence in an attack on "liberals" who protested the execution of members of Haile Selassie's government and of General Aman Andom, first leader of the Derg (Schwab 1976). Elsewhere, Schwab (1980/81) argues that human rights is a Western concept, both foreign to Ethiopia and inapplicable to revolutionary situations. This echoes a standard maxim of racist thought, as found in Lugard's (1923:82) manual of domination ("The negro . . . will never be fit for institutions which are not in some way a direct outcome of the negro character"). Furthermore, Schwab seems unaware of inconsistencies in his argument and is unconcerned that the socialism he detects in the Derg's policies was also a foreign ideology. As to the violence of revolution, this is surely to be regretted rather than valorized. Schwab's (1980/81:40) "hypothesis . . . that the Dergue is attempting to secure human rights and fundamental freedoms for the mass of Ethiopians through . . . whatever actions are considered necessary" is dubious, given the regime's demonstrated disregard for those rights and freedoms throughout the course of its tenure.

While apparently aberrant in its celebration of both Haile Selassie and Mengistu, Schwab's work does indicate what is at the center of hegemonic discourse: the relativity of violence and the fetishization of absolute authority. Violence is disregarded if the perpetrator observes the appropriate ideology; furthermore, the discourse is obsessed with sovereignty, identity, and authority and requires a powerful leader in the Horn. For U.S. policy makers, Haile Selassie provided such authority and was observant of the appropriate international hierarchy; therefore, the repressive aspects of his reign were acceptable. Despite the murderous actions of the regime that deposed their former ally, the U.S. was willing to increase its supply of arms to Ethiopia if the appropriate relations of power were preserved. It was Mengistu's alliance with the Soviet Union, not the Derg's violent character, which led to his demonization.

The symbolic significance of Ethiopia for Africans and African-Americans also was concentrated in the image of Haile Selassie. During the decolonization period Haile Selassie enjoyed a reputation as an elder statesman and skilled diplomat and had enormous respect among less experienced African politicians; Nkrumah, Senghor, and Kenyatta were all inspired by him (Wubneh and Abate 1988:1). The enormous prestige of Haile Selassie influenced African support for Ethiopia's position during the 1950 U.N. debates on Eritrea's future. In particular, Liberia gave strong support to Ethiopian claims. As had medieval Europe, Liberia found its own reflection in Ethiopia: Amhara dominance over other ethnic groups paralleled that of "the Americo-Liberian minority [that] imposed its norms and institutions upon the . . . sixteen or more ethnic groups" in Liberia, employing "all the mannerisms of an imperial power"; like the Amhara, this minority felt itself possessed of a civilizing mission over backward Africans (Liebenow 1986:95, 20).

Haile Selassie's mediation in conflicts between Algeria and Morocco in 1963 and in Sudan in 1972 also contributed to his reputation as a great African statesman, and he was instrumental in the formation of the OAU in Addis Ababa in 1963. His diplomatic skills were put to use at the OAU over the Eritrean issue. At its second meeting in Cairo in 1964, the OAU passed a resolution accepting boundaries established by colonial powers; however, Haile Selassie was able to keep the OAU from applying this to the Eritrean situation due to a previously adopted principle, that of noninterference in internal matters of states. Because Ethiopia had annexed Eritrea just before this motion was passed, the OAU refrained from applying the principle of observing colonial borders to the case. Indeed, during the long war between Ethiopia and Eritrea, many Africans opposed the idea of allowing Eritreans to determine their own future on that same basis. However, it is noteworthy that Abdul Rahman Mohammed Babu, formerly Foreign Minister of the Republic of Zanzibar and Minister of Economic Planning and Social Welfare for Tanzania, who presented the resolution on noninterference to the OAU, later criticized the organization's position on Eritrea, as well as his own role, which he attributed to his inexperience and to Haile Selassie's persuasiveness and prestige; Babu later became a strong advocate of Eritrean self-determination.

The symbolic importance of Haile Selassie remains central in contemporary discourse. Kaplan (1988b:10–11) transforms the emperor into a symbol not just of Africa but of the Third World generally. Echoing Farago's (1935:158) evocation of the "Dreamy Emperor," Kaplan's text situates Haile Selassie "like some figure out of a dream" taking his appropriate place in imperial iconography at President John Kennedy's funeral: "Millions of Americans, glued to their television sets that weekend, always will remember the marching emperor. Haile Selassie signified not only a distant, fairy-tale kingdom, but the very world beyond the United States and Europe in all its diversity."

In this text, Haile Selassie signifies not just Africa but the Third World in general, assuming a proper role in international hegemonic order. Haile Selassie is the "decent native" who respects Western interests and modernizes his nation accordingly. Just as the emperor represented appropriate allegiances, so the Derg's alliance with the Soviet Union symbolized potential loss of control over the Third

World: freed from the order imposed by Western hegemony, the Third World erupts into chaos, Africa's savage essence is unleashed, demons emerge from the heart of darkness, all with terrifying results.

A Black African military that ousted a U.S. ally and sided with the Soviet Union combined the two major demons of the political unconscious of Western capitalism: the native and the communist. It is impossible to understand discourse on Ethiopian famine without placing it in the context of these images that bracket it. The native has had a longer and more complicated history, signifying both terror and delight, elaborated in many specific manifestations. In discourse produced to explain African famine in the 1980s, many texts present Africans as backward and ignorant savages responsible for their own starvation. Anticommunism has provided ideological legitimation for the extension of U.S. power on a global scale and has functioned as a device to mobilize and police domestic populations (Chomsky 1991). With the end of the Cold War, the communist may be disappearing as a nightmare figure (apart from attacks on liberal intellectuals, evidenced during 1992 in condemnations of politically correct speech in most major mass-circulation periodicals). However, independent nationalism remains undesirable and the Third World will likely be a rich source of images and a ripe field for the production of useful external threats in the future. Before turning to the study of the discursive construction of more contemporary power relations in the Horn and of how Ethiopia has figured in discourse on the Third World, it is necessary to consider how the image of Ethiopia has been constituted and challenged from within.

3

NARRATIVE CONSTRUCTIONS OF HISTORY AND IDENTITY

Inventing the Past

The past is contested terrain. Selectively remembered, conveniently forgotten, or sometimes invented, it may be used to justify and legitimize actions in the present and to provide the model for a future which is to be created in accordance with certain traditions. Not simply a sequence of completed events, the past is a creation of the present, with traditions invented to serve particular needs (Hobsbawm and Ranger 1983).

Some historians argue that there can be no neutral collection of historical facts and no single representative account of any given phenomenon (Zinn 1970). Past, present, and future are not distinct periods but part of one interactive and endlessly self-reflecting process of imagination. In particular, nationalist historiography is part of an effort to create "imagined communities" (Anderson 1983; Barraclough 1979). Events in the past are emphasized in order to support a specific vision of the future. Nationalist histories tend toward a process of retrospective projection that defines the existing national self not as a created product of historical change but as the enduring and constant subject of history. Typically, such histories involve exclusion and silencing of certain voices and substitution of a hegemonic mythology. Official histories, institutionally authenticated and authorized, create particular visions of the past and provide instructions on how it should be perceived and revered. Elites frequently turn to history to develop justifications of their own power, and certain key historical events come to provide aspects of a group's image. Thus, history gives legitimacy to those in power and in turn defines that group's view of itself. Attempts to rewrite history from the point of view of subalterns, those excluded from power, may be opposed or suppressed, sometimes violently. Subnational entities cannot enforce their own histories, which are erased by the history-writing machine of the state (Tonkin, McDonald, and Chapman 1989:8).

In Ethiopia, competing narratives of history have been promoted by the state, by various opposition groups, and by nationalist movements seeking independence. Those who see themselves as Ethiopians, particularly those identifying with the Amhara culture, which has exerted hegemony over other peoples in the region, typically subscribe to a narrative of history that projects a unified territory and identity into the distant past. Other groups who live within the boundaries of the contemporary Ethiopian state but who reject their affiliation with Ethiopia and adopt other identities, such as Eritreans and Oromos, offer different versions of regional history. They reject a unified national identity and challenge the vision of an Ethiopian state that has endured since antiquity.

In addition, various other political movements, whose members identify themselves as Ethiopians but who opposed the Derg, have proposed their own narrative constructions of history that also challenge the hegemonic narrative of the Amhara. While offering conflicting or revised versions of the past, some of these groups propose that a unified but democratic Ethiopian state can meet the needs of all, regardless of identity. Others reject this and call for the establishment of new entities, such as an independent Oromia for the Oromo people. These alternative narratives of history have been rejected by various Ethiopian regimes and by expatriate Ethiopian intellectuals who have fled because of their own opposition to the government.

Finally, scholarly discourse, including that of Western intellectuals, is informed by and informs these narratives of history. The predominant tendency in this scholarly work has been to emphasize Ethiopia's cultural and historical unity, reflecting traditional concerns with Semitic ties, royal chronicles, the imperial state, and the Abyssinian Great Tradition (Rubenson 1976; Levine 1974). More recently, oppositional discourses have emerged that question this Great Tradition, offer conflicting versions of history, and proclaim other identities.

This chapter examines the broad patterns of such narratives, the metaphors employed, and the assumptions that underlie them. The contested nature and boundaries of the Ethiopian self point to broader questions about ethnic identity, about the essential elements and outlines of a culture, and about the authority to speak for cultural groups, questions that figure prominently in contemporary anthropological and sociological debates and which have been central to a rethinking of various academic disciplines.

The Narrative of Greater Ethiopia

The projection of contemporary borders backwards into time has characterized the historical narrative of Greater Ethiopia, as promoted by ruling elites. Ethiopian nationalist discourse emphasizes the deep historical roots of the contemporary state and continuity with the remote past. For example, in an undated manifesto of ENATAD (Ethiopian National Alliance to Advance Democracy, a monarchist group in exile), Prince Makonnen Makonnen states:

> Ethiopia is an ancient land and one of a few whose history as a nation-state can be traced back to antiquity. The Egypt of the Pharaohs called it Punt, or the Land of God. Later, the Greeks thought of it as the land of wheat and of the olive tree, and much later in the Middle Ages, Ethiopia was perceived as a remote kingdom shrouded in legend and mystery, the land of "Prester John." It's [*sic*] borders covered most of the Horn of Africa and the western portion of the Arabian peninsula. . . . For millennia, Ethiopians have preserved their independence and national integrity, and few countries over the centuries have so zealously protected themselves from foreign invasion.

Ethiopian nationalists trace their history to the ancient empire of Axum, which flourished from the first to sixth centuries and was based in what is now Tigray, a northern region of the present state. Weakened by Arab expansion, Axum fell under attacks from the Beja and Agaw peoples, was succeeded by the Zagwe dynasty, and, according to this narrative construction of history, was restored in 1270 by a descendant of the single survivor of Axum. According to the *Kibra Negast,* the Tigrean text which Donald Levine (1975) describes as Ethiopia's national epic, the origins of the Amhara ruling elite lie in the legendary union of King Solomon and the Queen of Sheba. The legend states that their son, Menelik I, was the first of a line of divine kings extending to the last emperor, Haile Selassie, a continuity that is a key theme in the Ethiopian narrative construction of history. This discourse proposes a fixed identity, deeply rooted in the ancient past, which has persisted to the present. Antiquity confers authenticity upon this identity, regarded as essential and unchanging throughout time.

Levine (1974:151), who supports this continuity of identity, states that beliefs codified in the *Kibra Negast* "assured the Tigreans [of Axum] and their Amhara successors of superiority" and presented "imperial expansion . . . as a kind of manifest destiny." During the fourteenth and fifteenth centuries, the Amhara expanded from the central Shoa region to conquer new territories. In the sixteenth century, their power declined during war against Ahmad Gran of Harar, who was supported by the Turkish empire then expanding into the Horn. With Portuguese support, the Amhara defeated Ahmad Gran's forces but their empire was weakened; this allowed the Oromo to spread from Bale region throughout most of what is now Ethiopia. A century of civil war followed as rival warlords struggled for power and no central government ruled; this period is known as the "Era of the Princes." In the mid-nineteenth century, under emperors Teodros, Yohannes, and Menelik, Abyssinian force was reasserted and the foundations of the modern Ethiopian state were established. The narrative of Greater Ethiopia characterizes the military conquests of these emperors and their expansion of territory as the reunification of the empire.

This empire resisted incursions by the Egyptians and by the Italians, who had established a colony in Eritrea on the Red Sea coast. After being defeated by Ethiopia at the 1896 battle of Adwa, the Italian army retreated to Eritrea and Emperor Menelik accepted the colonial border. Italy invaded Ethiopia in 1936, seizing control until its defeat by British and Ethiopian troops in 1941. In 1950 Eritrea was federated with Ethiopia, although Haile Selassie campaigned for what he termed a reunification of territory divided by Italian colonialism.

Ethiopian discourse asserts the essential identity of the two regions. In an April 1, 1950, radio broadcast in Addis Ababa, during the visit of the UN Commission of Inquiry to determine the future of the former Italian colony, Haile Selassie claimed that Eritreans had no separate identity but were culturally and linguistically identical to Ethiopians; the same assertions were made by Aklilou Abte Wold, the Ethiopian Foreign Minister. This exemplifies the tendency of nationalist discourse to employ invented facts to further its claims: there are a number of mutually unintelligible languages in Eritrea, as there are in Ethiopia, a fact noted by the UN Commission in its 1950 report.

Nevertheless, Ethiopian nationalist discourse has continued to assert the notion of unity, and this has been reflected in Western scholarship. Although an Eritrean nationalist movement emerged in the post–World War II period, it was not until 1980 that this oppositional discourse received a wider international audience with publication of a number of English-language works that challenged the idea of unity, rejected Ethiopian claims of continuous control, and argued for Eritrean independence (Bereket 1980; Davidson, Cliffe, and Bereket 1980; Pool 1980; Sherman 1980). This discourse questioned assertions of identity and continuity, presenting a more fluid situation characterized by the rise and fall of empires, invasion by different groups who exerted control at certain periods, and autonomy in areas where no Abyssinian king ruled.

Ethiopian writers rejected this oppositional discourse. For example, Addis Hiwet (1984:47) dismisses it as "obscurantist." Melaku Tegegn (1989:143) charges that it "ignores fundamental political and historical factors," such as his own assertion that Eritrea was ruled by Abyssinian kings from the Axumite period until the Italian invasion. Melaku assumes direct continuity from Axum to contemporary Ethiopia. Stating that "Eritrean politicians deny this fact and hopelessly argue instead that no part of Eritrea had ever been part of Ethiopia," he misrepresents claims of partial autonomy. Eritrean nationalist discourse rarely projects a unified identity into antiquity. Instead, it emphasizes a decisive transformation under Italian colonialism.

Ethiopian nationalist discourse refuses to acknowledge such a transformation and constructs Eritrea as inauthentic, opposing this to an essential Ethiopian identity. In 1950, Aklilou Abte Wold described Eritrea to the UN Commission as "an artificial entity . . . [requiring] artificial economic support" (United Nations 1950a:49). Deposition of the emperor did not modify Ethiopian discourse. Emphasizing the identity of the ancient Ethiopian state, Mengistu also dismissed Eritrea as "an artificial Italian-made entity" (quoted in Permanent Peoples' Tribunal 1984:369).

This formulation, contrasting essence to artifice, is problematic, however. In its appeal to an essential Ethiopian identity, it ignores the African context, in which all contemporary states are artificial creations of imperialism. Eritrean nationalists stressed the similarity of Eritrea's colonial experience with that of other now-independent states and appealed to the OAU resolution on observance of borders inherited from the colonial period. However, this appeal did not receive open support and the OAU, based in Addis Ababa, neglected the issue.

Following steady erosion of rights guaranteed by the federation arrangement, Eritrean nationalists launched armed revolt in 1961. The narrative of Ethiopian nationalism describes the movement as secessionist, inspired and encouraged by Arab states seeking the disintegration of Ethiopia and the transformation of the Red Sea into an "Arab lake." Efforts to crush the Eritrean independence movement have been presented within this discourse as attempts to defend an ancient Christian outpost encircled by hostile Muslim forces. Much like official Israeli discourse on the Palestinian issue, Ethiopian discourse rejects the idea of a distinct national identity among Eritreans.

The Derg maintained the same position and intensified the war against Eritrea, first with U.S. arms and then, following its adoption of Marxist-Leninist ideology, with support of the Soviet Union. From the 1950s to the mid-1970s, Ethiopia was presented in discourse as a pro-Western, modernizing nation with a benevolent and progressive ruler; by the 1980s, however, it was reviled as a communist dictatorship. Regardless of the ideological shift, however, both superpowers defended Ethiopia's territorial integrity. The Derg, dismissing Eritrean nationalists as bandits, insisted that political problems and ethnic inequalities be solved within a unified Ethiopian state. This position was shared by opposition groups, variously critical of the regime from a Marxist perspective or seeking restoration of the monarchy, and by both superpowers.

The Narrative of Eritrean Independence

Eritrean nationalists trace the origin of their separate identity to the experience of Italian colonialism, which carved out a distinct Eritrean territory in 1889. While acknowledging contact with Abyssinian kingdoms to the south, Eritrean nationalists claim that no Abyssinian king ruled the whole territory and that Turkish and Egyptian occupations contributed to the development of a separate regional history. However, it was Italian colonization that unified Eritrea, transformed the social and economic character of the area, and marked it off as a distinct unit. Whereas the narrative of Ethiopian history regards Italian colonialism as merely a temporary, artificial interruption of a preexisting cultural and territorial unity, Eritrean nationalism regards it as a definitive break that established a distinct identity among those who came under Italian domination. Crucial events of regional history are thus interpreted in directly opposing ways by the protagonists. Eritrean nationalist discourse contends that shared experience of Italian colonialism unified various ethnic groups in Eritrea and that this experience is comparable to that of other colonized areas that later became independent states. In contrast to the Ethiopian narrative construction of history, with its rhetorical emphasis on continuity, essence, and use of the remote past as validation of the present, a key theme of Eritrean nationalist discourse is the idea of a decisive rupture that created a new identity, authentic, legitimate, and fundamentally different from that of other peoples in the region. Whereas Ethiopian nationalism proposes a fixed transhistorical identity, Eritrean discourse suggests that identity is shaped and modified by changing historical circumstances. In asserting this more subjective and malleable definition, Eritrean discourse directly challenges fundamental assumptions of the Ethiopian narrative of national identity.

Federation and Self-Determination

In the debates over history and identity, much attention focused on pre-federation Eritrea. Kifle (1986:46), a former Foreign Minister of the Ethiopian government, claims that "in the immediate aftermath of the Second World War, there was in Eritrea a strong sentiment for union with Ethiopia." Getachew (1986:479) argues that "by all reliable accounts, the Unionist Party which advocated unconditional reunion with Ethiopia was supported by the majority of the Eritreans." The only "reliable account" cited is that of John Spencer, legal advisor to the Ethiopian government. Dawit (1989:77), former military governor of Eritrea, claims that "young Eritreans" formed the first political organization, Hager Fikre Mahaber, as the Unionist Party, which became "popular overnight" as the "single voice of highland Eritreans." Yet Markakis (1987:63) says the organization was formed to lobby the British on local issues and that Haile Selassie later sent Eritreans from Ethiopia to rename it as the Unionist Party, resulting in the immediate resignation not only of Muslim members but also of prominent Christian leaders such as Woldeab Wolde Mariam.

Whereas Ethiopian nationalists seek to emphasize Eritrean support for unification, Eritrean nationalist discourse regards the Unionist Party as a creation of the Ethiopian government. Whatever the degree of local support for unification, it is evident that Ethiopia funded the Unionist Party and that its tactics were coercive. For example, Colonel Negga Haile Selassie, the Ethiopian Crown's representative in Asmara, was implicated in bribery, intimidation, and violence. Terrorist attacks and assassinations were directed against supporters of independence. The Ethiopian government, through the Coptic Church, exacerbated existing tensions with anti-Muslim propaganda and weakened support for independence through threats of excommunication.

As well as assertions of full support for unification, Ethiopian nationalist discourse stresses divisions within Eritrean society. For example, Mesfin Araya (1990) critiques previous analyses of prefederation Eritrea for promoting conspiracy theories, emphasizing external powers, and ignoring local actors. Yet his "alternative explanation" merely restates standard themes of Greater Ethiopian nationalism. Mesfin concentrates on religious divisions to show Eritrean society as hopelessly fractured. It is reasonable to avoid treating colonized groups as inert and simply manipulated by external powers in favor of acknowledging resistance and local politics, and it is worthwhile to examine divisions in Eritrean society. However, Mesfin excludes the influence of external powers rather than examining their interplay with domestic forces. This is particularly problematic because external powers actively engineered the federation. Firm evidence exists; recently declassified documents clearly demonstrate that there was extensive U.S.-Ethiopian collaboration to attain shared objectives: guaranteed use of a strategic communications base at Asmara in return for securing Ethiopia's access to the sea (*Journal of Eritrean Studies* 1987, 1988). To ignore external influence, where this is amply documented, is not simply oversight but a polemical endeavor to show Eritrea as essentially divided.

Mesfin disregards these factors in order to emphasize internal divisions in Eritrea. This is a typical strategy of Greater Ethiopian nationalism, which seeks to obscure collaboration by external powers, the Ethiopian Government, and elements of Eritrean society to engineer federation. By emphasizing divisions and overlooking commonalities, it seeks to demonstrate the absence of a national Eritrean identity. Opposition to union with Ethiopia is depicted as having been restricted to Eritrean Muslims, overlooking involvement of highland Christians. Mesfin terms this "peripheral and largely confined to the educated urban youth," ignoring the fact that, typically, nationalism is promoted by the intelligentsia.

Here Mesfin minimizes involvement by prominent individuals from Christian backgrounds such as Woldeab Wolde Mariam. Woldeab's activities, maintained over four decades despite numerous assassination attempts, earned him acclaim by Eritrean nationalists as "the man who has walked the longest." Woldeab was a leading member of the Liberal Progressive Party, formed in the 1940s by Muslims and Christians who violated traditional norms of separation by eating together to demonstrate solidarity rather than sectarian identity. There is no doubt that religious factionalism has been significant in Eritrea and that such factors may continue to exert some influence, especially in the context of a resurgent Islamic fundamentalism throughout North Africa. However, Ethiopian nationalist discourse seeks to obscure any attempt, successful or not, to overcome these divisions. Ironically, this focus underestimates other differences, including those based on class, tribe, regionalism, ideology, and personal ambition. It does appear that independence was favored by most Muslims in Eritrea while the Unionist Party, which did seek integration with Ethiopia, gained support from the Christian population of the highlands. However, to conceptualize a strict division of political opinion along religious lines is to oversimplify the situation, as there were a number of prominent leaders in the independence movement who were Christians from the highlands.

Furthermore, the Eritrean nationalist movement did not characterize itself according to religious divisions. For example, the chairman of the delegation of the Muslim League, addressing the UN in 1950, stated that he spoke for Christian members of the Independence Bloc as well as Muslims in rejecting the "occupational yoke" of Ethiopia. Ethiopian nationalists such as Mesfin overlook this in order to argue that existence of religious divisions means there was no sense of national unity in Eritrea but only an idea of a state formed on religious lines. This division is too simplistic, reducing complicated relationships to a single binary opposition. For example, it overlooks ties of the Coptic Church with Eritrean elites threatened by the growing movement for peasant emancipation. Assertions that all differences are now resolved would exaggerate what unity has been achieved. Ethnic, political, and religious divisions exist in all states and will continue to play a role in Eritrea. Yet their existence does not negate nationalist consciousness.

Facts regarding support for unification are difficult to determine. The UN commission found Eritrean society completely divided, although the U.S. Embassy in Addis Ababa estimated that 75 percent of Eritreans wanted independence. All parties exaggerated support, to an extent that claims exceeded the country's estimated population. Neither of the two UN commissions that examined the case could agree on Eritrea's future, and the second commission eventually submitted separate reports that diverged even on basic facts. Assertions of full support for unification ignore problems encountered by the UN representatives, including protests by independence advocates that they were not informed of meetings. The UN Commission thought that many had no idea of the issues and found that many of those interviewed, particularly Unionists, responded in a "parrot-like" fashion, indicating they had been coached on what answers to give (Ellingson 1977:263–265). It is likely that the idea of a national identity, either Eritrean or Ethiopian, was not well-developed among some groups and, presumably, in remote areas much of the controversy would have been meaningless. It may be noted, however, that European powers originally favored a division of Eritrea that would have united part of the region with Sudan and part with Ethiopia. This proposal was rejected by all political parties in Eritrea, regardless of their position on independence or unification with Ethiopia, indicating some sense of Eritrea as a cohesive unit.

Federation was arranged by the UN in 1950; Eritrean nationalist discourse presents it as an imposition to further the joint interests of the U.S. and its Ethiopian ally. Most texts arguing for Eritrean independence reproduce the 1952 speech made by John Foster Dulles, later U.S. Secretary of State, to the UN Security Council: "From the point of view of justice, the opinions of the Eritrean people must receive consideration. Nevertheless, the strategic interest of the United States in the Red Sea basin and considerations of security and world peace make it necessary that the country has to be linked with our ally, Ethiopia" (quoted in Bereket 1980:58).

Clearly, independence for Eritrea was not in the interests of external powers. The U.S. sought to secure control of a strategic communications base in the Eritrean capital, Asmara, while Ethiopia wanted access to the sea. In the face of what it perceived as majority Eritrean support for independence, the U.S. pushed for federation to achieve its own goals in the region. Ethiopia regarded federation as a pretext for annexation and immediately began to violate the terms of the arrangement by banning language rights, political freedoms, and trade union activity in what had been intended as an autonomous Eritrea.

The historical narrative constructed by Ethiopian nationalists states that in 1962, the Eritrean Assembly voted to dissolve the UN federation and become fully reintegrated as a province of Ethiopia. Eritrean nationalists, however, challenge this and claim that Ethiopian authorities coerced the vote or that no vote took place at all and that a declaration was simply read out by representatives of the Ethiopian Crown. Whereas Ethiopian discourse claims that Eritreans approved of federation and then voted for its abolition a decade later to rejoin Ethiopia, Eritrean nationalists argue that federation was first imposed against majority opinion and later illegally abrogated so that Ethiopia could exercise direct control: "The mechanics were simple: the Eritrean assembly—many of whose members by this time were virtually handpicked—was pressured into accepting a speech from the throne that announced the federation was dissolved. The assembly was surrounded by units of armed forces and police, and there were machine guns inside the building when the 'vote' was taken. Those who stayed away, or walked out in protest, were arrested and beaten" (Bereket 1980:62).

Eritrean protests to the UN were ignored and an armed independence movement emerged as a response to increasing Ethiopian repression. Following a civil war created by ethnic, ideological, and regional contradictions, the Eritrean Liberation Front (ELF) was superseded by the Eritrean People's Liberation Front (EPLF), which formed the Provisional Government of Eritrea in 1991.

Recent works argue that Eritreans were denied the right to self-determination, that federation was improperly imposed and was a violation of the UN Charter; they demonstrate that Ethiopia consistently violated the arrangement and argue that annexation was illegal because only the UN could modify the federation (Bereket 1989; Fenet 1988; Keller 1988; Okbazghi 1991; Serapiao 1987; Semere 1987; Tekie 1983). Bereket (1983) notes the UN Commissioner's explicit stipulation that the UN had the right and duty to address violation of the federation and draws a parallel with Western Sahara, where the International Court of Justice ruled in respect of self-determination. The Permanent Peoples' Tribunal (1984) and the International Commission of Jurists (1981) concurred, but the UN continued to ignore Eritrea.

While some Ethiopian nationalists dispute this version of history and argue that Eritrean issues legitimately became an internal Ethiopian concern, others acknowledge irregularities. Yet many of the latter claim that, regardless, historical and cultural links require the two regions to remain united. For the most part, Ethiopian nationalists have ignored points of international law and concentrated on producing versions of the past which argue that Eritreans favored unification or that no national identity existed among Eritreans.

Support for independence did grow after 1974 among highland Christians who were formerly aligned with Ethiopia. However, Ethiopian nationalists ignore the existence of some earlier highland opposition to linkage and extrapolate from the presence of religious divisions to argue that no sense of national identity existed. This implicitly proposes that nationalist consciousness must emerge fully constituted and fails to recognize that it develops through various stages. Taking unionist supporters as an example, one finds a substantial shift in opinion after federation. Soon after implementation, much support for unity was lost and disillusionment with federation was evident at the highest levels among those who had advocated union with Ethiopia. Greenfield finds it remarkable that "one of the strongest nationalist parties in Africa could so shift in its fundamental emphasis, with the subsequent encouragement of separatism, to a degree which was later seriously to embarrass the Ethiopian government" (1965:305).

Mesfin does note the defection of Tedla Bairu, former Unionist Party leader, to the ELF but treats this as an aberration for which Tedla was execrated, rather than acknowledging that public opinion had changed dramatically. He says Tedla was ridiculed as "Sheik Tedla" but does not indicate where this name originated or who used it. As public opinion shifted, Ethiopian representatives likely would have attempted to portray Eritrean nationalism as ethnically based and exploit existing divisions. Similar tendencies have carried over into contemporary Ethiopian discourse. Yet regardless of whatever degree of nationalist sentiment existed before federation, it is clear that such a consciousness has developed now and cannot be disregarded.

Nationalist Mythologies

Nationalist movements create their own mythologies, organizing symbols and key incidents, real or invented, into narrative forms that evoke emotional resonance. In general, the narrative of Eritrean nationalism has a different, more recent historical emphasis than that of Ethiopian nationalism, with its emphasis on ancient history and its idea of a state that has existed for thousands of years. As noted, Eritrean identity is regarded as a product of the shared experience of colonial occupation; Eritrean nationalist discourse has emphasized creation of an independent state in the future rather than concentrating on the glory of the distant past.

However, while Eritrean nationalism generally has a more recent focus that concentrates on the history of the region since the Italian occupation, there are some examples of an appeal to a more ancient history. For example, the EPLF's monthly English-language publication, *Adulis*, takes its name from an ancient port on the Red Sea coast. The first issue, published in 1984, explains the publication's title:

> The choice of Adulis as the name for this magazine is befitting. Adulis is the historic name for the 3000-year-old ancient port built by the Ptolomaic Greeks on the Gulf of Zula, about 50 km. south of Massawa, the main Eritrean port on the Red Sea. The town that had emerged and flourished around it, today buried and in ruins, was the center of commerce and the meeting place of the old civilizations of the time.

> Within the framework of modern history, the name Adulis for the magazine that speaks in the name of the Eritrean struggle symbolizes civilization, that is, the ancient era, the origin and heritage of our people. This evocation of their distant past is significant for the Eritrean people, especially in view of the fact that the colonizers have, through the ages, sought to destroy their identity and expropriate the best in their history. In this context, the real struggle between Ethiopian lies on Eritrea and Eritrean nationalism is starkly visible in Adulis and what it symbolizes. For Eritrean nationalism is a potent force that delves into the columns of the past, unfolds its history and builds its future.
>
> In our present struggle, Adulis signifies a revolutionary beginning that links the old with the new while the lighthouse [depicted on the cover] symbolizes the way ahead for all Eritreans struggling for liberation and working for a better tomorrow in which future generations will live in freedom, peace, democracy and prosperity. . . . The independent and democratic Eritrea of tomorrow shall enjoy justice, peace and stability.

This exemplifies the deliberate and self-conscious selection of a national symbol rooted in the ancient past and its incorporation into a vision of the future. In the second issue (August 1984), the editors claim that Adulis both predated and survived Axum, which in Ethiopian nationalist discourse signifies the antiquity and integrity of the contemporary Ethiopian state. The editors also note the Greek origins of the name Eritrea, from Erythrea, given to the region around Adulis. This is posed in explicit contradiction to Ethiopian nationalist discourse: "And what about Eritrea as a name? Spokesmen and apologists of the Ethiopian ruling classes, whether the scribes of the defunct feudal regime or the theoreticians of the Dergue, claim that 'Eritrea is a colonial name given to the territory confiscated by the Italians from Ethiopia during the period of capitalist conquest.' This claim notwithstanding, Eritrea as the name and the land, if not the people as a defined entity, predates Italian colonization."

Here, Eritrean nationalist discourse constructs a distinct territory marked off from Ethiopia, while acknowledging that no distinct Eritrean people existed in antiquity. Use of Adulis as symbol and references to the antiquity of the name Eritrea are adopted in direct opposition to the Ethiopian narrative construction of history. Both narratives appeal to the ancient past to justify contemporary political goals. However, whereas Ethiopian nationalists claim that Eritrea has always formed an integral part of a continuously existing Ethiopian empire, contrasting claims for an independent Eritrean state traceable to antiquity are not typically put forward as a justification for independence. Some assert that not all of contemporary Eritrea was subject to Abyssinian rule and that this rule was not continual where it did exist. Yet appeals to antiquity are much less a component of Eritrean discourse than of Ethiopian nationalism. For example, apart from the first two issues, *Adulis* seems to have made no further reference to antiquity and thereafter consistently focused on contemporary events. Not all Eritrean nationalists find significance in such symbols; one EPLF supporter, questioned about *Adulis*, responded, "It's just a name they picked." Thus while there are some instances of attempts to refashion the distant past, they seem more an exception than a general tendency and defining characteristic of Eritrean nationalist texts.

Mesfin attacks Eritrean nationalist discourse for this very quality, asserting that its modern emphasis and lack of historical symbols of unity signify its illegitimacy. Believing "frequent reminders of past glories are indispensable" to nationalist movements, Mesfin claims that Eritrean "cultural displays are conspicuously devoid of examples of symbolic national history" and that their contemporary emphasis demonstrates the rootless character of Eritrean nationalism (1990: 92). Yet this argument is a misreading of Eritrean nationalism. It operates strictly within the parameters of Ethiopian nationalist discourse, insisting that nationalism is only legitimate if it can refer to symbols of an identity hallowed with age. Mesfin not only overlooks the symbols of antiquity that do occur in Eritrean nationalist discourse but also the fact that national identities are fluid and subjective; furthermore, his argument begs the question of what degree of antiquity would suffice to confer legitimacy.

Mesfin fails to recognize that nationalist mythologies take different forms. For new African states, there is a choice "between the recent history of the territorial state and its predominantly political myths, and the ancient histories of the many ethnic communities and their mainly cultural myths" (Smith 1983:126). Mesfin is unwilling to conceptualize discursive construction of nationalist sentiments in any form other than that of Greater Ethiopian mythology. Ethiopian elites have sought to legitimize hegemony by claiming descent from Axum and from Solomon and Sheba. This mythology proposes that a unified state has existed for 3,000 (in some versions 4,000) years, uses antiquity as legitimation, and obscures difference and disruption. Eritrean nationalism employs a different rhetorical style. Contemporary aspects of Eritrean nationalist cultural texts, which Mesfin reads as signs of artificiality, indicate not lack of authenticity but rather a unique identity created by struggle itself.

Rather than emphasizing the deeply rooted historical identity associated with Greater Ethiopian discourse, which conflates ancient and contemporary empires, Eritrean nationalism stresses the impact of Italian colonialism and the development, through several stages, of a new identity based on common experience. Divisions within Eritrea are recognized. For example, in 1986 I interviewed Issayas Afeworki, then EPLF Vice Secretary-General, who stated that colonialism created the basis of national identity. Issayas readily acknowledged that serious divisions have existed:

> The Eritrean Liberation Front was the only front until 1970; it was horrible, just a mess, it wasn't a national organization at all. In the towns things were more cosmopolitan. No one cared about tribalism or religion but when you came to the front you find people divided along these lines. There was no leadership, only regional commands and every regional commander was an emperor in his domain. . . . Within these regions you find the people divided on ethnic grounds or even narrower clan divisions. . . . In the towns no one cared about these questions of identity and we felt that upon joining the front our first task was to fight this sentiment and overcome the struggle within the ELF between these divisions.

Seeking only a discourse based on symbols of antiquity, Mesfin (1990:92) overlooks the very expressions of national integration that he himself lists: "[descriptions of] the beauty and richness of Eritrea, condemn[ations of] military repression by the Ethiopian regime, praise [for] E.P.L.F. fighters and long[ing] for or affirm[ation of] the inevitability of national independence."

Earlier forms of ideological mobilization have been superseded by new metaphors. To ignore developmental aspects of ideological mobilization and focus on forms employed in prefederation Eritrea is to fix these as timeless structures and overlook the transformation of symbolic forms in nationalist texts. Whatever metaphors of revival existed before federation were replaced by emphasis on the new society to be constructed. To dismiss Eritrean nationalist discourse as shallow because of an absence of historical symbols is a misreading of the future-oriented ideology that typifies it.

One example is the role of women. EPLF cultural shows often portray women engaged in traditional subsistence and production activities and emphasize ethnic identity through language, costume, and hairstyle. While intended to acknowledge and express appreciation for all ethnic groups in order to secure their support, these productions do not simply appeal to tradition by endorsing subordination of women. Instead, they emphasize emancipation and challenge patriarchal authority, stressing women's participation in health care, administration, and the military and offer new emancipatory symbols.

Arguments that Eritrean nationalism has no national hero both overlook the deliberate effort to avoid the cult of personality that is central to Ethiopian leadership and fail to note that such heroes have been acknowledged. This would include not only Woldeab Wolde Mariam but also the celebrated Tigre-speaking poet, Mama Zeinab. The decision that she be portrayed on the annual EPLF publicity poster in 1988 demonstrates the changing role of women in Eritrean nationalist discourse. Furthermore, the fact that a Muslim woman was chosen to symbolize national identity weakens arguments that identity remains fractured along religious lines.

Emphasizing persistence of religious divisions, Mesfin (1990:98) characterizes the EPLF as "Christian-dominated." This contrasts with more typical Ethiopian claims that Eritrean nationalism is an Arab movement. In fact, the EPLF never presented itself as sectarian, and its former Secretary-General, Ramadan Mohamed Nur, is from a Muslim background. One might argue that the later Secretary-General, Issayas Afeworki, is from a Christian background, that he is the EPLF's key figure, and that Ramadan's leadership was simply intended to demonstrate an all-inclusive character after prolonged civil war. Such an argument, however, overlooks that the EPLF has tried to bring all ethnic groups within its administrative structures, including groups such as the Rashaida, among whom the sense of a national Eritrean identity is little-developed; EPLF representatives I have interviewed acknowledge this situation with no attempt to claim that full participation has been achieved.

In a 1983 speech, Ramadan discussed "national unity" as an issue of "continuous concern" and encouraged cooperation toward common goals:

> It is not necessary for me to once again raise and discuss the pains of past experience. Let me however reaffirm to the world that the Eritrean People's Liberation Front strongly believes in the well-being of the unity of the Eritrean people and their national forces. I hope national unity will be achieved in the coming stage. The question of unity today should not be viewed in terms of the dominance or power balance of any organization in the Eritrean field. Rather, it should focus on the need to unite all Eritrean efforts, the need to coordinate foreign activities and the need to strengthen the link between the Eritrean people and their revolution in the face of recurrent challenges from the enemy. Realizing this, the EPLF has come up with a unity proposal that invites all national forces and elements to form a national coalition. The implementation of this proposal requires tremendous efforts and struggles on the part of our people, inside and abroad, particularly the National Union of Eritrean Workers, women, students and peasants and other people's organizations. (Ramadan 1983:8–9)

As a movement seeking to represent all Eritreans, the EPLF may be expected to minimize existing divisions and the ethnic differences in Eritrea may be more problematic than is acknowledged. However, the EPLF's efforts to create national consensus do not seem to have been purely rhetorical but involved practical attempts to form a unified movement. In 1987, the EPLF merged with the ELF Central Leadership. Although this group was small, negotiations with other ELF factions followed. Positions on the central committee were opened to ELF members. Some regarded this as "obviously intended to entice other groups into the fold as it is out of all proportion to their numbers or importance" (*Africa Confidential* 1987:2). Divisions still exist and, as the Provisional Government of Eritrea, the EPLF continues to appeal for national unity; if it has not been completely successful it has been so to a remarkable extent, given the violent circumstances of the past.

Misinterpreting Eritrean Nationalism

Many view the Eritrean case as an ethnic movement (Gamst 1986; Horowitz 1985; Smith 1983). However, Eritreans are not a single ethnic group and thus the term is inappropriate. Some argue Eritrea's ethnic diversity negates any claim for national identity, but the same argument applies to Ethiopia itself. Based on linguistic differences, the EPLF recognizes nine ethnic groups in Eritrea. This multiethnic quality means the case is more appropriately seen as territorial nationalism: "'Territorial' nationalisms start from an imposed political entity, and possess no common and distinctive cultural identity to protect. . . . the projected identity is really a total innovation. It is a politically fashioned and politically oriented identity. It turns its back resolutely on the small-scale cultural identities of the traditional social order for one which promises greater possibilities of group development" (Smith 1983:217–219).

Mesfin correctly states that the issue is one of state-building in a multiethnic situation but errs by insisting this process can only occur within Ethiopia and that no separate Eritrean state is possible. He argues that Ethiopian nationalism should be supported rather than a subnational Eritrean movement. This appeal is based on a particular value judgment and political allegiance: "More than terminology is at stake here, for the adoption of terms like 'subnation' (like that of tribe) indicates a political or ideological preference, in this case for the preservation of the political status quo, based on existing state boundaries" (Smith 1983:66).

As noted, there is a fundamental difference between Ethiopian and Eritrean nationalisms. Whereas opponents of independence typically refer to Eritrea's artificiality, Eritrean nationalists readily acknowledge that no unified self existed before colonialism, arguing that this is typical of other African states. Instead of promoting an ideology of ancient historical unity and essential identity, Eritrean discourse evokes territorial origins of identity, acknowledging its relatively recent construction and development through different stages.

Colonialism and Revolution

Failure to see Eritrea as territorial rather than ethnic nationalism raises questions of colonialism. Territorial nationalisms are seen as having been formed in resistance to European colonialism. Eritrean nationalists argue that Ethiopian colonialism replaced Italian colonialism. Ethiopian nationalists reject this, relying on a narrow definition that acknowledges only industrialized countries as colonialist, and argue that (semi-) feudal Ethiopia could not be a colonial power. Kifle (1986) and Melaku (1989) dismiss claims of Ethiopian colonialism, disparaging this argument as a recent tactic advanced in the 1970s, although actually it occurs in pre-federation debates. Assuming historical association, Melaku (144) argues that Ethiopia, at a lower level of socioeconomic development, could not have colonized "its own people" in Eritrea. Whereas Eritrean nationalists question federation and annexation in terms of international law, Ethiopian intellectuals have relied on Marxist texts to analyze the nationalities question. This curious argument acknowledged the right to self-determination up to and including secession but insisted that Eritreans could not actually exercise that right. Similar paradoxical formulations have accompanied the transition of Ethiopian nationalist discourse from professions of adherence to correct Marxist lines to enthusiasm for democracy.

Melaku (147) argues that the OAU does not support the Eritrean cause because of its resolution on observing international boundaries, and "Eritrea, whose federation with Ethiopia was decided by the UN General Assembly almost a decade before Africa's decolonization process, was also considered a natural Ethiopian territory." Yet this "natural" aspect is challenged by Eritrean nationalists. Asserting such "natural" associations, Ethiopian nationalists frequently refer to Eritrean secessionism, as do the international media. Yet the term is inappropriate and Eritrea is less comparable to Biafra and Katanga than to Namibia or Western Sahara, former colonial territories where self-determination was denied and which were not termed secessionist (Nzongola-Ntalaja 1987).

Thus, whereas Ethiopian nationalism presents the federation and its later abrogation as the reunification of a former coherent whole, Eritrean nationalism regards incorporation within Ethiopia as an unresolved colonial issue; doubly so, in fact, for not only was Eritrea denied the independence claimed by other former colonies but it became subject to Ethiopian colonialism. Eritrean nationalists argue that the situation was not acknowledged because Ethiopia's government was a black regime oppressing other black people. They argue that simplistic and racist definitions of colonialism, Haile Selassie's enormous personal prestige, the OAU's location in Addis Ababa, and the self-interest of other states wary of encouraging secessionist movements elsewhere (regardless of different historical circumstances) prevented other Africans from supporting their cause.

Ethiopian opponents claim that a charge of Ethiopian colonialism is invalid because it only has been made since 1974, because Ethiopia was not an industrialized nation and therefore could not be a colonial power, and because the definition of colonialism is subjective (Kifle 1986; Mesfin 1986; Andreas 1986). In fact, Eritrean nationalists had referred to Ethiopian colonialism since 1950 (United Nations 1950b: 7). With the adoption of Marxist-Leninist rhetoric by all protagonists during the 1970s, however, the interpretation of the Eritrean case as a national or colonial issue created intense debate, much of it directed toward finding correspondence or lack of correspondence between the Eritrean situation and prescriptions in texts by Lenin or Stalin. The thesis advanced by *Challenge*, the journal of the Ethiopian Students Union in North America, and also adopted by the Derg, argued that Ethiopian control of Eritrea could not be colonial because Ethiopia was precapitalist; from this perspective, it was therefore determined that calls for self-determination in Ethiopia under the Derg were counterrevolutionary. Ethiopian Marxist discourse on the issue is characterized by assumption of pure modes of production, reification of categories, and mechanical application of terminology (Jordan 1989).

Reports written from a pro-Soviet perspective not only denied Eritreans the right to self-determination but characterized the EPLF as a "tool of imperialism." For example, the *African Communist*, the journal of the South African Communist Party, took a stand against

Eritrean nationalism; although this suggested a contradiction with its support for the comparable situation of Polisario in Western Sahara, it may be explained by Ethiopian aid to the party. For example, Azad (1983:88) maintained that the Eritrean fronts had no political program but were simply motivated by hatred of the Ethiopian revolution and that independent Eritrea would "inevitably become a reactionary state dependent upon U.S. imperialism and Arab reaction." Similarly, Jabulani Mkhatshwa (1989) claimed that the Derg sought peace but was foiled in Eritrea by "imperialist conspirators" trained, armed, and coordinated by Western powers seeking to cut off Ethiopia from the sea and thereby undermine the revolution. Mkhatshwa (1990) also claimed that the EPLF presented the conflict as an Arab-African one, demonstrated by its efforts to elicit support from Arab countries that were "unquestionable partners of imperialism." Tesfatsion Medhanie (1986), formerly affiliated with the ELF and taking a U.S. Communist Party perspective, suggests that Eritrean nationalism was progressive until the Derg's ascension, at which point it became reactionary; the foreign agent in Tesfatsion's account is the CIA, invoked to explain the persistence of Eritrean nationalism despite a change of regime in Ethiopia.

While Addis (1984) and Clapham (1990b:17) state that Western Marxists were hostile to the Ethiopian revolution, Dasylva (1984), Davis (1988), and Schwab (1985) endorse the Derg, and Bush (1985) attacks those on the left who support the EPLF. Valdes Vivo (1977) endorsed the revolution from the viewpoint of the Communist Party of Cuba. However, there has been considerable debate over whether or not a socialist revolution took place in Ethiopia. While noting that it was not led by a socialist movement, Halliday and Molyneux (1981) conclude that a revolution did occur; although expressing some ambivalence about the violent character of the regime, they suggested the potential for a transformation to socialism. Addis (1984) acknowledged the Derg's repressive character but argued that a fundamental revolution had taken place, emphasizing rural transformation. Harbeson (1988) rejects claims that the Ethiopian state was based entirely on conquest and argues for a deeper foundation that allowed regional autonomy under absolute imperial authority; he contends that although the Derg did introduce fundamental changes, such as the 1975 land reform, results have been modest and the regime did not resolve basic conflicts that threatened the existence of the state. Harbeson thus prefers the term "transformation" to revolution. While noting that the Derg was a "martial dictatorship" of questionable legitimacy that "treated land reform, the centerpiece of the revolution, more as an instrument . . . to survive . . . than as the socioeconomic foundation for future political development," Harbeson (1990:88) remained optimistic about the liberating effects of the transformation.

A more negative assessment is made by Michael Chege (1979), who argues that a revolutionary movement in Ethiopia was supplanted by a military dictatorship. Markakis (1987) found that although the revolution expanded the apparatus and activity of the state, it did not change its nature and argued that the Derg had established "garrison socialism." Political opponents such as the OLF saw the Derg as imperialist, while the Ethiopian People's Revolutionary Party (EPRP), EPLF, and TPLF dismissed it as fascist.

Keller (1984:63), attempting to examine the question in depth, concluded that the Derg was a "radical military dictatorship with a socialist orientation." Keller (1988) also situated the Ethiopian revolution in the context of an international system of dependency, arguing that the Derg adopted Marxist-Leninist ideology to create a new social myth in order to replace that of the former regime, to build a stronger state apparatus, and to implement bureaucratic control; Keller concluded that the Derg was creating a new society based on an Afro-Marxist variant of state socialism.

Clapham (1990b) maintains that a revolution did occur in Ethiopia but, like Addis (1984), suggests that analysts on the left have been unwilling to acknowledge this because of the Derg's repressive character. Rejecting Marxist analyses, he suggests that the goal of revolution is not to destroy the state but to strengthen it and use it as a means of control. In his view, rather than betraying the revolution, the Derg followed its true course by seizing state power and bureaucratic control. Yet while rejecting Marxism for its emphasis on economic factors at the expense of political ones, Clapham himself notes economic causation of changes to social and political superstructures. Like Harbeson, Clapham emphasizes the continuity of the Derg with the imperial state, placing the regime's state-strengthening initiatives in direct succession to those of the nineteenth-century emperors. However, Harbeson (1990:89) criticizes Clapham's view of revolution as simple organizational change and suggests one must also analyze debates over the nature of the post-imperial state.

In contrast to those who emphasize continuity of the contemporary state with the former empire and who suggest that the Derg strengthened the state apparatus it inherited, Amare (1989) argues that a true state has never existed in Ethiopia. In his analysis, the state was only maintained by power and no national consciousness existed in history. Loyalty was expressed only in dynastic, religious, or ethnic terms; Clapham also notes this feature of power relations in Ethiopian society and indicates that the emphasis on personal power and instrumental loyalty has created difficulties for institution-building. Challenging the image of the antique state, Amare questions its autonomy in its alliances with foreign powers.

Encoded within these debates over the nature of the Ethiopian revolution are conflicts over the nature of socialism itself. Many of those expressing ambivalence or rejecting the notion that revolution took place in Ethiopia seem to conceive of socialism in terms of its possibilities for social justice, whereas Clapham, who asserts that a true revolution did take place, seems to find in the Derg's brutality itself the image of an inevitably repressive socialism.

Some of those who rejected the Derg suggested that the most significant social revolution in the Horn had been carried out by the EPLF and that it was in fact Eritrean nationalism which "became the source and catalyst for the disintegration of feudalism and the monarchy in Ethiopia" (Jordan 1989:195). Pateman (1990:224) notes a firm relationship between the EPLF and the peasantry that suggested success, while Babu (1986:16) finds a model for Africa's future in the EPLF's social revolution. Richard Leonard (1988) gives a positive assessment of the administrative structures of the EPLF, its programs and levels of popular participation. James Firebrace and Stuart Holland (1985) endorse self-determination for Eritrea, and, noting the EPLF's remarkable achievements in administration and public services, particularly in terms of education and health care, also suggest that Eritrea could serve as a new model for development. Thomas Keneally's (1989) novel *To Asmara* presented the EPLF as working to construct a just society in Eritrea.

In North America, however, progressive groups seemed uninterested in Eritrea or the Horn in general and no mass solidarity movement developed. With a few exceptions, such as the New York *Guardian* and *Z* magazine, the alternative press ignored Eritrea. The Marxist Institute in Toronto, which sponsors lectures on various Third World issues, said they had "no interest in discussing Eritrea." Refusal to engage with the Derg's repression or with the Eritrean case provided support for claims made by Kaplan (1988b) and others that a hypocritical "ultraliberal" atmosphere prevailed among aid and humanitarian groups, in government and in the media. However, Kaplan's claims were overblown and there was no lack of criticism of the

Derg in the mass media; what gave this criticism its unique characteristic was the lack of an opponent suitable for valorization.

The Resurgence of Oromo Identity

Conflict over Eritrea was not the only regional controversy over the nature of identity and the existence of the state. The Oromo movement, although it has attracted little attention in comparison with the Eritrean situation, may be decisive for the future of Ethiopia. The Oromo constitute approximately half of Ethiopia's population. Spread throughout the country, they are the largest group speaking a mutually intelligible language, Oromiffa, and sharing unique cultural traditions. The discourse of Greater Ethiopia has relegated them to an inferior status. Ethiopian historians have suggested that the Oromo are recent arrivals to the region from Asia or the Middle East, while mythological tales attribute to them a separate origin that makes them less human than the Amhara. They are presented as the antithesis of the Amhara: Levine (1974) characterizes the contrast as one of hierarchical individualism among the Amhara and egalitarian collectivism among the Oromo. Until very recently, the Oromo were known as the Galla, a term they do not apply to themselves and one that carries "overtones of race and slavery" as well as the imputation of a lack of civilization; according to myth, the Oromo were descendants of "a high-born Amhara lady and a slave" (Donham 1986:12).

Oromo nationalism contends that "the Oromo people have been enveloped by the Ethiopian colonialism since the late nineteenth century" and argues that this should be resolved by establishing an independent Oromo state, Oromia (Union of Oromo in North America 1990). Under Amhara domination, Oromo culture was devalued and degraded, central cultural institutions such as the *gada* system were banned, and even personal names of Oromo were changed to Amharic ones. Land was distributed to Amhara settlers and the Oromo became serfs. Under Italian occupation, Amhara control of Oromo areas was undermined and some saw this as liberation from Amhara domination. However, the British reimposed Amhara control by putting Haile Selassie back into power. Revolts followed throughout Oromo regions and were suppressed with the aid of British, Israeli, and U.S. forces. When the Emperor was deposed in 1974, the Oromo hoped that the new government would rectify the oppressive features of the old regime. By 1976, however, many Oromo felt that the Derg did not intend to change essential relations of power, and in 1976 the Oromo Liberation Front (OLF) formed to fight for independence.

While Ethiopian nationalist discourse has attempted to delegitimize Eritrean nationalism by arguing that Eritrea has historically been part of Ethiopia and that there is no distinct Eritrean identity, the Oromo have been excluded from discussion. Oromo history has been overlooked and what does exist is conjectural and obscure. Typically, the Oromo have been defined in negative terms by the chroniclers of Christian Abyssinia; these negative images were taken up by Western historians who, fascinated by the idea of a long-established Christian kingdom in the Horn, misrepresented regional history by adopting the hegemonic discourse of the Amhara and ignoring the primitive Oromo (Mohammed 1990). As Jordan Gebre-Medhin (1989) has suggested, scholarly attention to Ethiopia in general has been characterized by an antimaterialist Great Tradition paradigm in which the elite culture of the Abyssinian highlands was valorized to the exclusion and denigration of peasant cultures.

Challenging the image of the primitive Oromo, historians such as Mohammed Hassan (1990) focus on the territorial expansion of Oromo peoples throughout the region in the sixteenth century, following mutual destruction of the armies of Christian Abyssinia and the Muslim forces from Harar. Mohammed describes the establishment of five independent Oromo states in the Gibe region in the nineteenth century and claims that outlines of other states were emerging elsewhere but that these developments were interrupted by Menelik's conquests. Gadaa Melbaa (1986:33) suggests that various warring Oromo kingdoms were on the verge of forming a unitary state when the process was disrupted by Abyssinian colonialism. While Ethiopianist discourse has overlooked or disparaged Oromo culture, anthropologists have presented recent revisions to the image of the Oromo as the dark, destructive antithesis of the Amhara. Asmarom Legesse's study (1973) reveals the complexity of the *gada* system, simultaneously a calendrical system, an organization of age-grades, a device for retaining oral history, and a political system; Bonnie Holcomb (1991) and Sisai Ibssa (1990) argue that *gada* provides principles for a democratic society in an independent Oromia. Yet Gebru (1991) states that *gada* is only practiced in Borana now and that the geographic dispersal of the Oromo has entailed cultural differentiation and varying degrees of assimilation, while Clapham (1990b:26) suggests the "near impossibility of defining any conception of 'being Oromo.'"

Such interpretations do not simply assess the past but are contemporary political interventions. Ethiopian nationalist discourse rejects the idea of an independent Oromo state as a fantastic and unworkable notion, contending that since a state never existed in the past it cannot exist in the future. However, Oromo nationalism argues that an Oromo area was recognized by Amhara rulers and that this area can form the basis of a new state. Mohammed's effort to restore Oromo history is part of the contemporary struggle to create a new national identity, and although he appeals for unity and equality within Ethiopia, his historical revision has provided support to calls for establishment of independent Oromia. Gebru (1990:151) rejects these appeals as constructions erected in a "historical void" and dismisses Oromia as an abstraction relating to neither "recent past experience nor to . . . prevailing objective conditions." The EPLF and Ethiopian opposition groups such as the All-Ethiopia Socialist Movement (MEISON) accepted the Oromo right to self-determination, including the right to establish an independent state, but also indicated their preference for resolving the issue in the context of a unified, democratic Ethiopia.

Oromo nationalist discourse attacks the image of Ethiopia as a long-unified state that survived European colonialism. Holcomb and Sisai (1990) argue that European powers supported Menelik's rise to achieve their own aims and establish a dependent colonial state that would serve the ends of various imperialist powers. Their thesis is advanced in opposition to historical notions of Ethiopia as an exceptional African state that resisted colonialism. They maintain that European powers encouraged consolidation of an Ethiopian state because none could completely dominate the region and the created entity could serve as a buffer to prevent war and fragmentation while allowing access to resources and transport routes. As a dependent colonial state, Ethiopia was sustained and restructured according to European interests that encouraged conquest of weaker regions. As do Eritrean nationalists, Oromos reject the definitions of colonialism used by the Derg and Ethiopian Marxist intellectuals, arguing that these allow Ethiopian discourse to cloak historical subjugation of other peoples:

> Oromia is now a colony of Ethiopia. It is a colony because it has been conquered, and annexed by alien force. What does this mean exactly? It means that the occupying alien force, the Abyssinian colonial force, forcefully penetrated the country by military means, evicted the indigenous people, occupied the territory and built garrisons in the midst of the land. Once the conquest and occupation was accomplished, settlement was conducted from those garrisons which became subcenters for control. As settlement was carried out, institutions began to be developed: such as the legal system, the police, the courts, the school system and so on. Each one of these new institutions re-

placed specific functions of the indigenous Oromo socioeconomic system known as *Gada* and its institutions . . . but toward different objectives. The replacement was the *Neftegna-Gabbar* system, which was a dependent colonial form of social organization that combined some Abyssinian and some European features (Sisai 1990:3–4).

Triulzi (1983) notes that whether or not one accepts the colonial nature of the Ethiopian empire, it is perceived as such by those dominated by the state. Andreas (1986) summarily dismisses the experiential aspect as "a purely subjective criterion . . . [that leads to] anarchy." In addition to mechanical Marxism and denials of experience, such dismissals project colonial domination as specifically European, and both Oromos and Eritreans have charged that racism prevents accurate assessment and condemnation of black colonialism.

The rewriting of history entails reconceptualization of significant events such as the battle of Adwa. Rather than as a key symbolic event in African history—the triumph of Africans over a European colonial army—the event is reinterpreted as a proxy battle, an indirect confrontation between Britain and France. Processes of modernization and centralization carried out by successive emperors since the mid-nineteenth century are reconceptualized as creations of European powers acting in their own interests. The emperors themselves, elevated to semidivine status by the *Kibra Negast* and hailed as progressive modernizers in Great Tradition scholarship, are dismissed as mere functionaries. Ethiopian resistance is redefined as collusion. Even the central image of Ethiopian nationalist discourse, of Ethiopia as an ancient independent state, is here presented as an invention of European ideology, designed to support boundary claims and prevent expansion by rival powers.

The Tigrayan Struggle

Tigrayans, in northern Ethiopia, trace their descent from the ancient empire of Axum. Ullendorf (1973:33) regards the Tigrinya-speaking peoples of the highlands as "the authentic carriers of the historical and cultural traditions of ancient Abyssinia" and asserts a complete ethnic affinity on both sides of the Tigrayan-Eritrean border. While acknowledging use of the Tigrinya language in both Tigray and Eritrea, Eritrean nationalists claim that considerable cultural differences exist between the two regions.

Tigrayan nationalists dismiss claims of cultural uniformity and territorial integrity of Ethiopia as "forced unity"; in contrast to Levine's (1974) image of a culture area forming an organic whole, this discourse uses the image of "a mismatch in a patch work which is either due to incompatible patterns or the use of materials with different textures" (Solomon 1983/84:5). Rejecting the idea of "natural continuity and evolution," Tigrayan nationalism offers a version of history as constituted by breaks and disruptions, conquests and subjugation; in place of a continuously existing state, Tigrayan nationalism constructs "Ethiopia" as an ever-changing entity, a signifier with a number of historically different referents. This discourse asserts that "Tigray, with parts of Eritrea, had a separate existence from antiquity to the time of the fall of Axum" and that therefore there is no basis for referring to Axum as part of "Ethiopian" history: "The history of Axum is the history of Tigray and the southern part of Eritrea" (ibid.:7).

Tigrayan discourse argues that, following the defeat of the Zagwe king Ne-aukuto Le'ab in 1270 by Yikunno Amlak, supposedly a descendant of Axumite royalty and the founder of the Solomonid dynasty among the Amhara, there ensued centuries of warfare and only tenuous rule over areas conquered by the Amhara. Tigray is presented as autonomous in this period, apart from payment of tribute. Following the destructive wars of the sixteenth century, there was "an upsurge of Oromo nationalism" that caused the Amhara to retreat to Gondar, where they came under the authority of Tigrayan ruler Michael Sihul (ibid.:8).

During the Era of the Princes, no unified state existed and local warlords sought control; Emperors Teodros and Yohannes were both from Tigray, a rival for power with the Amhara of Shoa. Solomon claims that Menelik, king of Shoa, accepted Italian control of Eritrea and urged Italy to attack Yohannes, concluding, "It is a travesty of history that the Shoans who ceded Eritrea to Italy and recognized Assab as a colony purchased by Italy from the Sultan, should now be fighting to keep it as part of the empire" (10).

After Yohannes's death, Menelik took power and "was determined to destroy Tigray" (ibid.). The region came under Shoan control and was deliberately underdeveloped to weaken rivals. A 1943 revolt, known as *Weyane*, was launched by a coalition of local aristocrats, peasants, and pastoralists adversely affected by the centralizing initiatives of Haile Selassie, who suppressed the rebellion with British aid. In 1975 the TPLF was formed and began what it termed the second *Weyane*, using historical memory as a means of mobilizing against contemporary grievances and of constructing nationalist sentiment.

However, the goals of Tigrayan nationalism went through rapid evolution. In the midst of violent clashes with other opposition movements in the area, internal differences over the nature of the Tigrayan struggle as an issue of secession or regional autonomy, as well as over local representation, were resolved by executions (Gebru 1991:217).

Considering themselves Ethiopians, Tigrayans called for a united front to overthrow the Derg and install a democratic government. Several groups, particularly the OLF, remained wary, fearing that the TPLF sought to dominate this front and whatever government would follow the Derg. The OLF criticized the TPLF for creating its own organization among the Oromo; it saw the TPLF's actions as political ventriloquism, forming an organization it could manipulate for its own objectives, comparable to the earlier creation of the Oromo People's Democratic Movement and the Oromo People's Democratic Organization by the Ethiopian opposition movements, MEISON and the EPRP, respectively:

> On the nature of the Ethiopian state, the OLF holds that it is an empire in which the conquered Oromo have the status of colonial subjects and that they are entitled to the right of self-determination while the TPLF reckons Ethiopia from the conquest of the Oromo and thus opposed the OLF view. . . . To the OLF the exercise of the right of self-determination is an inalienable right of our people to the fulfillment of which our Front is committed as a matter of priority and it holds that it is the Oromo people and only the Oromo who should determine its own political future. The TPLF found this unacceptable and insisted that the OLF set its priority along the TPLF lines and to work for "unity" of Ethiopia as determined by the TPLF (Oromo Liberation Front 1990:19).

The EPLF (1985) and the TPLF (1985) also debated the issue of a united front and the right of nationalities within Eritrea to form their own states.

In 1989, the TPLF and some of its allies formed a coalition, the Ethiopian People's Revolutionary Democratic Front (EPRDF), and extended military activities into the highland regions of Gondar, Wollo, and Shoa. In 1991, the EPRDF took control of Addis Ababa and established a provisional government. While it announced a policy of democracy and self-determination for nationalities, some Oromo charged that the new government merely substituted Tigrayan rule for that of the Amhara. The politics of national identity also took a new twist in relations between the Eritreans and the Oromo. Whereas past relations had been mutually supportive, Oromo nationalists charged that the EPLF was assisting the EPRDF to oppress them, including restricting Oromos from key government posts, closing OLF offices and murdering OLF supporters. Writing in the Oromo publication *Qunnamtii Oromia*, Galaanaa Abbaa Gadaa (1992) charged that the EPRDF was actually an EPLF creation, while Falmattuu Biyyaa (1992) insisted that the Eritreans were "Abyssinians at heart," dedicated to asserting hegemony over the Oromo. The claims are ironic not only in ascribing to Eritreans the identity they had long contested but also because some Ethiopian nationalists had accused the EPLF of creating the OLF in order to divide Ethiopia. That is unlikely, although many Oromo acknowledge a key contribution to the resurgence of Oromo identity made by Eritrean anthropologist Asmarom Legesse's (1973) study of the *gada* system.

This presents the broad outlines of a number of conflicting narratives of history and identity, narratives that will structure the future of the region. These cases, however, do not exhaust the full array of such narratives. For example, some of the Afar people who live along the Red Sea coast in Eritrea, Ethiopia, and Djibouti have sought their own state; other Afars think their interests would be better served within a unified Ethiopian state while still others engaged in joint operations with the EPLF against the Ethiopian government. The Ethiopian government, in its 1976 National Democratic Revolution Program, resolved to create an autonomous Afar region, as well as autonomous areas in Tigray, Eritrea, an Amhara region, Oromo, and Somali regions. These resolutions were never fully implemented and were rejected by the nationalist movements in Eritrea and Tigray. The EPLF saw the Derg's creation of an Afar region as an attempt to split Eritrea and weaken the drive for independence. The tactic was compared to the Derg's manipulation of ethnic divisions elsewhere in Eritrea, by attacking Nara ("Baria") villages but not those of the rival Kunama, who sometimes assisted the Ethiopian military. The EPLF dismissed ethnic divisions within Eritrea as insignificant and argued that there is no case for establishment of an Afar state just as there is no historical reason for establishment of independent states in Tigray or by the Oromo.

Identity and History

Anthropology has recently turned to the examination of history and identity (O'Brien and Roseberry 1991; Tonkin, McDonald, and Chapman 1989). For example, James Clifford (1988), witnessing a

Boston court case attempting to determine claims of continuously existing tribal identity among the Mashpee Indians, noted the clash of two competing histories. Similarly, although in a much more complex fashion, nationalism in the Horn is contested in conflicting versions of the past and in different discourses of identity. The terms of the Greater Ethiopia discourse, the very basis of Ethiopian identity, are challenged by counter-discourses of Eritrean and Oromo nationalism and by some versions of Tigrayan and Afar nationalism. A number of these narratives are in direct opposition, each threatening the essential, authentic self that is the central aspect of the others. Concession or compromise threatens a loss of essence and endangers the authentic self. For example, Eritrean and Oromo nationalists do not wish to be incorporated within a broader Ethiopian identity, but the independence of Eritrea or Oromia is seen as a threat to the integrity of the Ethiopian self, an attempt to diminish and split the unity of the ancient state.

In particular, attempts to incorporate Eritrea within Ethiopia have led to a crisis of unity within Ethiopia itself (Hobsbawm 1990:154) and a questioning of national identity. As noted, Ethiopian nationalist discourse asserts complete cultural homogeneity between Eritreans and Ethiopians. This is clearly inaccurate, considering the various linguistic, ethnic, and religious differences in Eritrea itself, as well as in Ethiopia. Such assertions of shared cultural identity are part of a misreading of Eritrean nationalist discourse and an attempt to shift the basis of that nationalism from political to ethnic issues. If ethnic movements base their legitimacy on claims of cultural distinctiveness that mark them off from their neighbors and make the case that the establishment of a separate state is necessary for the survival of those distinct cultural traits, then a demonstration of shared culture may delegitimize claims for independence.

At the same time, Ethiopian nationalists reverse the argument to claim that there is no distinct Eritrean identity because Eritrea includes various ethnic groups. In rejecting claims for ethnic distinction and for independence based on such distinctiveness, some Ethiopian intellectuals argue that nationalism itself is a Eurocentric notion, which must be rejected as a foreign ideology (Andreas 1986). However, the characterization of nationalism in this case refers to ethnic nationalism derived from Herder's ideas, rather than territorial nationalism, and the argument is thus a misrepresentation of Eritrean nationalist claims. The Eritrean independence movement has not presented itself as an ethnic movement but instead promotes a panethnic national identity that is shared equally by all groups in Eritrea.

Therefore, the Ethiopian attempt to negate the Eritrean ethnic self is misplaced, an attempt to refute a claim that is not advanced by those to whom it is imputed. The Tigrayan and Oromo nationalist movements do have an ethnic dimension, although the former moved through several phases from stressing a distinct Tigrayan identity to the need for an integrated, multicultural Ethiopia. As noted, the latter has been interpreted by Oromo nationalists as an attempt to crush the expression of their own cause through a variant of the same Abyssinian hegemony the EPLF and TPLF claimed to oppose.

Adding further irony, Ethiopian nationalist discourse, having stressed the Ethiopian character of Eritrea in order to dismiss claims of ethnic distinction, itself conjures up such a distinction in order to delegitimize the independence movement from another perspective, by emphasizing the Arab character of the Eritreans. As noted, the core of the Ethiopian Great Tradition has long been linked with Christianity. In the discourse of Ethiopian nationalism, notably in a famous circular letter of 1891 issued by Menelik describing Ethiopia as "a Christian island surrounded by a sea of pagans," identity is defined in religious terms and presented as threatened by encircling Muslim cultures (in Rubenson 1978:393). As part of the attempt to negate its validity, Eritrean nationalism is represented as an Arab-inspired attempt to destroy the integrity of Ethiopia. The argument not only invokes the historical unity of Greater Ethiopia but also emphasizes the element of Christianity as a defining characteristic of the state.

Yet this creates a paradox within the discourse: while Ethiopian nationalist texts stress that it is the alien, Arab character of Eritreans that causes them to wage secessionist war, this character must be simultaneously shown to be superficial so that Eritrea can be presented as having been an integral part of the state throughout history. The Arab dimension is consistently stressed so that Eritrean nationalism can be portrayed as invalid, externally created and, above all, "artificial"; but it is also denied in order to preserve the idea of a national Ethiopian essence. Whereas Italian influences must be dismissed as superficial in order to reject Eritrean claims of a fundamental transformation and creation of a new identity, the Arab influence is stressed in order to prove the nonauthentic character of Eritrean nationalism and to play upon Ethiopian fears concerning the Muslim threat to Christian identity. Thus there is a tension created in the discourse that simultaneously insists on the sameness and the difference of the Eritreans.

Similarly, racism and cultural arrogance shown toward the Oromo, long regarded as primitive, backward, and inferior to the Amhara, is cloaked by assertions that Oromos are fully accepted as Ethiopians so that claims for a separate Oromia can be delegitimized. Here the essential opposition has been posed as order and chaos. In Amhara narrative constructions, victory over the Oromo is presented as the establishment of order, while Oromo versions of the conquest portray it as the imposition of an alien culture. Scholars such as Levine (1965) and Clapham (1990b) emphasize the permeability of Amhara identity, the ease with which one can pass as Amhara by speaking Amharic and adopting an Amharic name, and suggest that Amhara culture furnishes an open, unifying mechanism for the creation of a national identity. Yet those whose cultures have been devalued by Amhara hegemony emphasize the power relations inherent in such a national identity, the necessity to commit cultural suicide, and the inability for non-Amhara to ever fully succeed.

Whereas Ethiopian nationalism asserts essential similarities in the case of Eritrea, dismissing nationalist sentiments as alien and superficial impositions, the Oromo have been conceived as radically other. The Amhara have seen themselves as engaged upon a civilizing mission among primitive peoples; the Oromo have been regarded as savage and warlike invaders, the antithesis of Amhara culture. Until recently, this has been accepted in Western scholarship. Levine (1974) argues that the Oromo (to whom he applies the derogatory term "Galla") had no sense of unified identity as Oromos, let alone as members of a multiethnic state, but rather that their loyalties were to their own particular "tribal" group or even to a particular unit within their system of age-grades.

Just as nations are assumed to go through stages comparable to periods in the life of individual people, nationalism is typically accompanied by assumptions of a characteristic personality type somehow believed to be associated with the nation itself (Handler 1988). In the Horn, numerous stereotypes of self and other are promoted. For example, Donham (1986) lists derogatory Amhara proverbs about the Oromo; at least one of these ("Even if you wash them, stomach lining and a Galla will never come clean") is also used by Eritreans in reference to Amharas. Ethiopians may regard Eritreans as selfish troublemakers, while the latter describe the former as untrustworthy, compulsively deceptive liars. Both Korten (1971) and Levine (1965) suggest that the Amhara personality is motivated by a strategy of advancing oneself at the expense of others and that this personality type shows limited scope for cooperation and compromise. Babile Tola (1989:4) argues that violence is the traditional method of rule in Ethiopia at every level, between Emperor and subject, men and women, parents and children, and that "murder or violence has been inculcated into the system, into the national psyche and socio-cultural heritage." At a 1990 Oromo conference in Toronto, one participant suggested that Amhara are warlike and aggressive because they are beaten by their parents, while Oromo are peace-loving and egalitarian, an inversion of the Amhara stereotype of the Oromo. Some Amhara informants are enraged at such suggestions, rejecting the idea that parents beat their children and so on; others agree with the assessment but point out that such an orientation is necessary to survive in a harsh world. Quite apart from any validity to such generalizations, the point is that these discourses of national identity encourage the tendency of opponents to essentialize the other.

Ethiopia in Academic Discourse

Contrasting narrative constructions of history and competing versions of identity in the Horn have spawned external discourses. In turn, nationalists seize upon these discourses to legitimize and further their own claims. Examination of competing historical narratives used by Ethiopians and by those who reject Ethiopian identity cannot ignore the Western images of Ethiopia and the significance that Ethiopia has had for other Africans. Ethiopian and foreign discourses have fed upon each other and have been formed in opposition or reaction to one another.

Academic discourse on the Horn, growing out of philological concerns, a focus on the Semitic roots of the Great Tradition of highland Abyssinian culture, and the hagiographic chronicles of the royal court, accepted and reinforced the narrative of Greater Ethiopia, as exemplified in some key texts. For example, Edward Ullendorf's study emerges from the tradition of Semitic studies and is firmly fixed on the role of the highland Abyssinian peoples; he dismisses the Oromo:

> The Gallas had little to contribute to the Semitized civilization of Ethiopia; they possessed no significant material or intellectual culture, and their social organization differed considerably from that of the population among whom they settled. They were not the only cause of the depressed state into which the country now sank, but they helped to prolong a situation from which even a physically and spiritually exhausted Ethiopia might otherwise have been able to recover far more quickly (1973:73).

The Oromos are portrayed as drawing a reign of darkness over Ethiopia, a time of isolation, stunted intellectual development and xenophobia. They are essentialized as pure negativity, contrasted with the purposeful expansion of the Amhara: "Not until the advent of King Theodore in the mid-nineteenth century does Ethiopia emerge from her isolation. Only then, in her rediscovered unity under the Emperors John, Menelik, and Haile Sellasie, does the country find its soil and genius again, its spirit and its sense of mission" (ibid.:75).

Rubenson's work, significant in modern Ethiopian historiography, accepts as given the unity of Ethiopian national identity and argues that it was this ideology, rather than features of its geography as earlier historians had claimed, which allowed Ethiopia to remain independent during the European "Scramble for Africa."

Echoing Ethiopian officials who justified federation with Eritrea on claims of cultural uniformity, Levine (1974) argues that cultural differences within Ethiopia are superficial and that more factors unify the people of Ethiopia than divide them. Adopting an implicit psychological model that mirrors that of Africanist discourse in general, Levine acknowledges enthusiasm for Amhara culture, portraying it as the ordering genius of Ethiopian civilization and representing the Oromo as agents of chaotic, darker forces. Levine's theoretical approach displaces key issues of power, conquest, and domination. Regarding the nineteenth-century Abyssinian conquests, he argues that "the question whether this imperial expansion was basically a subjugation of alien peoples or an ingathering of peoples with deep historical affinities" is best answered by the latter possibility. This perspective, he feels, corrects the idea of an "arbitrary empire" and indicates the long history of interaction among those included in the boundaries of the present Ethiopian state: "Traumatic though they were for most of the peoples subjugated, these conquests have been judged beneficial in several respects: they bolstered Ethiopia's position as an independent African power, greatly reduced the intertribal warfare and brigandage that had prevailed in the conquered areas, and paved the way for bringing an end to the slave trade in Ethiopia" (1974:26).

Levine conceptualizes Ethiopia as a single cultural area with a unified identity. He notes thirty-two shared cultural traits to justify this characterization. However, these traits are extremely general (e.g., "Annual calendar of religious ceremonies") and are found throughout a much broader region ("Practice circumcision," 'Strongly pejorative image of women,") so that delineation of a culture area corresponding to the boundaries of the Ethiopian state is questionable. In acknowledging that these cultural affinities also occur outside the state's borders, Levine does indicate the "arbitrary" character of the empire.

The assumptions underlying Levine's analysis are challenged by discourses produced by subjugated peoples. Eritreans, Oromos, and Tigrayans insist that they have been dominated by the Ethiopian empire and that their histories and cultural traditions have been suppressed by the Amhara. Narratives of nationalism constructed by these groups reject any notion that their incorporation into the empire should be described in so neutral a term as an "ingathering." For example, Amare (1989:492) describes "an empire created and preserved by violence, seething with hatred and tormented with conflict." Similarly, the "beneficial" aspects of conquest detected by Levine have been less apparent to those subjugated: "Under the colonial system Oromo people have been arrested and tried in Amhara courts. Many were convicted and sentenced to death. The brutality displayed in putting them to death is unbelievable. No people have ever been subjected to persecution that the Oromo have undergone as a result of Ethiopian colonialism" (Union of Oromo in North America 1990:1).

In general, works challenging traditional assumptions of a historically unified Ethiopia have been dismissed as polemical tracts unworthy of serious consideration. Yet the ostensibly objective discourse of Greater Ethiopia is rooted in an antimaterialist paradigm with its own political orientation:

> Camouflaged as an academic problematic, the Greater Ethiopia thesis is a brilliant intervention at the ideological level for justifying the continued existence of the Ethiopian empire. If the core of Ethiopian civilization was originally located in Eritrea, then Eritrea can be regarded as an organic unit of Ethiopia. In turn, the struggle for Eritrea's independence can be termed "unnatural" and secessionist. Further, the expansion of the Shoan-Amhara rule to the south can be viewed as a positive step. In this view, Ethiopia's Great Tradition was only confronting and destroying the endless reproduction of the prehistoric *Gadda* system; absorbing and introducing the Oromo people to a higher civilization. (Jordan 1989:8–9)

Only recently has academic attention turned to consideration of other cultures in the region and begun to question fundamental assumptions of traditional scholarship. However, texts that question Ethiopia's essential unity remain under suspicion.

Rhetoric of Authenticity

Appeals to an essential Ethiopian identity are used not only to vilify Eritrean nationalism and to reject the colonial argument but are a rhetorical tactic to dismiss inconvenient interpretations. Ethiopian nationalists deploy notions of identity and difference to reject any challenge to unity and territorial integrity. Just as Eritrean nationalism is portrayed as an Arab creation, skeptical scholarship is dismissed as illegitimate interference. Andreas (1986:60) castigates "foreigners" for promoting Eritrean nationalism. Mesfin (1990:79, 100) attacks "foreign commentators" who "cynically . . . [and] thoughtlessly preach the break-up of Ethiopia." Negussay (1988:111–120) berates "ballpoint mercenaries . . . lumpen academics [and] lying 'historians' abroad . . . who made a case for Eritrean rights to independence." While "western observers" are cited approvingly if they endorse Ethiopia's territorial integrity, unacceptable conclusions are dismissed as alien impositions and plots to divide Ethiopia. Underlying such arguments are appeals to authenticity and xenophobia. Eritrean nationalism is characterized as artificial, as contagion, a foreign virus threatening the (Ethiopian) national body politic.

Relying on the same conspiracy theories to which he ostensibly offers an alternative, Mesfin demonizes western observers as capriciously advocating Ethiopia's disintegration. He exclaims, "Let the continent write its own history!" (1986:16), appealing for an authentic narrative, written by an African subject uncontaminated by foreign ideas. Yet subaltern discourses are themselves divided, and the notion that there exists a single African subject with one vision of the past or the future is untenable. Mesfin does not want Eritreans to write their own history. They must allow Ethiopian intellectuals to write it for them or reinscribe those statements by accepting membership in an Ethiopian state. After an extended critique, Melaku (1989) recommends that Eritrean independence be supported because of its expediency, but few Ethiopian nationalists agree. Demands for Eritrea's inclusion within a future Ethiopian "democracy" are more typical and the term is frequently used by those who seem to have no intention of guaranteeing democratic freedoms. For example, Dawit (1990) characterizes his work in the Derg as being "in the front line of the struggle for freedom, democracy and unity in Ethiopia," but clearly his priority is on "unity," even if this must be forcibly imposed on those who do not wish to partake of it.

This "democracy" permits no decision making on basic issues but allows only acceptance of a single possible future and a single (Ethiopian) identity. In the past, few Ethiopian proponents of "democracy" supported calls for a referendum in Eritrea on national identity, as held in Quebec concerning its relationship with Canada. The EPLF appealed for such a referendum, which would allow Eritreans to vote on independence, federation, or full unity, but the Derg consistently rejected it until its collapse in May 1991. The EPLF, as the provisional government, decided to proceed with a referendum after a two-year period rather than immediately declaring independence. Despite their professed enthusiasm for democracy and assertions that most Eritreans felt themselves part of Ethiopia, some Ethiopian nationalists still refused to countenance such a referendum. Yet a democratic solution requires voluntary participation, not forced unity.

Identity Crisis

Andreas (1986:25) finds nationalism essentially absurd because national identities can be internally fragmented and split into ever-smaller groups that each demand autonomy; in fact, the Derg did attempt to exploit such divisions to weaken Eritrean nationalism. Nationalism may be irrational, but this applies as readily to Ethiopian as to Eritrean identity. Despite additional challenges by Oromos, Tigrayans, and others, Ethiopian national identification remains unquestioned by many. The irrationality of nationalism is recognized only where the form of identity promoted by others is unacceptable.

Clearly, all peoples of the Horn would benefit from some type of friendly association that would replace the conflicts which have ravaged the region. The EPLF acknowledged this and stated that it would maintain equitable economic relations with Ethiopia in the future and that it had no intention of choking off Ethiopian access to the sea. While the provisional government of Ethiopia formed by the EPRDF accepted what was in fact if not in name Eritrean independence, others still insist on "unity" and "territorial integrity."

After major victories by the EPLF and TPLF in 1988, there was a surge of Ethiopian nationalism in response to what seemed the imminent disintegration of Ethiopia. This appeal was not restricted to Ethiopia's own borders; throughout North America and Europe expatriates called for mobilization in support of the motherland. There was furious activity as monarchists, remnants of the left-wing opposition, and late defectors from the Derg jockeyed for power as the regime crumbled. A myriad of coalitions and meetings formed, featuring surprising alliances as the appeal to nationalism contended with other ideological commitments. For example, one meeting held in Ottawa included representatives from MEISON, EPRP, the Ethiopian Democratic Union (EDU), and the Ethiopian government. The

EDU is dedicated to restoration of the monarchy, while the other groups share both Marxist-Leninist rhetoric and a history of violent rivalry, including gun battles in the streets of Addis Ababa.

Some Ethiopian intellectuals suggested renewed federation as a compromise that would meet the demands of both parties. The U.S., which consistently opposed Eritrean independence and supported Ethiopia's "territorial integrity," did encourage such a solution. Yet while offering a form of continued association that might mollify Ethiopian claims to some degree, the proposal had little appeal to Eritreans. Federation failed under Haile Selassie, and the Derg's attacks against the civilian population of Eritrea intensified anti-Ethiopian sentiment. Many Eritreans feel they have no reason to trust any Ethiopian government and no desire for close association.

Narrative versions of history in the Horn of Africa are in direct opposition, bringing into question the nature of Ethiopia and its continued existence. Ethiopian nationalist history, claiming a link with the ancient kingdom of Axum, emphasizes continuity, unity, and cultural identity. Opposing narrative constructions challenge these themes and emphasize conquest, subjection, and difference. History and identity are thus conceived in conflicting narratives. Ethiopian nationalism insists that identity is unchanging, that it has persisted for thousands of years, and that it must be maintained at all costs. Independence for Eritrea or creation of an Oromo state are regarded as threats to the Ethiopian national self. The narrative of Eritrean nationalism insists that identity is changing, that different identities can be created at different points in history. Oromo identity now seems to have adopted a more essentialist form, stressing cultural distinctiveness, expressed in opposition to Ethiopian identity, but this has not always been the case. The overthrow of Haile Selassie offered a chance to resolve the various national and ethnic issues but this opportunity was lost as the Derg insisted on the same claims of Ethiopian nationalist discourse.

Thirty years of continuous warfare have brought devastation to the Horn of Africa. In addition to those killed in the conflict, war exacerbated effects of drought and created massive famine, affecting millions. Such appalling events have brought Ethiopian identity to a state of crisis. Compromise is seen as a threat of annihilation of the collective self, a fear of "a dilution and eventual loss of national identity, a negation of boundaries and distinctions" (Handler 1988:49). At the same time, arguments for Eritrean independence have been rejected by other Africans who sense that a modification of Eritrea's status would be a threat to their own identity. Counter-discourses to Ethiopian nationalism have been strengthened to the very extent that the latter rejected their claims; chauvinism, rigidity, and refusal to share power exaggerated existing differences. While the TPLF sought the overthrow of the Derg, both the Oromo and Eritrean movements have been oriented toward independence. The call for establishment of an independent Oromo state is fairly recent and the extent of its appeal is not certain, but clearly it grew in response to the Derg's intransigence regarding social justice for the Oromo. While the Derg's collapse seemed to offer a second chance for Oromo participation within Ethiopia, many were disappointed by what they saw as continuation of previous policies under the new regime and doubted that a serious social transformation could be implemented that would meet their aspirations within the borders of the present state.

4

MEDIA, FAMINE, WAR

A New Discourse on Ethiopia

In October 1984, a new strand of discourse on Ethiopia was initiated by the BBC broadcast from the relief camp at Korem. Reporter Michael Buerk described the scene as "hell on earth," and televised images of famine victims gave graphic confirmation of that assessment. Following the broadcast, international media acknowledged the situation as a major news story, although the food crisis had preceded and would outlast the temporary publicity it received. In the popular imagination, Ethiopia became inextricably bound with these media images of famine.

Crisis-oriented coverage encouraged a view of famine as an event that had struck unexpectedly. In reality, it was the culmination of a slow-building disaster that had arisen over a period of years and had been predicted long before starvation occurred. Although relief agencies had approached the media repeatedly throughout the previous year, urging them to publicize the impending disaster, there was little interest in Africa, and warnings of imminent starvation were ignored. Photographic documentation of famine was available in the U.S. in September 1983 but was considered too bleak for audiences. Writer-producer David Kline's film was rejected by all major U.S. media; CBS rejected the film because the images were not strong enough and did not depict people actually dying of starvation. In Britain, David Cairns's photographs of famine victims were rejected by his editor at the *Daily Express* as "mere Oxfam posters of no news value or interest." Mohammed Amin, whose film of starving Ethiopians finally appeared on BBC and sparked unexpected public response, delayed his trip to go on safari with Brooke Shields for an episode of "Lifestyles of the Rich and Famous" (Harrison and Palmer 1986:97, 28, 100–101).

In general, Africa receives little attention from North American mass media, and the very nature of the media selected against coverage of famine. Media corporations are saturated with the values of entertainment, a category that demands the transformation of disaster into spectacle and the packaging of events into an easily consumable form determined by a repeatable cycle of meanings. In this context, Africa occupies only a peripheral position, and a complex, slow-onset African phenomenon is regarded by the media as inherently uninteresting. Thus, famine in Africa was dismissed from the news agenda because it was considered low in entertainment value.

It was only when a crisis had been reached and when truly horrifying scenes of actual starvation were available that the situation was judged significant. As with the Sahel famine in the 1970s, the media ignored available information until an established channel (BBC) acknowledged the crisis as newsworthy. At that point, there was a sudden and intensive production of texts—newspaper articles, television documentaries, radio broadcasts, books, and international pop concerts. Public response generated a demand for graphic images of starvation, which were immediately integrated into ideological discourse.

Such shared assumptions and conventions about which events are newsworthy create a standardized approach to news production. Various factors influence media coverage. Based on Herman and Chomsky's propaganda model, ideological suitability can be judged most significant; other factors include the entertainment value of mass starvation, possibilities of simplification into story form, with good and bad agents, and, for television, visual appeal. Galtung and Ruge (1965) suggest a formula for Western media coverage of foreign news. An item is most likely to become news if it concerns elite nations or elite people, if it can be seen in personal terms, and if it is negative in its consequences. Distant events are made to seem important by their relation to the West, and such events must be sensational and capable of capturing attention of viewers. Therefore, foreign news usually concerns natural disasters, violence, or changes of government. Typically, foreign events are not recorded unless they build to a crisis, in which case they function to reinforce the image of the Third World as dangerous and unpredictable. The more distant an event is, the less ambiguous it must be, requiring simplistic terms of explanation. All of these characteristics of foreign news reporting apply to coverage of the Ethiopian famine.

Accounts of television coverage of the famine suggest that the BBC film was originally selected on the basis of its visual appeal and shock value, that is, on the basis of aesthetic criteria; thus starvation was immediately aestheticized. Amin's original footage, narrated by Michael Buerk, set the terms for the discourse. For example, Buerk notes "the biblical business. People looked like those depicted in the colour illustrations in my old school Bible. Sort of sackcloth colour and a certain nobility of features. . . . Ethiopians' distress . . . engage[d] people's sympathy because they're such fine-looking people" (quoted in Harrison and Palmer 1986:118–119). Biblical associations were consistent, serving as ideological signifiers in the construction of famine as political narrative.

Similarly, the general manager of foreign news at NBC said that the "tremendous images" of starving Ethiopians led to coverage: "In other countries the situation may be just as desperate but it's not quite as graphic" (*Newsweek*, November 26, 1984). Much of the photographic coverage of the famine concentrated on sensational close-ups of the most emaciated and desperate individuals, lingering near death and too weak to brush away the clouds of flies settling on their faces. Media emphasized visual and human interest aspects of famine, excluding structural causes and explanations. Reports emphasized individual victims; generally the focus was on immediate suffering, with great demand for heart-breaking images of emaciated children.

The initial emphasis in these images was that of Africans as victims, consigned to a cruel fate in awesome numbers, helpless, and in need of the West's charity. Some Ethiopians living abroad were so embarrassed by such images that they sought to conceal their identities. Defending the sensational aspects of coverage of famine, journalists have argued that it was only these dramatic images that sparked public response. Arguably, concern might have been inspired by an earlier presentation of the situation, with a different emphasis. In any case, this intense focus on the plight of the starving at camps like Korem did have a positive effect in generating urgently needed emergency relief; unfortunately, the very nature of media coverage ensured that the focus was not a sustained one. These sensational images were also incorporated into fund-raising appeals of various charities and aid organizations. Some agencies continued to broadcast scenes of starvation long after the crisis had subsided in the areas they serviced and were accused of exaggerating the number of famine victims in order to maximize donations. Such images did create an emotional response and encouraged public donations but also helped to construct famine as an emergency that struck without warning and could be rectified by short-term relief. By continually stressing the emergency character of the famine and overlooking long-term aspects of development, such appeals may have created unrealistic expectations and the "donor fatigue" about which the same agencies would later complain.

Media insist upon novelty, or rather the semblance of novelty, as it has long been recognized that culture industries depend on "the constant reproduction of the same thing," and news items, regardless of content, are typically structured according to standard rhetorical techniques, some of which will be examined below (Horkheimer and Adorno 1972:359; Epstein 1973; Gitlin 1982; Nimmo and Combs 1985; Parenti 1986). The sensational images from Korem meant that a new discursive configuration was constructed around a situation formerly deemed to be of no interest or news value.

Therefore, a key process in the discursive construction of famine in the Horn is that of aestheticization, the packaging of famine as a shocking and dramatic crisis. Immediately after the BBC and U.S. television networks broadcast the "tremendous images" of famine victims, the mass circulation periodicals devoted cover stories to the crisis, typically featuring close-up photographs depicting the desperate faces of starving children. Fashion photographer David Bailey mounted an exhibition of photographs of starving Ethiopians at a London art gallery, and in the Ethiopian relief camps camera crews jostled for the most sensational snapshots of the famine victims. Gill (1986) describes one photographer hovering about a dying peasant, attempting to capture on film the very instant of her death. While Ethiopian peasants died in a photogenic manner and thus were considered suitable for inclusion on the news, media largely ignored famine elsewhere. Although it was a continental problem at the time, Ethiopian famine eclipsed African famine and became the focus of news reporting. In effect, Ethiopian famine became a kind of miniseries featuring a specific narrative structure and arresting images of mass starvation. However, it was not merely the visual appeal of starving Ethiopians that made Ethiopia the focus of media attention. While it may appear self-evident that television news depends on dramatic images, it is actually the case that many televised news reports feature mundane images such as politicians climbing into automobiles, so that the images themselves cannot entirely explain the nature of media coverage.

Galtung and Ruge suggest that news coverage of distant events requires unambiguous explanations. Several studies argue that media emphasized natural disaster and ignored more complicated political aspects of mass starvation. This tendency to exclude the political character of famine involves a rhetorical process that may be termed "naturalization"—a process that typified a number of reports in which famine was attributed mainly to drought. Murray (1986:3), examining 572 press reports on the Horn, finds that 59 percent "dealt only with food or famine-related issues and did not mention conflict or engage in political analysis." A further 33 percent "had food or famine-related issues as a primary focus" while referring only "in a cursory manner, to conflict or political, historical or military analysis." Thus famine is seen as a result of natural disaster in 92 percent of the articles surveyed. Investigating CBC television reports of the famine, Black (1986:7, 27) finds natural disaster portrayed as the main cause and concludes that political, social, and cultural factors "which contributed to the devastating famine were given scant media attention and for the most part were systematically omitted." Journalist Robert Kaplan (1988b) argues that the media misrepresented the situation by concentrating on drought. In his view, the media failed to recognize the political character of the famine and criticized neither the Derg's agricultural policies nor its use of famine as a weapon against its enemies.

Many reports did present famine as a result of natural disaster. For example, *Time* (November 26, 1984) described Ethiopia as suffering from "a desperate thirst for water." However, *Time* failed to point out that drought frequently occurs elsewhere but does not necessarily create famine. Naturalization ignores conditions of poverty, repression, and conflict that allow drought to be translated into famine. Reports explaining famine as a natural disaster are reductionistic and overlook a growing body of work which recognizes multiple causation of famine (e.g., Ball 1976; George 1977; Lofchie 1975). Media coverage failed to bring the long-term economic and political issues underlying famine into clear detail. However, the suggestion made by Kaplan and others that the media explained famine exclusively as a natural disaster and excluded political aspects of the situation is not accurate. Rather, coverage was arranged according to a number of identifiable rhetorical techniques and themes that constructed an ideological version of war and famine.

Contrary to Kaplan's argument, an examination of the original BBC report reveals that a political message was imbedded in the very origins of the discursive configuration. Buerk, the journalist who reported the story, comments, "[The film was] edited . . . to indicate fairly forcefully . . . that this famine was a result not only of a black government, but of a Marxist, military, black government, in a way that made me a little bit angry" (Harrison and Palmer 1986:133).

Anticommunism has been a consistent theme in Western mass media. Herman and Chomsky (1988:2) include anticommunism as an essential feature of their propaganda model of media and refer to it as "a national religion and control mechanism." Given this context, all news items are already structured by a complex of preconceptions and assumptions. It is unnecessary to invoke a model of the media as ideological apparatuses that impose new beliefs on audiences; instead the media confirm existing beliefs. During the intensified Cold War atmosphere of the 1980s, therefore, even a cursory reference to "the Marxist-Leninist government of Ethiopia" structured the interpretation of any media report. There were no corresponding references to, say, "the capitalist government of Canada." Therefore, it is clear that an ideological message exists in those media reports which, as Murray says, only refer to political issues in "a cursory manner." Lack of coverage of famine elsewhere linked famine exclusively with Ethiopia and its government. The Derg did use famine as a weapon against political opponents, but famine also gave the West a means to discredit its own enemies. Such ideological messages were not all constructed through a simple process of labelling the Derg as a Soviet ally. Analysis of coverage from a mass-circulation weekly magazine indicates some other techniques used to construct discourse on Ethiopian famine.

"An African Nightmare"

Analysis of a cover-story feature from *Newsweek* (November 26, 1984) reveals mythologizing of famine and imposition of a narrative structure. Ostensibly critical of international relations that negatively affected African food production, *Newsweek* actually emphasizes African culpability: Africans are depicted as either incompetent or greedy and the West is portrayed as a generous benefactor. The article has a pronounced anticommunist theme, asserting that "Soviet-style" agricultural policies brought disaster.

Media coverage of famine obscured actual causes of the food crisis, portrayed Africans as agents of their own disaster, and constructed African famine as an ideological parable. One objective of this version of famine and war was to delegitimize the Mengistu regime. However, lack of an alternative, ideologically acceptable ally prevented use of the standard "conflict" narrative favored by the mass media. Therefore, a variety of rhetorical devices were used to vilify the Derg and its enemies.

Newsweek's cover photograph depicts a mother and emaciated child, and names the famine "Africa's Nightmare." Inside, the title is transformed to "An African Nightmare," a slight change of emphasis but one expressing the character of the discursive configuration. Gibbon's (1929, 5:176) famous lines ("Encompassed on all sides by the enemies of their religion, the Aethiopians slept near a thousand years, forgetful of the world by whom they were forgotten") might suggest that Ethiopians would have unique susceptibilities to nightmares, but famine was no dream to its victims. Rather, the Horn has been a favored locus for Western dreams and nightmares: Herodotus's headless Ethiopians with eyes in their chests, the medieval obsession with Prester John, explorer James Bruce's rapture over what he mistakenly assumed was the source of the Nile, Rimbaud's nihilistic "nightmare" life in Aden and Harrar, where he feared becoming "an animal" like the inhabitants. In the 1980s, famine too became a nightmare for the West; however, it was not simply a particularly horrifying image of the Third World as disaster zone but also a fragment of the dreamwork of imperialism. Famine in the Horn of Africa became a sign of impending apocalyptic disaster, but this warning was interpreted in relation to the West, not for Africans.

Essentially, this nightmare involves deep anxieties over loss of control. Kaplan (1988b) makes Haile Selassie ("like some figure out of a dream") signify not just Africa but the Third World in general, assuming its appropriate place in the world order. The Derg's overthrow of the emperor and its alliance with the Soviet Union was a disruption of this order. Ethiopia, formerly one of the West's most reliable allies in Africa, was now equated with Angola, Cuba, Mozambique, and Nicaragua, and seen as another portent of loss of control in the Third World.

At this point, however, let us examine how *Newsweek* presents this "African Nightmare." News reporting constitutes a specific type of discourse with its own codes and conventions. Despite an ethic of impartiality professed by journalists, many theoretical and empirical studies conclude that news discourse is not ideologically neutral. Mass media are huge corporations, controlled by wealthy people, drawing profits from advertising revenue and sharing values with the corporate community and government (Bagdikian 1983; Herman and Chomsky 1988; Parenti 1986). Messages produced within this context have a distinct ideological orientation and are manufactured according to a number of rhetorical processes that include fragmentation, simplification, condensation, and repetition, functioning to reproduce a hegemonic vision that invites readers and viewers to recognize common sense constructed by elite authority.

Fixing the Blame

Ideology functions by establishing common sense. *Newsweek* creates this through construction of significant absences in the text and by repetition of a particular rhetorical device: a problem is raised, tension is created, then resolved by the solution offered. *Newsweek* also employs the rhetorical technique of inoculation, the admission of accidental evil to conceal continuing structural inequalities (Barthes 1972:150). The tone throughout suggests fairness and objectivity, a desire to address problems, admit to mistakes, and encourage reform. This tone of omniscience constructs the transcendental authority of mass media. Speaking authoritatively, *Newsweek* ostensibly takes an objective position, mildly chiding the West for unmet responsibilities but consistently placing the blame for famine on Africans themselves. *Newsweek* describes hordes of "lame, gaunt Africans trudg[ing] through the bush," estimating 500,000 dead in Mozambique and Ethiopia ("but the numbers are little more than guesswork") and concedes, "there is something hideously wrong about people dying of famine when others have more food than they know what to do with [and there are] mountains of food piled up in our silos and warehouses" (Watson et al. 1984:50–52). Inoculation here consists of presenting this imbalance without examining its foundations. Reassurance is immediately offered: "last week the mountain was finally moving [as] a vast outpouring of concern and generosity" flooded relief agencies. Africans are presented as passive victims and North Americans are constructed as active, charitable, and responsive to crisis.

In *Newsweek,* inoculation operates by a process in which the influence of external factors appears to be acknowledged but is actually refuted and displaced. *Newsweek* states that "in the past it was convenient to blame outsiders for Africa's problems—and with some reason" (Ng'Weno 1984:55). The slightly rueful admission that African complaints were made with "some reason" seems to indicate objectivity, balance, and willingness to acknowledge mistakes. However, this admission is defused in advance by pointing out how "convenient" it is for Africans to avoid responsibility and blame outsiders (who go unnamed). Reference to "convenient" assignations of responsibility to external factors introduces doubt about their validity. *Newsweek* consigns such indulgences to "the past." Although "it has taken African leaders quite a long time to come around to accepting the fact that many of the continent's pains are self-inflicted," *Newsweek* suggests that they now accept responsibility. Through repeated assertions that African troubles are "self-inflicted," *Newsweek* minimizes external responsibility. Essentially, Africans are presented as being to blame. *Newsweek* briefly notes that African goods bring low prices and face import barriers and chides (but again leaves nameless) "predatory multinational corporations" that dumped obsolete technologies in Africa; similarly, unspecified aid organizations are rebuked for incompetence (ibid.).

Inoculation dehistoricizes and depoliticizes discourse (Barthes 1972). Having alluded to a number of external factors, *Newsweek* leaves them unexamined: "technology" is a euphemism that frequently stands for capitalism itself; behind the signifier, "technology" is the myth of the Green Revolution and the system of neocolonial dependency. There is no specification of which technology is needed, nor any demonstration that new technology will benefit Africa more than that which is now obsolete. Absent is any discussion of how African countries are to acquire and maintain this technology. Also ignored is the question of how the poorest of Africans will be affected, as they are unable to purchase such technology; clearly, the result will be to widen the gap between rich and poor. Ostensible criticism of unnamed multinationals actually encourages increased activity to replace obsolete technology with new models. Similarly, the vague criticism of aid agencies overlooks consideration of whether negative aspects of aid relationships are matters of competence or policy. There is no mention of which agencies failed and no discussion of why warnings and appeals by some of them were ignored.

Briefly alluding to such factors, *Newsweek* negates their influence by blaming Africans: outside factors could have been mitigated if Africans had demonstrated a greater "commitment to development." The type of development to which this commitment ought to have been made remains unspecified, as do the means by which Africans might effect this, and the obstacles they might encounter. Pointing out their lack of "commitment" emphasizes the unappreciative character of Africans who have sought "convenient" scapegoats. *Newsweek* obscures external influence throughout Africa.

The passivity of unappreciative Africans who blame the West and fail to demonstrate "commitment to development" is supplemented with incompetence, dishonesty, and savagery; *Newsweek* tells readers that drought is normal in Africa but it is worsened "because of Africa's deepening poverty, booming population and abuse of the land itself. Some Africans agree that part of the damage is self-inflicted—that mismanagement, corruption and civil strife aggravate the natural disasters that have always beset their societies. . . . It is no coincidence that some of the nations suffering most from the current famine—Ethiopia, Mozambique, Chad, Angola—have been embroiled in civil war for years (Watson et al. 1984:52).

In the *New York Times* (May 12, 1990), Jane Perlez echoed the view that it was "no coincidence" that famine had struck countries "mired in long civil wars." These explanations are only partial: effects are transformed into causes, and famine is dehistoricized. Both *Newsweek* and the *New York Times* overlook the nature of the "civil wars" they disparage, including the role of superpower intervention. They also ignore Europe's underdevelopment of Africa, overlooking the process by which Africa provided cheap raw materials and labor for the West. This discourse severs current problems from their historical context: the fundamental transformation of Africa's economy under colonialism and its underdevelopment within the context of neocolonial relationships. For example, Portugal forced reductions in agricultural production in its colonies and pressured African farmers to produce cotton for sale to Portuguese companies at artificially low prices, laying the foundations for unbalanced economies that occupied precarious positions within the international economic order. A comparable instance is the French subsidization of groundnut production in Senegal to the exclusion of a diversified agricultural economy. The result was cheap oil for France but soil depletion and vulnerability to world market fluctuations in Senegal. *Newsweek* ignores persisting neocolonial relationships, local class contradictions, and the massive debt crisis that drains African foreign exchange.

Although *Newsweek* correctly notes "mismanagement, corruption and civil strife," these remain unexamined and dehistoricized, as if they are an inherent part of Africa's primitive chaos and collective masochism, its urge to inflict damage on itself, or an example of the incompetence of Africans lost without their former colonial masters. *Newsweek* fails to explain why Africa is poor, why its poverty is deepening, or why African land is abused. Having inoculated readers through an admission of imbalances that remain unexplained, *Newsweek* uses the rhetorical technique of ventriloquism to blame a dehistoricized African essence. "Some Africans" (left unnamed) "agree" that the damage is partially "self-inflicted" (Watson et al. 1984:52). The agreed-to proposition is not directly stated but exists as an unavoidable precondition imposed on discourse through a transcendent authority, reaffirmed by the same common sense it perpetuates and by unproven consensus. The African "self" that inflicts this damage goes unexamined and is presented as monolithic and undifferentiated, essential, without history. All Africans are implicated in "mismanagement, corruption and civil strife" in the absence of discussion of external influence, difference, or resistance. *Newsweek* correctly states that "it is no coincidence [that famine is worse in areas which] have been embroiled in civil war for years," but leaves unexamined the causes of these conflicts. War, like poverty, is presented as eternal in Africa, part of the essential African condition. The absence of explanation naturalizes the situation, making it part of common sense: Africa is poor and violent and will continue to be so.

Use of the technique of ventriloquism ensures that African self-incrimination continues relentlessly through *Newsweek*'s presentation of famine. A boldface section heading, "All Our Fault," is excerpted from a statement made by a Mozambican refugee in Zimbabwe, referring to Zimbabwean border patrols who must turn back the ever-increasing number of refugees: "They treat us as though the drought is all our fault" (ibid.). The difference in meaning between heading and quote is obvious; *Newsweek* transforms complaint into confession, an admission of guilt. Identification of Africans as victims and villains and North Americans as charitable benefactors is a major priority. In a section entitled "Placing the Blame" (accompanied by a photograph captioned "A pro-Mengistu mural in Addis Ababa: Many of Africa's pains are self-inflicted"), *Newsweek* says Africa's leaders "mismanaged economies, squandered national wealth and literally threw away the future as they jostled with one another for personal power and gain. When it was not greed that moved them, it was folly and gullibility" (Ng'Weno 1984:55).

Although famine was a continental problem, the media consistently condensed it into an Ethiopian issue. All African leaders are collapsed into the image of Mengistu and readers are again reminded that the Derg is "partly to blame for the severity of the disaster." This is true; however, truth is put to ideological use. *Newsweek* points out that Mengistu ignored reports of impending disaster, spent nearly half Ethiopia's gross national product on arms from the Soviet Union, and delayed famine relief until after celebrating the tenth anniversary of Haile Selassie's deposition. What *Newsweek* overlooks is that Ethiopia had issued appeals for emergency aid since 1978, that the World

Food Council and the Food and Agricultural Organization verified the crisis (although the FAO ignored the conclusions of Ethiopia's Relief and Rehabilitation Commission, and, after long delay, minimized the required amounts of emergency food), and that the Reagan administration delayed its steadily decreasing emergency relief and in 1984 attempted to stop emergency supplies to Ethiopia entirely, in keeping with its explicitly stated objective of using food aid to support foreign policy. After long delays and attempts to affix amendments that would supply aid to the Nicaraguan contras in Central America to bills on emergency relief to Ethiopia, the Reagan administration did eventually channel large amounts of food aid to the Derg. Both the Derg and the Reagan administration used famine as a weapon, a tactic apparently unacceptable to *Newsweek* only when employed by ideological enemies. *Newsweek* uses Ethiopian famine to reinforce Cold War polarities: "[Mengistu's agricultural policies] concentrated on building Soviet-style state farms—hardly a promising model, in view of the fact that the Soviets can't even feed themselves" (Watson et al. 1984:54).

Criticism of Soviet agricultural policies is a consistent anticommunist theme of the mass media (Parenti 1986:142–143); *Newsweek* neglects to mention U.S. food imports or the fact that millions in the U.S. are starving or sick because they are too poor to adequately feed themselves (George 1983:30). Through the rhetorical processes of inoculation, ventriloquism, repetition, condensation, and construction of significant absences, the message is hammered out within the ambit of racist and anticommunist discourses: Africans, particularly those who have adopted socialist policies, have only themselves to blame for the famine.

A Humanitarian Response

Having consistently stressed African culpability in creating disaster, *Newsweek* praises U.S. charity and famine relief efforts. The magazine's cover stresses that "The World Reaches Out" to solve "Africa's Nightmare," and a full third of the feature concerns the U.S. response. Several examples of individual generosity are given and *Newsweek* constructs famine as a sudden disaster to which the public responded immediately. The concern of many individuals was genuine and should not be belittled, but by emphasizing immediacy and personal solutions, the media encouraged a programmed, consumerist response, the same response generated by the Live Aid charity spectacle. *Newsweek* positions readers in a particular relation to the Third World and to the international hegemonic order by constructing Africans as victims or villains and the West as a source of charity and aid.

Having criticized Africans for bringing starvation upon themselves by deviating from established order and embracing socialism, *Newsweek* mythologizes Western humanitarianism and reaffirms hegemony by depicting the U.S. as the most active and influential agent in the crisis. The notion of charity celebrated by *Newsweek* is an important thematic constituent of common sense in the U.S., deriving from interpretations of the New Testament that see charity as a sign of the Elect, who will be hated for their efforts: "The burden placed on the recipient of charity is not only one of gratitude, it is also one of recognizing the 'despised' donor . . . as one of the Chosen" (Augelli and Murphy 1988:44). *Newsweek* includes a "Five-Point Plan for Action" by Dr. Jean Mayer, president of Tufts University, who congratulates the U.S. on the "great honor" earned by its generous response to famines (except Biafra; Mayer ignores U.S. obstruction of aid intended to relieve critical food shortages in Cambodia, Laos, and Vietnam, as well as the Reagan administration's attempt to block aid to Ethiopia). *Newsweek* adds a final note to the ideological construction of charity by pointing out that "the one conspicuous deadbeat . . . was the Soviet Union."

Employing the rhetorical technique of inoculation, *Newsweek* does acknowledge that the U.S. initially blocked relief aid to Ethiopia on the grounds that starving children there were simply "little Commies" (echoing policies in Southeast Asia) but stresses that grain is now on the way. There is a tacit admission of the political objectives underlying humanitarian concern: "The political overtones, however, are loud and clear. 'The word is out that the West delivers the food,' boasts AID administrator M. Peter McPherson" (Watson et al. 1984:54). Thus feeding "little Commies" is deemed more efficacious than starving them. Aid to Ethiopia was a response to public concern but it also reaffirmed basic founding principles of foreign aid. For example, rebuilding European capitalism in subordination to U.S. interests was a principal objective of the Marshall Plan (Kolko 1972). Similarly, Chomsky (1987:18) quotes a 1947 Joint Chiefs of Staff report advising restriction of aid to strategic countries, "except in those rare instances which present an opportunity for the United States to gain worldwide approbation by an act strikingly humanitarian"; he also notes that in 1950, Secretary of State Dean Acheson suggested "that should starvation break out in mainland China the United States should give a little food aid—not enough to alleviate the starvation, but enough for a psychological warfare advantage."

The Mutual Security Act of 1951 stated that all foreign aid must be tied to anticommunism; only Western-aligned countries were eligible. In 1957 Senator Hubert Humphrey expressed the objectives of U.S. food aid: "If you are looking for a way to get people to lean on you and to be dependent on you, in terms of their cooperation with you, it seems to me that food dependence would be terrific" (in Carty and Smith 1981:115). In 1974, Secretary of Agriculture Earl Butz acknowledged that "food is a weapon . . . one of the principal tools in our negotiating kit," a sentiment echoed by John Block, Secretary of Agriculture in 1980: "Food is the greatest weapon we have for keeping peace in the world" (Shepherd 1985a:4). Frank Carlucci, National Security Advisor and later Secretary of Defense under Reagan, described aid as an "indispensable contribution to achieving foreign policy objectives" (Bandow 1985:xii). Clearly, the Derg was not alone in using food as a political tool.

Discussing the media's role in such disasters, *Newsweek* employs the technique of inoculation, noting that "the first warnings of impending disaster, issued two years ago, were largely ignored by Western governments, relief agencies and news media—and by the Ethiopian regime itself" (Watson et al. 1984:52). *Newsweek* admits that media ignored famine, but defends this by noting that others did the same, a defense partially contradicted by the text itself: "For months relief organizations had barraged the news media with press releases, phone calls, photos and even filmed footage of the developing disaster" (Anderson et al. 1984:56). *Newsweek* resolves the problem through inoculation: although media ignored famine for years, it was the BBC that finally "alerted the world to a tragedy" and thus inspired charity from the Elect. Once again, as *Newsweek* elucidates, it is Africans who are to blame: "The lack of press attention may have been due in part to the Ethiopian government's refusal to allow foreign journalists to tour the country prior to the massive anniversary celebration in September of Haile Selassie's ouster" (ibid.:57).

Yet, as *Newsweek* admits, relief agencies offered to obtain visas, freelance journalists had reports, and U.N. documentation was available. Furthermore, other drought-affected nations suffering from severe food shortages were accessible but famine in those nations never became a major news story. An African problem was condensed into an Ethiopian disaster, primarily for ideological reasons but also as an aesthetic decision. *Newsweek* suggests the aesthetic aspects of Ethiopian famine made it newsworthy, noting that even excellent press coverage could not compare with the power of televised images. *Newsweek* does not consider how the ideological orientation of famine-stricken countries might be reflected in differential media coverage.

Reference to graphic images indicates the internal logic of news production and the importance of entertainment aspects. Ethiopian famine became a major news story because of aesthetic values as well as ideological utility; internal and external constraints on discourse (i.e., the visual aesthetics of mass starvation and the ideological orientation of the Derg) allied to make Ethiopian famine an issue. Famine was circumscribed within the limits of the system that imaged it. Captivating images of starving Africans kept media attention only temporarily until it moved to new events, simultaneously creating and fulfilling the need for spectacle.

Discourse on famine in Ethiopia evoked the grim consequences of loss of hegemony and suggested that what was happening there could happen elsewhere if control was not maintained. A black African military regime that ousted a U.S. ally and sided with the Soviet Union combined the two major demons of the political unconscious of the West: natives and communists. Discourse on famine in Ethiopia elaborated existing racist and anticommunist mythologies. The loss of Ethiopia, along with the loss of other former colonies, was consistently interpreted in the context of other imperial myths, such as the Vietnam syndrome. Famine in Ethiopia became a parable of betrayal of the civilizing and charitable Elect by communists and savages. Themes of Christian mythology also contributed to these representations of Ethiopia. The formerly pious kingdom, beloved of the gods, was now ruled by what some saw as the Devil himself, in the form of Mengistu Haile Mariam (Harris 1987).

These inversions and reversals were deeply troubling. Whereas formerly Ethiopia served as a sort of mirror image for the West, offering completion and stability against the threat of Islam through the figure of Prester John, in contemporary discourse Ethiopian famine would come to function as a warning of chaos, dissolution of hegemony, and impending nuclear apocalypse. Ethiopia became a nightmare, a site of shocking hegemonic transpositions, locus of continually shifting significations in which no identity remains certain, and all is inverted: Ethiopia simultaneously is and is not Africa and Europe, blacks are whites, superpower alliances are reversed, and "Arab-inspired" Eritreans become "Africa's Israelis" (Kaplan 1988a:

62). In this discourse, military domination becomes the only means of protecting against a contagion that threatens to erode identity, undermine the civilizing mission, and subvert racial essence.

Modernization and Anticommunism

Themes and rhetorical processes employed in *Newsweek* are elaborated upon in a major feature (three articles) in the *New Republic* (January 1985). The articles share assumptions about modernization, in part derived from a discourse of development rooted in Rostow's *Stages of Economic Growth* (1960). Rostow invokes an evolutionist paradigm in which all societies evolve from a traditional condition to a modern one through a sequence of stages. Within this paradigm, the U.S. signifies modernity and its political allies are posited as modernizing agents. The *New Republic* suggests that both Ethiopia and Sudan had been on the road to modernity but their progress was interrupted by communists and Islamic fundamentalists, respectively. Modernity remains undefined; it invokes a rhetoric of replication but involves practice designed to ensure subordination. What is clear, however, is the relation of the modernization paradigm to key elements in the discourses of racism and Christian mythology (e.g., hierarchy, evolution, the civilizing mission). Rostow subtitled his work "An Anticommunist Manifesto" and was a fervent cold warrior who encouraged Kennedy's adoption of a widespread counterinsurgency program directed against nationalist movements in the Third World. The doctrines of development and counterinsurgency are two sides of the same coin, designed to shape the world according to Western economic interests, and both are thoroughly permeated with and shaped by the three discourses identified above. Although Africa had a minor role in the projected global system and, for the most part, was assigned to the European sphere of influence, the Horn was viewed as having a more significant strategic value. Contemporary discourse on famine in Ethiopia must be read in the context of this hegemonic design for world order.

Myth operates through a process of distortion (Barthes 1972:129). The *New Republic* effects this process through the assembly of facts within a particular ideological structure; through construction of significant absences the causes of famine are obscured and falsified. The editors of the *New Republic* situate starvation in ideological terms by the subtitle of anthropologist Allan Hoben's article: "The deadly mix of civil war, socialism, and depleted soil." Hoben provides some facts on Ethiopian history and agricultural techniques; these are embedded in the modernization paradigm. For example, discussing Haile Selassie's rule, he states:

> But during the '50s and '60s the pace of investment in roads and agriculture, as well as in education and health, steadily increased. There was rapid agricultural development along the roads in favored regions to the south and west of Addis Ababa. New agricultural technologies were introduced by Swedish, American, and World Bank projects. Large scale commercial plantations producing cash crops were established in several locations. Private Ethiopian investment in coffee, oil seeds and grains, often organized by urban entrepreneurs, grew rapidly. Trade flourished. (Hoben 1985:17)

This is the image of modernizing Ethiopia, taking its appropriate place under Western tutelage, a bustling capitalist land providing a model for Africa. Hoben paints an optimistic picture of a developing Ethiopia, under U.S. ally Haile Selassie, drawing on already existing discursive fragments concerning the Emperor that suggest benevolence, wisdom, and acceptance of U.S. hegemony. Hoben proposes that Haile Selassie was leading Ethiopia into prosperity until the march to modernity was ambushed by communists who plunged the country into chaos. Whereas *Newsweek* constructed the ideological character of famine through association, juxtaposition, and condensation (e.g., the photograph of a "pro-Mengistu mural" absorbs the generalized corruption and mismanagement of African governments described in the text), the *New Republic* performs this operation through falsification and construction of significant absences.

For example, according to Halliday and Molyneux (1981:69), Ethiopia's agricultural output was growing but only at a rate of 2.5 per cent yearly, roughly equal to population growth; Griffin (1987) and Robinson and Yamazaki (1986) state that the agricultural growth rate actually was in steady decline during Haile Selassie's rule. The rapid industrialization of the 1960s was extremely costly and Ethiopia, like other African nations, was weakened by monocrop dependency. Little assistance was available for small producers, and larger-scale landowners took advantage of programs intended to benefit the former. Analyzing the centrally planned programs of the 1954–1970 period, Keller (1988:127) finds that "not much progress" was made. Hoben lauds "large scale commercial plantations producing cash crops," without mentioning that mechanization programs such as those in the Awash Valley created pollution problems, reduced employment, pushed peasants and nomads off their land and into peripheral areas that quickly became overpopulated and overgrazed, and forced others into the cities where they became a cheap labor force. Hoben also neglects to mention that 80 percent of the land was owned by 2 percent of the population. In 1974, when Haile Selassie was deposed, inflation had risen to 80 percent. Industry accounted for only 4 percent of the GNP and was confined to import substitution. Approximately 75 percent of manufacturing was foreign-owned. Ethiopia was the poorest country in Africa and one of the poorest in the world. "Ethiopia had a permanent deficit on its foreign trade, and exports were dominated by primary commodities" such as coffee, ensuring precarious dependency on world market price changes, while the rapidly growing cash crop investments mentioned by Hoben were "meagre" ($300 million annually) (Halliday and Molyneux 1981:69).

In addition to championing large-scale commercial farming of cash crops in a situation where huge numbers of peasants were starving to death at least in part due to lack of access to land, Hoben praises "new agricultural technologies" as agents of modernization. This emphasis on technology was a major thrust of the Green Revolution, a strategy that has increased crop production in some cases but that leaves unaddressed social relations of production. Typically, only wealthier farmers could afford such technology; using it often increased pollution and the emphasis on cash crops put many countries at the mercy of fluctuations in world market prices. These factors cast a different light on Hoben's claim that "trade flourished." Hoben does concede that in addition to these benefits there were "problems"—a widening gap between rich and poor, evictions, and finally, famine, but this occurred "not surprisingly" because of "the quickening pace of change" (Hoben 1985:17). Striking here is the complete evaporation of responsibility: famine during the rule of a U.S. ally is presented as an unsurprising (i.e., natural) occurrence and a product of the "pace of change," an impersonal, quasi-natural process unrelated to human agency. In contrast, famine during the 1980s is depicted as the direct result of socialist policies imposed by corrupt leaders. As in *Newsweek*, African famine was condensed into an Ethiopian problem; whereas Ethiopia had once signified the antiquity and independence of African civilization, it here functions in inverted form as a symbol of African degradation.

Transforming African famine into Ethiopian famine involves a process of falsification. For example, Hoben claims that "with the partial exception of Mozambique, the drought has not been translated into famine in other countries" (ibid.). This "partial exception" refers to the fact that only 200,000 people starved to death in Mozambique during 1984 as opposed to 300,000 in Ethiopia. The suggestion that famine did not occur in other countries is plainly false. Even *Newsweek* acknowledged that 50,000 people had died of starvation in Senegal. In 1984–85 the FAO estimated that twenty-one African nations faced exceptional food supply problems and even in countries where thousands of people were not literally dropping dead from starvation, malnutrition was widespread, as were livestock losses and epidemic diseases due to displacement of populations into crowded and unsanitary feeding camps. Not all of these nations had a government allied with the Soviet Union, however, and thus did not present the same opportunities for incorporation into a narrative form based on Cold War ideological polarities.

Like the *Newsweek* reports and Harris (1987), Hoben criticizes collective farms, stating that they reduce peasant incentives to produce. No proof is offered, and Griffin (1987:190) suggests that some form of collective arrangement could be vital for Ethiopian agricultural recovery. As Griffin points out, however, collectivization was imposed rapidly and forcibly and incomes were appropriated through high taxation and compulsory sale of produce at low prices. In general, the Derg's agricultural policies were disastrous. Despite the priority placed on large, mechanized state farms, these did not yield a substantially higher agricultural output than smaller peasant farms that were more or less neglected. The agricultural situation worsened under the Derg but to attribute famine to socialism is an oversimplification based on ideological objectives. In a comparative study, Pateman (1989) provides a more balanced analysis of the performance of state farms. In part, the food crisis of the 1980s reflects the cumulative impact of an agricultural decline that was already in progress under the former regime.

Robert D. Kaplan's accompanying article for the *New Republic*, "Ethiopian Exodus," which concentrates on Sudan, also adheres to the modernization paradigm. Writing before the 1985 coup that ousted Nimeiri, Kaplan critiques the former's imposition of Islamic law but lauds him as a U.S. ally whose modernization plans were threatened: "[*Shari'a*] wrecked whatever hope there was for a viable economy here. Foreign banks aren't exactly encouraged to do business in a place where it's illegal to charge interest. Moreover, guerrilla attacks have put an end to several projects vital to Sudan's further development: Chevron's oil explorations in the south, a proposed oil pipeline crossing the country to Port Sudan; and the Jonglei Canal scheme, needed to provide both Sudan and Egypt with more usable Nile water" (Kaplan 1985:22).

Both Kaplan and Hoben construct significant absence in the text by ignoring historical details. This technique makes disaster appear as the result of immediate causes rather than of long-term processes. It was not simply imposition of Islamic law that wrecked the Sudanese economy but rather a long history of inappropriate development planning. Sudan's attractive anticommunist stance, seen as a counter to Libya and Ethiopia, brought huge Western loans and financing from conservative Middle Eastern regimes for large-scale development projects. Nimeiri planned to use Arab financing and Western technology to transform Sudan into a regional breadbasket. However, a drop in cotton production, increased imports of oil to fuel imported machinery, and sugar subsidies created deficits that were paid off by foreign loans. Due to lack of private investment, a policy of industrialization for import substitution became the responsibility of the government, which financed this through acquisition of agricultural surplus at low prices and more foreign loans. Inefficiency, misplanning, and corruption, as well as lack of infrastructure, finance, and equipment, led to production losses. Sudan became one of Africa's most indebted states; its high ratio of debt service to export earnings meant that the country earned less foreign exchange than was required to pay its interest on principal payments.

Like Hoben, Kaplan promotes a development model based on large-scale capital intensive projects. The very projects Kaplan promotes as "vital to Sudan's further development" are among the main causes of the country's problems. Other large-scale projects, such as the Kenana sugar factory near Kosti, were equally disastrous. The Kenana factory was a joint venture between the Sudanese government and foreign capital. Estimated at $125 million, the factory's actual cost was $750 million. In addition to having to import all necessary products and equipment, Sudan found itself facing both plummeting world sugar prices and rising oil prices, which meant that the Kenana project was costing more than it earned. The Kenana factory also was an impetus toward construction of the Jonglei canal. The factory plantation requires huge amounts of water, but due to the canal scheme the drainage of southern marshes could create environmental disaster, climatic change, less rainfall, further drops in agricultural production, and famine. By draining water from the south, the government disrupted the livelihood of the Dinka people and further contributed to social problems, repression, and armed conflict (Korner et al. 1986:91–97).

As in Hoben's article, myth operates in Kaplan's text through distortion and incorporation of facts into an anticommunist parable. Kaplan (1985:20) refers to the "barbarity of Colonel Mengistu Haile

Mariam's Marxist regime in Addis Ababa"; by any standard, the regime was barbarous, having acquired one of the world's lowest rankings for human rights from Amnesty International and other observers, but the media identify some atrocities in ideological terms while never designating others as actions of capitalist regimes. It is only through its ideological affiliation that violence acquires meaning within hegemonic discourse and, therefore, existence. Herman and Chomsky's (1988) propaganda model indicates the distinction between "worthy" and "unworthy" victims, building on the earlier conceptualization of "benign," "constructive," and "nefarious" bloodbaths (Chomsky and Herman 1979). Atrocities by enemies may be condemned, but those committed by Western allies and business partners, such as Indonesia's genocidal attacks on East Timor, are ignored. Indeed, this had been the case with Ethiopia itself. Not only was repression under Haile Selassie accepted but, prior to its adoption of Marxist-Leninist rhetoric, the Derg's human rights abuses were overlooked. Alliance with the Soviet Union made the regime's violence suitable for condemnation.

The Subversion of Charity

In their formula for media coverage of foreign news, Galtung and Ruge (1965) stress the importance of a demonstrated relation of events to the West and construction of events in such a way as to allow audiences to interpret them in terms of a personal relation. Having selected which atrocities are ideologically suitable for condemnation, the media must then construct the proper subject position for audiences. *Newsweek* does this by devoting a third of its coverage of African famine to the U.S. response. Ignoring African efforts to deal with the crisis, *Newsweek* celebrated the West's charitable impulses and relief efforts. The *New Republic* replaced celebration of charity with warnings that the West was a dupe of Third World villains, emphasizing a lack of appreciation shown by the undeserving poor for the Elect (Augelli and Murphy 1988; Chomsky 1989b). The idea that sentimental Westerners are misled by emotion and exploited by the Third World is a dominant refrain in a discourse that inverts the effects and purposes of foreign aid.

Kaplan (1985:20) warns of "the naivete of the Western public, which has goaded various governments into an overly hasty response." Public response did encourage action from governments that preferred to let "little Commies" starve to death, but to claim that the action was "overly hasty" is pure invention. Warnings were issued years before famine reached a point of crisis and then were ignored. The Derg did not act effectively to save the Ethiopian population (Dawit 1989); it used famine as a weapon in Eritrea and Tigray and repeatedly was accused of diverting relief aid to its troops. Less widely reported, however, were the Reagan administration's efforts to stop food aid to Ethiopia entirely in this period. Rather than being too eager to respond, the U.S. delayed for months before answering emergency appeals with inadequate supplies. Providing a trickle of aid to Eritrea and Tigray was a means of maintaining the fronts to bleed the Derg; since none of the opposition movements were ideologically acceptable, however, quantities remained minimal to ensure that Ethiopia's territorial integrity would not be threatened when the Soviet Union departed. This was not an unusual strategy; as noted, use of food aid for political ends is a basic and consistent aspect of U.S. policy.

Kaplan notes that relief aid did enable the Derg to concentrate on war against Eritrea and Tigray. Looking at wounded refugees who had survived an Ethiopian bombing attack on a water hole, Kaplan muses that the attack might never have occurred "had the West continued to follow its tough but sensible course in dealing with the Ethiopian regime" (1985:20). These remarks on "naivete" and the "sensible course" are issued in tones of understated authority and common sense; Kaplan presents himself above the emotionalism of an easily misled public and encourages a more aggressive U.S. policy.

Anticommunism is Kaplan's main theme, expressed clearly in his warning that providing food to Ethiopia will not only assist a "pro-Soviet government bent on inhuman tactics of resettlement to prosecute its various wars [but will] further destabilize what for America is one of the most important countries—anti-Soviet Sudan. While the West has its eyes focused on the human drama in Ethiopia, it is liable to get whacked over the head by the geostrategic consequences next door" (ibid.:21).

In Kaplan's view, the real priority for the U.S. was to maintain a pro-Western regime in Sudan. Although Sudan suffered widespread corruption, poverty, and repression under Nimeiri, Kaplan finds these acceptable because they are conducted by a U.S. ally and not an "inhuman" pro-Soviet government. Here, the U.S., portrayed as naively humanitarian and preoccupied with the "human drama" of mass starvation, risks being "whacked over the head" by those less scrupulously concerned with human rights; the Elect are shown to be at the mercy of those in the Third World who do not share their charitable impulses and high standards.

In order to emphasize Nimeiri's importance as a U.S. ally needing support, Kaplan delves into the mythology of nineteenth-century imperialism to suggest an unusual equation with General Gordon, who died "fighting Islamic extremists" in Khartoum in 1885; despite Nimeiri's own connections with Muslim fundamentalism and his imposition of Islamic law in Sudan, including the south, where Christianity and traditional religions predominate, he "represents Western political interests now as clearly as Gordon did then" (ibid.).

Having criticized the naivete of the public that would supply food to a pro-Soviet government and threaten a U.S. ally, Kaplan suggests that the U.S. could regain control over the region by providing aid to "guerrilla groups": "This might not be a bad idea: doubtless they would siphon some of it to buy arms, but at least it might provide the West with a little more leverage over Mengistu" (ibid.). Here the humanitarian gloss is dropped; Kaplan did not argue for provision of aid because it was needed or because the organizations who would distribute it in Eritrea and Tigray had proven themselves effective, but because it would provide "leverage" for the U.S. against the Derg. *Newsweek*'s construction of U.S. charity is transformed in Kaplan's text (particularly in his book, *Surrender or Starve*) into a warning against liberalism and exhortations for a more interventionist anticommunist stance in the Third World.

Later discussions of Ethiopian famine shared the same rhetorical processes of falsification and construction of significant absence as employed in the *New Republic*. Columnist Lubor Zink, writing in the *Toronto Sun* (April 15, 1988), ignores 100,000 deaths from starvation under Haile Selassie's reign in 1974 and asserts that Ethiopians took drought in stride for centuries until communism made them vulnerable to famine. Arch Puddington, writing in *Commentary* (1986), also ties famine directly to communism. Identical claims are made in *Reason* (June 1988), which announces its ideology in its motto "Free markets, free minds"; Karl Zinsmeister, a consultant at the American Enterprise Institute, writes, "Ethiopia was once considered a potential granary for Africa. During Selassie's reign, the nation was an agricultural exporter, small farmers prospered, large plantations growing food and cash crops sprang up, an extensive network of private traders and investors took root. But all that was thrown away" (Zinsmeister 1988:30).

Zinsmeister, drawing on both Kaplan and Harris (1987), also ignores famine under Haile Selassie, expressing moral outrage over starvation only when it occurs under communist regimes. Echoing complaints by Kaplan (1985:20) that the West was "overly hasty" in aiding Ethiopia, and by journalist Jonathan Power (*Winnipeg Free Press*, December 22, 1987) that "too much effort" was made to help Eritrea and Tigray, Zinsmeister (1988:30) warns that the Elect must not be manipulated by the undeserving poor and prescribes tougher action: "[Only] belatedly [has the West realized] that the only sensible use for its aid (outside of emergencies . . .) is as a carrot or a stick, to induce structural change." However, as statements of U.S. policy makers explicitly demonstrate, the political use of aid was not a belated realization but one of its fundamental purposes.

Through a rhetorical process of inversion, in which the actual circumstances of U.S. response to famine are reversed and the political use of food aid is presented as an exclusive practice of the Derg, these texts serve a hegemonic function on two levels. First, they present a humanitarian response as naive, encourage belief that the U.S. administration is more "sensible" than an easily misled and overly generous public, and attempt to manufacture domestic consent for the regime's policies. Second, they invoke hegemonic order by advocating a more confrontational and interventionist role in the Third World. Rejecting the sentimentality of the public response, Kaplan (1988b) calls for application of the Reagan Doctrine, urging military intervention to restore hegemonic order. Other texts, discussed below, transform what he offers as expressions of common sense into a narrative incorporating discourses of racism, anticommunism, and Christian fundamentalism: the simple "naivete" of the too-charitable West is transformed into a betrayal of racial mission and a prelude to apocalyptic confrontation caused by relaxation of hegemonic global order.

Spectacles of Charity and Betrayal

Foreign news items are depicted largely in terms of their relation to the West (Galtung and Ruge 1965). The narrative structure of discourse emphasized this relation not only by depicting Ethiopian famine as the inevitable result of abhorrent policies adopted by ideological enemies but also through depiction of charitable efforts of Western nations. Much coverage concentrated not on Ethiopia itself but rather on Western relief efforts. The Live Aid concert serves as an outstanding example of the switch of emphasis. What began as a spectacle of suffering, the "tremendous images" of the famine victims at Korem, was transformed into a spectacle of celebrity and charity, as the world's richest pop stars performed in novel combinations and jetted from London to Philadelphia to participate in what was regarded as a media marvel. Carried by thirteen satellites, the concert was seen by an estimated two billion people. This second media spectacle extended the longevity of the "mini-series" of African starvation by providing an all-star, predominantly white cast, but it also tended to eclipse it. For example, a *Newsweek* feature (July 22, 1985) concentrated on the stars exclusively and devoted only one sentence to "hunger—the devastating hunger that has swept Africa in the wake of searing droughts."

Live Aid and its coverage in the media not only focused on the various pop stars who performed but also emphasized the role of the West as savior of helpless African peasants. Celebrities told viewers that with the provision of charity dollars, "after today, the world may never be the same." Recognizing that the Live Aid concert did generate some relief assistance does not require a dismissal of its negative consequences. Not only was the image of Third World passivity emphasized, but once again unrealistic expectations were created, and the promise of immediate solutions helped to undermine a long-term response.

The spectacle of Western charity also incorporated a narrative of African betrayal. Just as Africans were shown to have rejected benefits of the civilizing mission and brought famine upon themselves by the pursuit of foolish policies, so was Western charity shown to have been manipulated by the ruthlessness of African Marxists. There were numerous charges of misuse of food aid. For example "The Horn of Africa," a film written and directed by Robert Roy of Stornoway Productions and broadcast on Canadian television in August 1990, credits the media with alerting the world to a disaster that the Derg tried originally to disguise and then to manipulate for its own ends. It overlooks the fact that the media originally ignored the famine despite abundant information and that the West also attempted to use famine to discredit ideological enemies. Assembling commentators such as Myles Harris and Paul Henze (both discussed in subsequent chapters), Hannah Yulma (a founder of the CIA-funded Ethiopian People's Democratic Alliance [EPDA]), and former Ethiopian government officials, the film attacks the Derg for misusing international humanitarian aid in order to retain power while dismissing the EPLF as "kinky Marxists." Canadian journalist Peter Worthington repeatedly charged the Ethiopian regime with the misuse of food aid. Roy Pateman (1988:171) gives details of "conclusive evidence of Ethiopian misuse of food aid."

In April 1989, Berhane Deressa, formerly Deputy Commissioner of Ethiopia's Relief and Rehabilitation Commission, told me that he had personally diverted food aid to the military. Another defector, Goshu Wolde, formerly Foreign Minister, agreed this was common practice. Both stated there was no choice in the situation, that the soldiers themselves were starving peasants who had been conscripted, and that the military would have taken the food in any event. A third defector, Dawit (1989), denies that food was used as a weapon and says the EPLF and TPLF invented reports of refusing food to Eritrea and Tigray to discredit the Derg; Dawit himself attempted to block aid to Eritrea by pressuring agencies working there (Pateman 1988: 174).

While there is not much doubt that diversions of aid did occur, these were interpreted in strikingly different ways. For the commentators in the Stornoway film and for Worthington, both of whom have fairly explicit affiliations with right-wing ideologies, the abuses provided clear proof of the nefarious character of socialism. Others, such as Pateman, recognized the misuse of food aid as a practice of the Derg rather than as the conclusive refutation of a variegated philosophy.

Although famine in the Horn was a major news story of 1984 and 1985, and despite the fact that serious food shortages have continued, the nature of media discourse determined that coverage would be of limited duration. The Horn did receive sporadic attention afterwards as the liberation fronts won significant victories. Many of the same rhetorical techniques were applied. For example, the technique of neither-norism was widely applied following an EPLF attack on a truck convoy in October 1987. Food aid was destroyed in the trucks, which the EPLF charged were also carrying weapons. The EPLF's version of the story and its subsequent efforts to ensure that future relief shipments would not be interrupted received little attention and were overshadowed by a massive show of international indignation. Similarly, following the EPLF's victory at the port of Massawa, CBC television blamed both sides for the disruption of food supplies in May 1990. Canada's Minister of External Relations, Monique Landry, also attacked both sides for holding the civilian population hostage. Conservative Member of Parliament and Minister of Employment and Immigration Barbara McDougall stated in an August 2, 1990, letter to the author that "both parties have clearly placed their military and political priorities above humanitarian concerns." Such judgments rest upon the construction of significant abscence and obscure the historical context of conflict in the Horn. The international community had consistently failed in its responsibility to address the

Eritrean case, and the conflict had been encouraged by massive military inputs from both superpowers. As well, these assessments do not acknowledge the fact that Massawa was a principal point of entry for the arms the Derg was using to attack Eritrea. Furthermore, these statements must be viewed in the context of the imbalanced provision of emergency relief supplies. The Canadian government refused to acknowledge the extent of famine in EPLF-controlled areas and channeled most of its aid through the Ethiopian government even though the latter did not have access to many of those in need. Despite the existence of an effective cross-border route from Sudan, Canada resorted to expensive and inadequate airlifts to Asmara. The commitment of Western governments to maintain the territorial integrity of Ethiopia guaranteed that the cross-border route would not be fully utilized, regardless of the fact that this meant placing "political priorities above humanitarian concerns."

5

EXPLAINING FAMINE

Beyond Natural Disasters

Emphasis on natural causes of famine is not limited to the media. Causal linkage of drought and famine in institutional and academic studies has been noted (Lofchie 1975; Torry 1984; Watts 1983). Governments, including Ethiopia's, typically favor climatic explanations in order to deflect criticism of their policies. However, such versions of the causes of famine can only be maintained in deliberate ignorance of a growing body of research that looks beyond natural explanations. Numerous studies indicate that drought may affect wide regions but create famine only in areas of relative poverty. Furthermore, famine may occur where climate barely deviates from the norm. Recognition of multiple causation of famine has existed for centuries (Byron 1982b:63). Drought may be the most important natural cause of famine but other factors include population pressure, disasters such as earthquakes and locust infestations, war, and misplaced agricultural policies (Aykroyd 1974). The distinction between drought and famine is often overlooked; the former need not create the latter. The link is mediated by political and economic conditions. For example, one can distinguish between drought as a natural process and famine created by exploitative agricultural policies, often benefitting external interests (Meillassoux 1974).

Access and entitlement are as important as food shortages (Liebenstein 1982). Famine may result not from food shortages but rather from differential availability. Discussing the Ethiopian famine of 1972–1974, Amartya Sen (1981) finds no major crisis of food production, only a small decline. Food moved from areas like Wollo into the cities, indicating that market entitlement, not absolute shortage, caused famine; Wollo residents were too poor to draw food into the region and the poorest groups were the most affected. Expansion of commercial agriculture drastically reduced pasture for nomads, increasing their vulnerability to environmental changes. Thus, structural changes to the economy exacerbated the impact of drought.

Famine does not result from environmental causes alone (Ball 1976; Dando 1980; Glantz 1987; Golkin 1987; Palmieri 1982). No serious study of famine can attribute it solely to drought or other natural causes. Yet other monocausal theories have been advanced; Paul Ehrlich (1968) and Sudhir Sen (1982), for example, tie famine to overpopulation. Such theories are rejected in general terms by George (1977) and Amartya Sen (1981), by Vaughan (1987) for Malawi, and by Watts (1983) for Nigeria. It is also useful to distinguish between overpopulation and rates of population growth (Timberlake 1985:38–39). Neo-Malthusian and Social Darwinist paradigms of population theorists may conceal a political agenda that blames the poor for their own problems (Carty and Smith 1981:77–79, 185). Unwillingness to acknowledge a broader political context and an endeavor to blame Africans rather than considering historical and structural conditions for famine characterize discourse on the Horn.

Despite numerous charges that the media placed undue emphasis on natural explanations of famine and overlooked political elements, a political message was embedded in the initial BBC broadcast. As reporter Michael Buerk indicated, the film from the camp at Korem had been edited in such a way as to convey a clear ideological message and attach the blame for famine on the Mengistu government.

Even reports that did not overtly criticize the Derg contained implicit political messages. The focus on environmental conditions and the failure to consider historical factors that transformed African environments and made certain populations more vulnerable to environmental changes are themselves political constructions. Many reports contain little overt discussion of political factors related to famine, but this does not mean they are apolitical. Historical, political, and economic conditions that structured African famine are excluded by construction of significant omissions in the text. In the absence of historical contextualization, readers are invited to attribute famine solely to the actions of Africans.

Colonialism and Famine

Discussing famine in general, Sudhir Sen (1982) employs this rhetorical technique, claiming that there is no point in "blaming" colonialism for famine since it is "essentially postcolonial." To characterize famine as a postcolonial phenomenon Sen must ignore it in India, Ireland, and Nigeria under colonial rule. Christopher Clapham (1990b) has also rejected colonialism as a factor in Ethiopian famine. Before addressing his argument, however, it is useful to note the impact of colonialism on African food production in general. As noted, one method of politicizing famine was to limit discourse to the situation in certain areas: although famine struck many African countries in the 1980s, the media concentrated almost exclusively on Ethiopia. Information on starvation elsewhere was ignored or falsified to make Ethiopian famine serve ideological ends. Although the Horn has a unique history, famine there is part of broader historical, economic, political, and environmental processes.

Food production in Africa has been declining since the 1950s, barely keeping pace with population growth. Although drought has afflicted Africa throughout this period, the decline was not part of an overall agricultural failure but rather a structured imbalance. By the late 1960s production of export crops was rising by 4 percent annually, and in countries where mass starvation was imminent, tens of thousands of tons of agricultural commodities were exported to Europe and North America. Across Africa, export crops flourished while food production deteriorated (Lofchie 1975:555).

Franke and Chasin (1980) describe how African governments were encouraged to place low priorities on food production for local consumption: cotton production rose in Burkina Faso while sorghum and millet cultivation declined; in Mali, while drought ravaged the Sahel and thousands starved, cotton production soared. During Tanzania's 1973–1974 drought, tobacco production increased as maize sales fell by a third. Both crops require the same amount of water but tobacco was a priority: 62 percent of loans from the Tanzanian Rural Development Bank (1978–1979) went to tobacco, while only 19 percent went to maize.

In the 1970s, USAID, the World Bank, and the IMF promoted large-scale, highly visible, mechanized projects that emphasized Western expertise and technology but overlooked local food production. In general, there is clear indication of agricultural dualism with success in export crops achieved at the expense of food production, although some studies identify the problem as a pattern of uneven commercialization (Vaughan 1987; Watts 1983). This structural imbalance was created under colonialism, and post-independence African governments inherited it. In Africa, colonialism created economies geared to external interests. Infrastructural development was directed toward resource extraction, such as railways organized for collection of export commodities.

Colonial policies encouraged production of what was most immediately profitable and discouraged other crops, rapidly transforming African economies. Foreign capital did not diversify these economies by adding investments in new areas to already existing sources of foreign exchange; instead, it replaced them. This led to shortages in food crops and population displacement as new farming methods and systems of land tenure brought uneven regional development. Land expropriations forced peasants to the cities.

Emphasis on export crops, reinforced through incentives and sanctions, created inadequate supplies of food (Gakou 1987). Claude Ake (1981) has shown that the monopolistic nature of capital in Africa restricted competition and resulted in few benefits in terms of development of productive forces. With little indigenous capital for investment, the colonies were dependent for currency, technology, and external trade. Manufacturing was generally ignored and was rudimentary where it did exist. The colonial state acted in the interests of capitalists to manipulate production in the precapitalist sphere through formation of laws concerning production and by imposing agricultural development programs requiring imported fertilizers and technology, thereby speeding integration of commodity relations.

The best land went to export crops, with full government support for infrastructural development to deliver these crops to ports. Regarded as backward, the peasant agricultural sector received little government support; there was little development of infrastructure such as roads and storage facilities, no marketing boards for food crops, a lack of scientific inputs, and the lowest use of fertilizers on any continent. This was not neglect but rather a continuation of policies from the colonial period (Lofchie 1975). These policies were designed to deprive support for food-producing areas and to keep market prices low to make labor necessary and transform peasants into wage workers. Interested mainly in export crops and needing a supply of cheap labor, African governments have refrained from improving living conditions for peasants.

Africa's resource base remains narrow and undiversified, providing little opportunity for change. Dependence and a disarticulated economy are mutually reinforcing. Dependence on external control limits opportunities to restructure the economy, thus maintaining Africa as a producer of primary products within an international division of labor and discouraging industrialization.

The postcolonial development of Africa converted the continent within three decades from one that could feed itself into one increasingly dependent on grain imports, particularly from the U.S. Inappropriate development projects have had adverse effects, and even provision of food aid has sometimes undermined local production by maintaining prices at an artificially low level. International borrowing for large- scale development projects was encouraged, but a drop in market prices and establishment of quotas against some African products, accompanied by the strength of the U.S. dollar against other currencies, made it difficult for many African nations to pay their debts; at least 60 percent of the total African export economy goes to debt repayment. The combination of low export prices, high interest rates, the strong U.S. dollar, and growing imports of oil contributed to a situation in which development funds received by African nations are actually channeled into debt repayment and purchases of imports, not only of oil but also of food. Africa's balance of trade is worsening: prices for export crops plummeted from the levels of the 1960s (accompanied by a declining rate of food production of 2 percent per year), the cost of grain imports rose tenfold, and the cost of oil imports jumped 757 percent, so that by 1981 Africa faced a balance of payments deficit of $54.3 billion (Shepherd 1984).

Explanations that posit famine as solely the result of natural disaster cannot be accepted in the light of extensive information concerning continuing effects of colonialism on disarticulated economies inserted into a world system and subjected to inappropriate development. Despite this, rhetorical techniques of naturalization and dehistoricization provided ideologically acceptable explanations of famine.

Colonialism and Famine in the Horn

Clapham (1990b) seems to support the natural explanation of famine. His argument is similar to Sudhir Sen's, but it is inverted to suggest that because famine prefigured European colonialism, one cannot discuss effects of Ethiopia's involvement in a world economy, especially when contemporary famine occurs in remote areas. Recognizing the historical existence of famine, however, does not require one to ignore effects of colonialism.

Initially, Clapham's argument seems plausible, The first recorded famine struck the Horn in the ninth century. From 1540 to 1700 there were ten major famines, many lasting several years. Another ten struck in the eighteenth century followed by eight more in the nineteenth century, ending with the Great Famine of 1888–1892 (Pankhurst 1961). In the Great Famine thousands of people died and 90 percent of the livestock was wiped out. Interspersed with famine were smaller cycles of hunger, droughts, crop failures, cattle plagues, epidemics, and locust infestations. Contemporary famine seems simply the latest manifestation of a seemingly endless cycle of natural disasters, unaffected by recent political and economic events, apparently justifying Clapham's conclusion. However, the conclusion is erroneous. It overlooks differential effects of drought: climatic changes may affect a broad region but bring famine only to areas of poverty. Absolute food shortages are less an explanation for famine than reduced accessibility due to pricing, inflation, and transportation. Famine is a catastrophe caused by human agency although often triggered by environmental factors (Torry 1984). People starve not because food is unavailable but because they cannot afford it (Sen 1981). Therefore, it is necessary to examine the structural and historical conditions of famine.

John Markakis (1987) provides a useful overview of the historical transformation of the Horn under colonial impact. The impact was most evident in Sudan, where the colonial economy was based on cash crop production for export. Over a million acres were put into cotton production, which accounted for over half of Sudan's exports. Irrigation, mechanization, and introduction of new crops accompanied new social relations geared to international markets.

Transformation was less extensive in Eritrea, where Italian colonialism did not establish a significant cash crop export economy. Nevertheless, commodity production transformed social relations and private ownership and accumulation encouraged class stratification. Confiscation of the best land caused overcrowding and conflict and, particularly after the invasion of Ethiopia, there was rapid urbanization as labor demands in housing, transportation, and manufacturing soared. The trend continued under British administration as factories geared to wartime production needs were established.

Colonialism affected pastoralist groups whose movements were determined by rainfall patterns and sparse grass cover. The transformation to capitalism gradually restricted movements across colonial borders, although this was not particularly significant until the end of World War II. Increased cultivation pushed pastoralists further from water sources, creating ecological and social changes. Simple veterinary care increased herd size (tripling the livestock in Eritrea from 1905 to 1948) in these restricted areas, resulting in overgrazing (Jordan 1989; Markakis 1987).

Colonialism also accelerated deforestation. Forests were burnt to dispel animals and insects or to deprive enemy troops of protection. In the 1870s the forests of Shoa were destroyed for charcoal and pasture; Baron Leopoldo Franchetti, supervising Italian colonization of Eritrea in 1890, complained that soldiers had changed Asmara into a treeless plain (Pankhurst 1968:244). Clapham (1990b) argues that the extent of deforestation in Ethiopia has been exaggerated, but it is clear that, where it occurs, deforestation exacerbates drought, leads to soil erosion, and contributes to the spread of diseases such as bilharzia (Roundy 1973:434).

In Ethiopia, Italian occupation had limited impact but changes had already occurred due to Amhara expansion, encouraged by overpopulation, disease, drought, and locust infestations. Even though Ethiopia was not directly under Italian control, colonial activity worsened the Great Famine of 1888–1892. Building for the planned invasion of Ethiopia, the Italians imported cattle from India to Eritrea; the animals, however, were infected with rinderpest virus, which devastated African herds. By 1899 it spread throughout Ethiopia, combined with limited grazing and malnutrition resulting from the unusually high temperatures and low rainfall of the previous year. Virtually all the cattle died except a few isolated herds in Gojjam. Drought continued for three years but the lack of cattle needed for ploughing and harvesting also had a significant effect. The cattle plague was followed by diseases associated with chronic food shortages, and approximately 15 to 20 percent of the population died, although in some areas the death rate was 50 percent. In the twentieth century there have been four major famines as well as regional droughts. During the Long Famine of 1965–1974, hundreds of thousands of people starved to death.

The situation in parts of Ethiopia worsened under the impact of capitalism and cash crop production. In the Awash Valley, Afar nomads subsisted mainly by cattle herding. In 1962, with UN assistance, the Ethiopian Government established the Awash Valley Authority; it controlled administration, land and water use, and power schemes. Hydroelectric stations were established and by 1973 "there were a total of twenty-seven large and medium size agro-industrial enterprises functioning in the valley" (Gilkes 1975:132). These included the Metahara and Wonji sugar plantations, operated under near-monopoly conditions by Handels Vereniging Amsterdam (HVA), which began business in Ethiopia following its expulsion from Indonesia, and the Tendaho Plantations Share Company for cotton production, the latter managed by the British firm Mitchell Cotts, which had 51 percent of shares. Also operating were "Melka Sidi farm—52 per cent Italian-financed; three farms . . . owned by ex-Agricultural College graduates; and Abadir farm which has Israeli finance" (Bondestam 1974:435; Gilkes 1975:132). Firms such as HVA operated under conditions of virtual monopoly, with complete tax exemption, and brutally exploited the labor force (Markakis and Nega 1986). Production under "optimum conditions for investment" was "spectacular" and also "attracted local entrepreneurs" so that Ethiopian capitalists owned one-third of the plantations (Markakis 1987:96). Class differentiation grew as larger farmers formed a local elite and the poorest became seasonal laborers. Development of sugar and cotton plantations utilized the flat plains and low river beds that had provided grazing for Afar herds; by 1970 a quarter of the land was under cultivation, mainly in cotton, and the Awash River was polluted with industrial waste from the plantations and sugar factories. Extremely favorable arrangements allowed foreign companies to take capital out of Ethiopia, but the general impact was less positive within the country. Displacement of the Afar led to violent clashes with the Issa Somali people to the east, and in 1973 disaster struck the nomads. Official explanations for the disaster emphasized drought and large herd sizes.

Colonialism also affected areas not directly tied into the cash crop and commodity production economy. McCann (1987) has described this process in Wollo. There, subsistence was based both on agriculture and the area's intermediate position in trade routes from Eritrea to the interior. Population increase led to intensified cultivation of marginal areas, reduction of pasture, and subsequent environmental decline. This was combined with an inheritance system in which land was subdivided and redistributed after the death of the male head of a household, as well as with the growing power of the Amhara state, which diverted both taxes from local elites and profits from interregional trade while suppressing cattle raiding. These factors combined to create disaster for the peasants. Haile Selassie's new policies eroded the traditional economic base of local elites and created dependency on urban administration. Relations of production were altered in rural areas, although forms of autonomous household production remained unchanged. In this context, oxen were critical; ownership of oxen determined social status so that within an overall regional decline impoverishment was not equal. Instead, there was an emergence of classes in which land was claimed by those who possessed the means of production while the poor transferred their land rights for access to oxen, seeds, tools, and food and increasingly had to sell their labor for food. The state and the local elite demanded labor from the peasants, among whom impoverishment was further divided by gender. In conditions of worsening impoverishment even a slight environmental change brought disaster to the poor.

Despite its brevity, colonialism had substantial and lasting effects in the Horn. It disrupted both pastoralist and subsistence agriculturalist strategies, and the inflow of capital and technology created new modes of subsistence and social relations. Italian colonialism introduced a market economy and wage labor through industrialization and establishment of large plantations; this modernization benefited the indigenous middle and upper classes at the expense of traditional agricultural and pastoral modes of production. As communal landowning systems of the highlands disintegrated, there was growing dependency on wage labor among the peasantry. Agricultural development introduced by the Italians was not promoted by the British or the Ethiopians; both contributed to a degeneration of the Eritrean economy through deliberate policies that effectively established preconditions for mass starvation. Seen in this context, Clapham's effort to dismiss any connection between colonialism and famine seems misplaced.

Yet arguments like those of Clapham and Sudhir Sen recur throughout discourse on Ethiopian famine. By ignoring the structural conditions for disaster that had been established during the previous regime, such arguments were used to attack the Derg. To employ such techniques, it is necessary to avoid understanding famine as the result of combined factors. Frequently, excision or falsification of historical detail is required unless, as in Clapham's construction, history can be invoked to show that colonialism is not to blame for African problems. Despite the long history of famine and changing weather patterns in the Horn, it is incorrect to assume that colonialism did not affect the region or that famine is a strictly natural disaster. Nevertheless, environmental factors should not be dismissed entirely. Recurring drought plagues the Horn and famine cannot be attributed to colonialism alone. It is as simplistic to attribute famine solely to incorporation within a global capitalist system as it is to blame only environmental factors (Gartrell 1985). Rather, it is necessary to see famine as the product of a dynamic interaction of climatic factors, agricultural technology and production systems, demographics and population growth, property relations and indigenous social institutions, politics, and warfare (McCann 1990). Famine in the Horn must be seen in the context of the colonial transformation of the entire continent, but it is also necessary to note the effects of militarization on the region.

Militarization and Famine

The famines that plagued the Horn in the 1980s were worsened by the war that had afflicted the region for a quarter-century. Generally, the media ignored or understated the relation of militarization to famine. Given the duration and extent of conflict in this significant region, and the involvement of both the Soviet Union and the U.S., media coverage is surprisingly limited. This is partially due to the absence of an ideologically acceptable opponent to the Derg and concomitant difficulties of reducing the war to a standard conflict narrative. U.S. strategists had always regarded Soviet influence in the Horn as superficial; criticism of the Derg therefore was limited by support for Ethiopia's territorial integrity.

The media viewed the Horn according to either a famine or war frame, which were consistently kept separate. Of 640 news articles written from November 1984 to June 1988, 195 articles (30.5 percent) were concerned solely with drought, famine, and/or relief issues, a further 27 (4.2 percent) mentioned war in a cursory manner, and an additional 125 (19.5 percent) noted the interrelationship to varying degrees, while 88 articles (13.7 percent) were concerned mainly with war; 126 articles (19.6 percent) attempted analysis, although of varying quality and with a high degree of superficiality. Discrepancy between my survey and Murray's (1986) analysis is partially explained by the fact that I used a wider range of sources (including newspapers from North America, Australia, Africa, Britain, and the Soviet Union) and included material from 1988, (when the EPLF launched a major offensive). Generally, the war received more attention after 1988, although important developments, such as withdrawal of government troops from Tigray in March 1989, were ignored. The war's importance was belatedly acknowledged: Michael Yellin, writing in *Africa Report* (January-February 1988), stated that war could not be ignored as it was in 1984; David MacDonald, formerly Canadian ambassador to Ethiopia, told the *London Free Press* (April 2, 1988) that conflict was now "front and centre." Increased coverage of conflict did not necessarily mean more sophisticated analysis. For example, the *Toronto Globe and Mail* (April 14, 1988) continued to refer to "secessionist rebels" in Eritrea and Tigray, equating two struggles under a term appropriate only to one and ignoring that the TPLF saw secession only as a last resort.

The Horn is one of a number of Third World conflict zones in which arms supplied by both superpowers intensified and shaped the conflict. The region's strategic value may be less important than its ideological value: presented as part of a system of defense of strategic interests, increasing arms production and sales can be presented as a priority to the U.S. public (Luckham and Dawit 1984). While Kagnew station was considered vital in the 1950s, its significance declined in the 1970s when a U.S. Senate Subcommittee charged that for the Department of Defense and the Secretary of State, Kagnew was merely a pretext to supply arms to Ethiopia in order to allow it to retain colonial control over Eritrea. Assistant Secretary of State for African Affairs David Newscom rejected such charges, defended Ethiopia's territorial integrity, glossed over the annexation of Eritrea, and disclaimed U.S. responsibility for atrocities, stating, "What they do with the bombs within their own country is a matter for their decision and their policy" (United States Senate 1970:1922).

As Soviet aid to Somalia increased, the U.S. provided higher levels to maintain its own position (Lefebvre 1987:474). This created inter-institutional conflict; the Department of Defense sought a build-up of the Diego Garcia base, while the State Department criticized this confrontational stance (Dougherty 1982:27). The importance of the Berbera base in Somalia to the Soviet Union may have been "exaggerated by a military lobby strenuously engaged in persuading a reluctant U.S. Congress to vote the large sums required to develop the Anglo-American installations at Diego Garcia" (Legum and Lee 1977:12).

Militarization was not imposed by external powers on unwilling allies. Regimes in the Horn were eager to amass arsenals. Prior to the coup U.S. interest in Ethiopia was declining, and in 1973 President Richard Nixon denied military aid to Haile Selassie, the same year that Egypt distanced itself from the Soviet Union. The U.S. was not immediately hostile to the Derg on the basis of ideology, and the Derg's shift to the Soviet Union appears at least partially based on a U.S. refusal to provide arms in quantities demanded by the regime to pursue its wars in Eritrea and the Ogaden. Also, in 1974 the terms of arms transfers changed significantly. Previously, commercial sales comprised only 3 percent of U.S. arms transfers to the Horn, but from 1975 to 1982 this rose to 92 percent, as the U.S. urged allies to pay for arms (Luckham and Dawit 1984).

War between Eritrea and Ethiopia continued for three decades, making it one of the longest wars of the twentieth century. While not the only cause of starvation, war did have a disastrous impact on the entire region, both directly and indirectly (McCann 1990). There were thousands of casualties on both sides and vast numbers of refugees fled to Sudan or Somalia or to camps for the displaced in remote valleys of Eritrea, where overcrowding and unsanitary conditions spread infectious diseases, not to mention the psychological stress created by such conditions. Most of the fighting took place in Eritrea, where crop fields and livestock were destroyed, tools were lost in flight, and the constant threat of aerial attack made it impossible to plant crops when rain did come, or to undertake effective water conservation measures or irrigation to lessen effects of drought. Villages and crop fields were abandoned for long periods of time due to continuous harassment by the Ethiopian military, and significant farming areas were left unused because of placement of mines. A Leeds University evaluation of Eritrean food needs estimated that 40 percent of arable land was uncultivated due to war, along with shortages of labor, seeds, tools, and oxen, the presence of pests, low-market prices, and lack of rain (Agriculture and Rural Development Unit 1988).

War also disrupted the pastoralist economy. Animals were targets for bombing and strafing attacks while curfews and harassment disturbed grazing patterns; land mines will continue to restrict grazing in the future. Both agriculturalist and pastoralist economies were disrupted by the war and the Leeds study suggested that the entire Eritrean society was affected at the household level, particularly because of extra burdens placed on women. Additionally, many communities were isolated from essential trading networks.

In the cities, the flight of technicians, near-total dependence on relief supplies, periodic water shortages, restrictions on movement and communications, and a virtual state of siege prevented any effective development. Later, all-out attacks on cities such as Massawa destroyed necessary infrastructure. Ethiopian-imposed marketing policies negatively affected food production by keeping prices low and restricting trade. The Leeds study noted definite discrimination against both Eritrea and Tigray in allocation of agricultural budgets, but even if the Derg had encouraged development in Eritrea there were no resources to support it. By 1981 Ethiopia's military expenditures ($378 million) exceeded its total value of exports by $4 million; Ethiopia's debt to the Soviet Union for arms eventually rose to more than $4 billion. Costs of militarization not only impoverished Ethiopia but plunged the entire region into economic chaos.

Politics of Famine

Just as opposing nationalist discourses created conflicting versions of history and identity in the Horn, famine was reported in different ways by the Ethiopian government and its antagonists. The Derg claimed that it could distribute food to famine-affected populations in Eritrea, Tigray, and Wollo, and its claims were accepted by donor governments, who channeled most of their aid through Ethiopia's Relief and Rehabilitation Committee (RRC). In contrast, the Eritrean Relief Association (ERA) and the Relief Society of Tigray (REST) stated that most famine victims were located beyond government-held areas and could only be reached by their cross-border operations from Sudan. Several Western nongovernmental organizations (NGOs) verified the reports of ERA and REST, but relief aid to Eritrea and Tigray was limited because foreign governments accepted Ethiopian claims of sovereignty. Most food aid was delivered to the government, despite claims that the Derg was using it to feed its troops and attempting to starve Eritrea and Tigray into submission. While donor governments provided support for development programs in government-controlled areas, none would assist rehabilitation or development in Eritrea and Tigray. Such programs are necessary to prevent the recurrence of famine, and donors were clearly contributing to an unbalanced situation by providing this type of aid only to certain areas. While justifying this on the basis of observing Ethiopian sovereignty, few donors raised the issue of Ethiopia's annexation of Eritrea or the fact that the regime was starving those it claimed to represent and protect through such sovereignty.

The Derg clearly intended to use famine as a weapon. Relief supplies intended for Eritrea were confiscated; for example, in January 1985, six thousand tons of food and a water drilling rig were taken from the ship *Golden Venture* at Assab. Food convoys were attacked and destroyed, limiting supplies to the civilian population. In contested areas, relief supplies had to be transported at night by pack animals to avoid detection, and it was very dangerous for peasants to attempt to reach ERA and REST distribution centers. In April 1988, the Derg expelled foreign aid workers from Eritrea and Tigray, citing security risks; it was clear that any disruption in relief efforts at that time would have a devastating effect in Eritrea, reeling under renewed drought and total crop failure. The EPLF said the Derg's objective in expelling aid workers was to remove witnesses and avoid international protest over atrocities against civilians. In April the TPLF reported that Ethiopian planes napalmed Wukro to destroy food supplies that had been delivered to relief agencies before the TPLF took the area. Reports of atrocities continued, including arbitrary executions, use of napalm and cluster bombs, and burning of villages and crops. In May the EPLF reported that Ethiopian troops massacred four hundred people in the village of She'eb, some of whom, it charged, were herded into a pit, then deliberately run over and crushed to death by tanks.

One of the more controversial development policies of the Ethiopian government was the resettlement program in which people were moved from Wollo and Tigray to the south. The Derg insisted that the land was depleted and that people had to move or starve. The Soviet Union, Canada, Italy, and the UN supported the program; OXFAM, however, achieved success in agricultural rehabilitation in the area and argued that resettlement was purely political and intended to deprive opposition forces of civilian support. The organization Cultural Survival reported that resettlement was coerced, brutally implemented, and itself a cause of famine in southwestern regions. Western aid was used to lure people to distribution centers where they were captured and forcibly moved to other areas.

While it was clear that the Ethiopian government had an appalling record of human rights abuses and that it was using famine to attain its political goals, its claim to sovereignty blocked utilization of other channels of assisting the rural population in Eritrea and Tigray. Because ERA and REST were associated with the EPLF and TPLF, both were considered too political by the UN, donor governments, and many NGOs, all of whom refused to work with them. Clearly, the power to distribute food in such a context bestows legitimacy and wins allies, and many regarded ERA and REST as mere tools of the liberation fronts that would help them acquire control over local populations. However, both ERA and REST were extremely effective in saving many lives. Furthermore, as I have argued, such criticisms tend to be selective and to overlook the political objectives of all parties. Many agencies refused to see their own interventions as anything but charitable operations and angrily rejected suggestions that they also played a political role by working only in government-held zones while most of the famine-affected population lived outside those areas. Some did acknowledge that ERA and REST played "central roles" in relief efforts and regarded ERA as the most efficient aid operation in Africa (Brodhead 1986:876). Even Dawit Wolde Giorgis, former military governor of Eritrea and head of Ethiopia's RRC, acknowledged the efforts of ERA and REST. However, the work of African organizations went unrecognized in other reports. For example, Kurt Jansson, who had headed the UN's emergency operations, makes no reference whatsoever to ERA in his book and mentions REST only in a dismissive way (Jansson, Harris, and Penrose 1987). The fact that the UN bore a historic responsibility for the Eritrean case made Jansson's omission all the more striking. However, it was not merely a matter of not giving credit to ERA and REST; the UN's mandate to work only with member governments encouraged it to rely on government information only and to dismiss other sources as unreliable, a practice that resulted in greater fatalities. Donor governments such as Canada also refused to accept information from ERA and REST, or from NGOs working in Eritrea and Tigray, or to assess their claims by sending its own observers to these regions.

Unbalanced aid provision continued even after 1989 when Ethiopian government forces retreated completely from Tigray and controlled only urban garrisons in Eritrea. The EPLF and TPLF victories meant greater access for ERA and REST but also placed greater strain on their supply and distribution capacity, and despite the fact that even greater numbers of people came under the direct responsibility of these organizations, Western donors continued to insist on routing supplies through government channels. For example, Canada emphasized an inefficient airlift operation that maintained Ethiopian troops in Asmara but did not supply the rural population. Consistently, Ethiopian officials regarded Western aid as a means of implementing their policies, and the provision of humanitarian assistance did give significant support to the Derg, allowing it to continue the war in Eritrea and Tigray.

Discourse on famine in the Horn places it outside history, particularly colonial history, transforming it into a product of Africa's essence. Two interrelated rhetorical techniques are used to achieve this: naturalization and dehistoricization. Within discourse, famine is naturalized through exclusion of historical and political explanation. However, the exclusion is partial: the elision of historical details is a selective process that advances a specific economic and political agenda. Discourse on famine contained a critique of the Mengistu regime's policies and its intention to use starvation as a weapon. However, there was little criticism of Western attempts to manipulate famine for political objectives, such as the deliberate 1982 decision by the U.S. National Security Council to withhold food from Ethiopia in order to destabilize the Mengistu regime and force changes in its policies (Clay 1989). Thus, naturalization and dehistoricization construct an ideological version of famine.

Ideological discourse ignored the long-term structural causes of famine and the effects of militarization and argued that the disaster was the direct result of the Derg's socialist policies. The anticommunist emphasis in the mass media ensured that socialism would be presented negatively and seen as monolithic and undifferentiated. Thus, criticism of Ethiopia's Marxist-Leninist regime and its opponents is unremarkable. However, the discursive construction of famine was also influenced by a rhetorical approach particular to Africa.

A key aspect of this discourse is racism. Agricultural decline in postcolonial Africa is frequently depicted as being the fault of Africans themselves. Historically, it was a consistent belief among European colonialists who were contemptuous of Africans and unfamiliar with farming conditions in Africa that all indigenous agricultural practices were backward and destructive (Vaughan 1987). Agricultural collapse is attributed to some African essence rather than to structural conditions inherited by the postcolonial states and the specific historical circumstances of Africa's integration into a world-market system.

Assumptions of the primitive character of Africans carried over into discourse on Ethiopian famine. It was assumed that African peasant farmers were unable to feed themselves because they were ignorant of basic agricultural methods. For example, in the television documentary "African Calvary," Margaret Thatcher shouldered the White Woman's Burden by stating that the West had to "teach [Africans] the basics of long-term husbandry" (Gill 1986:96). This is simply a contemporary restatement of the Civilizing Mission, one which cancels out history by ignoring the massive economic and social transformation of Africa in the colonial period. Although Ethiopia occupied a peculiar place in the hierarchical structure of racist mythology, it was inserted within a general discursive configuration on Africa determined by these racist concepts. As Thatcher's comments indicate, Ethiopia was still regarded as part of a Dark Continent that would have to be led into the light of modernity by the West.

6

AUTHORITY AND DELEGITIMIZATION

Delegitimizing Eritrean Nationalism

Discourse on famine incorporated anticommunist themes in order to launch an ideological attack on the Derg. Unlike the Contras in Central America, however, there was no military force in the Horn that was both opposed to the Derg and ideologically suitable for valorization as "freedom fighters." The complexity of the Eritrean case limited its ideological utility. For example, in Eritrea one journalist told me that it was extremely difficult to interest North American media in the Eritrean case in 1983 due to the perception of the conflict as a complicated squabble between Marxist groups. Following the popularity of the 1984 mini-series on mass starvation, however, there was some recognition of ideological utility in the conflict; the same journalist said that he had been sent to Eritrea by NBC television to get "anything which could be used against the Soviet Union." This ideological aspect of media coverage was recognized by many in Eritrea. For example, in an interview with the author, EPLF Secretary General Issayas Afeworki suggested that negative media reports on the Derg were simply a response to failures in U.S. policy to detach the regime from its Soviet alliance.

Extrapolating from the propaganda model, one would expect media to employ an ensemble of rhetorical techniques intended to delegitimize both the Derg and its opponents. As other opposition forces in the Horn were rarely mentioned in media accounts of conflict, we may consider the application of these techniques to Eritrean nationalism. As noted, the most consistent rhetorical technique employed to delegitimize Eritrean nationalism was to characterize it as a secessionist movement. Some other techniques are demonstrated in a report by Jonathan Power, who writes on Third World issues for the *Herald-Tribune*.

Power's argument is summarized in a headline warning that the "West Should Not Meddle," a suggestion that obscures the central role of the U.S. in negotiating the 1950 federation of Eritrea and Ethiopia (*Winnipeg Free Press*, December 22, 1987). Power uses the construction of significant absence to obscure the historical background and to erase U.S. involvement. Whereas Kaplan (1988b) argues that the media overlooked the Derg's brutality, Power employs a standard model of conflict to claim that media coverage is actually biased in favor of the Derg's opponents: in his view, the EPLF enjoys "media favour as the underdogs in Mariam Mengistu's Marxist horror state, the downtrodden rebelling good guys against the militaristic dictatorial bad."

Initially, such opposing interpretations of media bias appear to contradict the propaganda model. In fact, they offer further confirmation of its validity. Following a series of military victories in 1988 that indicated a turning point in the war and the possibility of Eritrean victory, the EPLF did receive more positive press coverage. However, a survey of reports prior to 1988 demonstrates the same pattern exhibited in Power's text: Ethiopia's alliance with the Soviet Union made it a target of anticommunist discourse and the Eritrean movement was useful to the extent that it signified opposition to the Mengistu regime, yet the EPLF itself was ideologically unacceptable and could not be endorsed. For example, the U.S. State Department found the EPLF "as Marxist-Leninist as the Ethiopians" (Connell 1987:30).

In such cases, the rhetorical tactic of neither-norism is employed (Barthes 1972:153). Where no ideologically acceptable ally is available, conflict is presented as senseless brutality between savages, and charges of bias in favor of either opponent thus encourage skepticism about both. One example of neither-norism is Jonathan Dimbleby's description of the war in the *Spectator* (March 5, 1988): "a suicidal stalemate where the self-righteous rhetoric of both sides about 'our just cause' floats ludicrously back and forth over the corpses." Dimbleby insinuates that the EPLF cannot be trusted, dropping hints about Issayas Afeworki's "unyielding" eyes, the EPLF's "seductive performance," and the "touch of Pol Potism" present in Eritrea, providing no basis for such aspersions. The references to Pol Pot are entirely gratuitous, presenting the EPLF as a band of bloodthirsty fanatics.

Clapham (1991:246–247) also proceeds by innuendo, suggesting the degree of support for opposition groups is unclear and arguing that "all are organised, like the Ethiopian government which they oppose, on 'democratic centralist' lines, and both the EPLF and TPLF are said to operate ruthless internal security systems." In several works, Clapham emphasizes the "ruthless internal security system" of the EPLF, basing his assessment on remarks made by Markakis (1987) but giving them greater emphasis and ignoring the fact that it would be suicidal for the EPLF not to have had a security system in the context of such a war. He presents the EPLF as the Derg's mirror image, opposed to the Ethiopian regime but matching it in evil. There is no need to romanticize the EPLF or to overlook its use of violence, but Clapham's efforts to equate it with the Derg seem based more on a commitment to the image of Greater Ethiopia and an ideological abhorrence of socialism than on any knowledge of the EPLF itself.

Clapham (1990a:225) furthermore suggests that most writing on Eritrea and Tigray is biased, produced either by the fronts themselves or by "observers who are . . . heavily committed to their cause" (in contrast to "politically uncommitted social scientists" who write about Ethiopia). The distinction between committed observer and uncommitted scientist remains unclarified but seems based on Clapham's own ideological commitments; the studies he recommends are among the most clearly biased and, with no proven justification, he dismisses virtually all research on Eritrea as "propaganda." Clapham (1990b:17) claims that those who write favorably on the social revolution in Eritrea are victims of a tendency to romanticize and overlook the repressive character that he finds inherent in revolution. However, he provides no evidence of any falsification but simply creates suspicion through insinuation. His assertion that researchers could work freely in Ethiopia but not in Eritrea overlooks not only efforts by the Rome-based Research and Information Center on Eritrea to encourage study but also the fact that much of Eritrea was a battlefield where movement was restricted to darkness to avoid aerial bombardment, hardly a setting conducive to academic investigation. Behind assertions of objectivity, Clapham's text functions to police the production of discourse and narration of regional histories through an inclusive but unproven condemnation.

Similarly inducing suspicion, Power suggests media exaggerated the famine in Eritrea and Tigray, while overlooking Wollo where most starvation occurred: relief agencies "operating out of the Sudan were able to get food in using the rebel relief organizations. Although the Ethiopian government huffed and puffed and threatened retaliation it did not follow through."

The idea that Ethiopia did not "follow through" with "threatened retaliation" is refuted by the fact of its continuing aerial and artillery bombardment of Eritrea, including attacks on relief convoys, feeding centers, and civilian encampments, as well as the destruction of crop fields, confiscation of relief material, and later, in April 1988, the expulsion of relief workers from Eritrea and Tigray.

Power claims Eritrea and Tigray were "better off . . . because of the extra efforts that had been made to get clandestine supplies in." In contrast, Paulos Tesfa Giorgis, Chairman of the Eritrean Relief Association, stated in the *New York Times* (November 25, 1984) that less than 11,000 tons of grain were being distributed in Eritrea, "scarcely enough to feed 500,000 people for a month." (In a spring 1984 appeal, the Eritrean Relief Committee of New York estimated that 1.25 million people were affected, while in October 1984 the Eritrean Relief Association in Canada stated that the number had climbed to 1.5 million. Two months later in Khartoum, ERA's Emergency Relief Budget Request stated that 2 million people were affected but asked for assistance for 42 percent of the required amount in order to feed 750,000 people, which it evidently felt was the limit of its delivery capacity at that time.) In the same article, Dan Connell of Grassroots International estimated a daily death rate of 200 to 400 people in Eritrea and Tigray; Smith (1987:33, 37n31) placed the death rate in Tigray as high as 1,500 per day, estimating that only 5 percent of emergency food needs were being met in Eritrea and Tigray, and concluded that a total of 1 million famine-related deaths from 1984 to 1986 "appears realistic if not conservative." In November 1984, 69,200 tons of food were distributed through the Ethiopian Government (U.S. Senate 1986:10); however, EPLF and TPLF representatives charged that the Derg deliberately withheld food from Eritrea and Tigray.

In fact, Wollo may have been the area most severely affected by famine (Smith 1987:33; Jansson et al. 1987:49). However, this is a relative assessment, and even if one doubled the highest estimated ratio of provision to need in Eritrea and Tigray, it would still leave half the population there facing starvation, a ratio that hardly bears out Power's contention that "donors were concentrating too much effort in Eritrea and Tigray."

Power addresses the "tempting" idea of providing support to Eritrea. Apparently, this temptation is not based on humanitarian concern since he argues that by allowing (at least) half the population to starve, "too much effort" had been made. Like Kaplan (1988b), who argued for support to the EPLF as a counter to the Derg, Power observes that the EPLF is "a thorn in Mengistu's side," and this seems to be the basis of its attraction. Similarly, Peter Worthington, a Canadian journalist known for support of right-wing causes, described the EPLF as a "Thorn in a Tyrant's Flesh" in *Reader's Digest* (December 1988), and advocated support to Eritrea. Worthington also warned of the EPLF's "disturbing affinity for Marxist terminology, a reminder that the Soviet Union originally backed the Eritrean independence movement before switching sides." Unlike Kaplan and Worthington, Power does not argue for increasing support to the EPLF as a proxy in a regional Cold War struggle.

Power hints that Eritreans "have a case in their demand for independence" but warns "it is by no means watertight." He does not identify any leaks but merely introduces suspicion to delegitimize Eritrean nationalism. Similarly, ignoring the fact that only a trickle of aid was reaching Eritrea and Tigray and that most went to the Derg, Power warns that "this time round the Western countries pouring in aid need to keep some perspective," suggesting that the West had been duped by Eritreans and Tigrayans in some nefarious but unspecified way. Instability of meaning pervades discourse on the Horn, but this is not a product of the literary tropes involved. It is constructed through purposeful absence and generated for ideological ends: conflict is presented as meaningless, without legitimacy or understandable motive, and Marxists are shown fighting Marxists, suggesting essential opportunism and encouraging apolitical attitudes among the domestic news audience.

Another technique of delegitimization is to minimize the historical context of Eritrean nationalism. For example, Power states that Eritrea was colonized by Italy for forty years. Even if one ignores the purchase of parts of Eritrea by Italian companies in 1869, there were fifty-one years from Italy's formal recognition of the whole of Eritrea as a colonial possession in 1890 to the establishment of British administration in 1941. Power thus not only shortens Eritrea's colonial history but distorts its character within the context of African history: "Before that Eritrea had not existed as a separate political entity." This is true, but Power uses it to construct another significant absence in the text, the fact that this situation was typical of the colonial creation of new entities across the continent. In Power's text Eritrea is evanescent, without history or identity, an artificial creation, a freak. Employing a rhetorical technique used by the Derg (Permanent Peoples' Tribunal 1984:368–369), he occludes the historical context of colonialism, which carved Africa into its present national configurations; rather than an exception, Eritrea was a typical, albeit unresolved, case of decolonization. Power refers the Eritrean case to mediation by the OAU, which observed a principle of inviolability of colonial borders—except in the case of Eritrea.

Other distortions of history occur; Power suggests that the Italian invasion of Ethiopia was "in the image of the old Amharic rule, bringing Eritrea again under the authority of Addis Ababa." This indicates that what Italy divided by colonizing Eritrea it reunited by conquering Ethiopia. To what extent Eritrea had ever been "under the authority of Addis Ababa" is questionable since the new capital was only named by Menelik in the late nineteenth century when the Italians were establishing their colony in Eritrea. Certainly it was not the case following May 9, 1936. At that point, the King of Italy became Emperor of Ethiopia, Haile Selassie having fled a week earlier; therefore, Eritrea was not "again [brought] under the authority of Addis Ababa," but rather Ethiopia, too, was annexed by Italy and both Eritrea and Ethiopia came under Italian authority. Even then, control was not centralized in Addis Ababa; instead the region was divided into four autonomous districts that formed "a disunited federal state. Each governorship was in essence a separate entity; each region was an independent republic and acted autonomously. Individual governors ignored the problems of the neighbouring governors and had no interest in co-operating with them, fearing that their difficulties would cross governorate boundaries" (Sbacchi 1985:43). Perhaps in this unintended sense, Power is correct in asserting Italy's reproduction of an image of Amharic rule: the creation of a fragmented collection of separate entities.

Ignoring British plans for partition, Power notes how Britain and the U.S. "favoured federation," failing to mention any motive for such aims. Discussing federation, he admits that the "relationship . . . could never be easy" (again dispensing with explanation) but then states, "Eritrean separatists continued to up the ante and in 1962 the federal government cracked down, abolished the federal institutions and integrated Eritrea fully into Ethiopia." Power implies that Eritrean demands became unreasonable, that Haile Selassie lost patience and simply "integrated" Eritrea. Yet Haile Selassie began undermining the federation almost from its inception, and if Eritreans in any sense "up[ped] the ante" it was only by demanding the constitutionally guaranteed legal rights that the Ethiopian Government was determined to deny them.

Power's conclusion further obscures the causes of the Eritrean nationalist struggle and attempts to cancel the validity of Eritrean claims: "This is one of those situations outsiders would do well to steer clear of. In international law the central government probably has right on its side. But the Eritreans, and their fellow successionists [*sic*], the Tigrayans, whose case is even weaker, will continue to try and pull on the heart strings of the Western world." The suggestion that "outsiders . . . steer clear of" the situation ignores historical reality (i.e., decades of superpower involvement following European colonialism). Power's reference to international law not only contradicts his previous statement that Eritrea had a case for independence, but is unaccompanied by any evidence demonstrating that Ethiopia had "right on its side." Characterization of Eritrean and Tigrayan struggles as secessionist ignores selective application of the term, as well as considerable evidence that abrogation of the federation violated international norms and the TPLF's more consistently stated objective of replacing the Derg rather than forming a separate country. Conflation of goals confuses the situation and overlooks debates between the fronts on such issues. As for a tendency of Eritreans or Tigrayans "to try and pull on the heart strings of the Western world," the above-mentioned statistics demonstrate the past effectiveness of such attempts. Importantly, Power implies that appeals to humanitarian concern are illegitimate, and evil purposes underlie emotional pleas that might seduce the charitable Elect. Not simply an inconsequential report by a misinformed journalist, Power's text displays configurations typical of discourse on the Horn. It echoes the familiar threat of contagion from Africa. Too kind, too liberal, too charitable, the West is swayed by Africa, seduced by the pulling of its heart strings and lured toward disaster.

Foreign Agents, Headless Chickens

External discourse on the Horn of Africa does not simply reproduce that of local protagonists but is produced from within sites which have their own interests and objectives. An important aspect of the propaganda model suggested by Herman and Chomsky (1988) is the reliance on institutional sources, including state and business elites and the work of various experts who are funded by those elites to provide information that supports their interests. The media typically rely on opinions provided by present or former government officials, by conservative think tanks as well as by other journalists. Government and corporate sources spend millions of dollars annually on propaganda campaigns, subsidizing mass media, providing routine and prestigious sources and actively excluding alternative viewpoints.

One of the experts whose work is examined by Herman and Chomsky is Paul Henze, who also has been a prolific contributor to the production of discourse concerning the Horn. Although Henze identifies himself as an independent scholar, Herman and Chomsky (1988:145) identify him as "a longtime CIA officer and propaganda specialist," stating that his CIA career began under a cover of Foreign Affairs Advisor in the Defense Department in 1950, followed by six years as policy advisor to the CIA-controlled Radio Free Europe in Munich. In 1969 he became CIA Station Chief in Ethiopia, then assumed a similar post in Turkey in 1974 before becoming a National Security Council representative in the White House in 1977 (Herman and Brodhead 1986). Afterwards Henze was a Wilson Fellow at the Smithsonian Institution and then became a consultant for the Rand Corporation, a U.S.-military allied think tank. Herman and O'Sullivan (1989:86–87) charge that Henze's move to the Rand Corporation provides a veneer of scholarly objectivity to what are in fact CIA propaganda and disinformation operations.

In his writing on the Horn, Henze makes no reference to any CIA background, stating only that he has "travelled, lived and worked in Ethiopia over the past two decades" (1986a, 1:7). This experience allowed Henze to become a prolific commentator on the region and thus be acclaimed as an expert. For example, at a Michigan State University conference on the Horn, Henze was welcomed as "a former government official who has built an impressive new career as a scholar." Yet Henze's work has been sharply criticized. Discussing his book on a purported Bulgarian plot to kill Pope John Paul II, Herman and Chomsky (1988: 147) find "complete absence of credible evidence, a reliance on ideological premises, and internal inconsistencies." Similar assessments have been made of Henze's work on Africa. Aseffa (1989/1990:53) remarks that although Henze "provokes serious issues," his writing is "elitist, paternalistic, complacent, and based on a biased premise."

While Henze's other work has been closely analyzed, a review of his extensive contributions to discourse on the Horn is in order. Essentially, his writing exemplifies the manner in which regional hegemonic discourses are incorporated into global strategies. Antiquity, essence, and identity are dominant themes in his writing, as Henze reiterates legends propagated by Ethiopian elites to legitimize their rule over the empire and integrates them into a Cold War framework. This ideological complex traces the descent of rulers of the modern state to Solomon and Sheba; a related element in Ethiopian hegemonic mythology is the claim of direct links between ancient Axum and the contemporary state. Henze (1986a, 1:5) endorses such claims: "Like China, Egypt and Iran, Ethiopia is one of the oldest countries in the world. Its beginnings are still shrouded in mystery." In a Rand Corporation report, Henze (1985:3) terms Ethiopia "one of the oldest states in the world," implying correspondence with Axum. However, contemporary Ethiopia is not one of the world's oldest states; emperors Yohannes and Menelik expanded their territory through arrangements with European colonial powers in the nineteenth century, and contemporary borders were only attained by annexation of Eritrea in 1962. The "mystery" shrouding the origins of the contemporary state is introduced by Henze himself, in order to authenticate claims for the antiquity of the Ethiopian empire and legitimize U.S. support.

Emphasis on Ethiopian antiquity is a consistent rhetorical technique in Henze's work. Incorporating mythology used by the Amhara elite to justify their rule in Ethiopia into contemporary ideological struggles, Henze portrays the Soviet-allied Derg as inimical to ancient traditions. He suggests that in toppling traditional authority and breaking ties with the West the Derg cut itself off from Ethiopia's people as well as from the country's essence and historical identity. The betrayal is portrayed as both political and ontological. Whether expressed in terms of racial or ideological destiny, the trajectory is fixed and deviation means disaster. For example, Henze complains that the new museum in Addis Ababa is too small to display Ethiopian history, noting that the Soviets "have made no effort to get into serious archaeological or historical research in Ethiopia. . . . Evidently other interests have preoccupied the Kremlin" (1986a, 1:7). Henze depicts the Soviet Union as unappreciative of Ethiopian antiquity, therefore disconnected from its essence. In contrast, the U.S. is linked with traditional authority and the antiquity of the Solomonic throne, emphasizing the aberrant nature of the Soviet alliance while simultaneously reinforcing and naturalizing a timeless U.S. global hegemony. At a time when Ethiopia, one of the poorest countries in the world, was gripped by deadly famine and several wars, "other interests" might well have made sensible priorities. Sadly, the Soviet Union's priorities did not include initiatives for a negotiated solution to the Eritrean issue or assisting the population of Ethiopia but instead were to sustain Mengistu in an unwinnable war.

Consistently, Henze (ibid.) stressed the superficiality of Soviet influence and of Ethiopia's adherence to Marxism-Leninism: "Like the Ethiopian regime's official espousal of Marxism-Leninism and adherence to the Soviet-Cuban political fraternity, which is propagandistically intense but seems to lack real depth, the Soviet approach to Ethiopia seems to lack genuine commitment."

Even descriptive passages are constructed in such a way as to emphasize the superficiality of the alliance: "The gaudy arches and obelisks—constructed of plywood and tin, painted in the national colors, which were set up for the lavish celebrations of the tenth anniversary of the 1974 revolution—have already peeled" (ibid.:5).

Henze's suggestion that the Soviet Union was not fully committed to Ethiopia seems to contradict his view that Russians had engineered Haile Selassie's deposition and had sought hegemony in the Horn since at least the nineteenth century. Henze manipulates the Cold War framework, sometimes arguing that a long-term Soviet plot had created regional crisis and other times that the Soviet presence was superficial, transient, and likely to be replaced by a return to the proper relationship within a framework of U.S. hegemony.

Haile Selassie was the most enthusiastic U.S. ally in Africa. After World War II, the U.S. helped him acquire Eritrea and access to the sea, securing in return guaranteed use of a strategic communications base in Asmara, which allowed the U.S. to relay messages from the Mediterranean to the Indian Ocean and to monitor Moscow radio transmissions. Henze portrays Haile Selassie sympathetically, minimizing abuses: "[He provided] dynamic leadership for nearly 50 years. His style of leadership was far from dictatorial; it was paternalistic and mildly authoritarian . . . neither notably corrupt nor (by Third World standards) particularly oppressive" (ibid.:8–9). This constructs the Third World as inherently brutal, a zone of endemic corruption and oppression. Reference to "Third World standards" excuses famine during Haile Selassie's reign, as well as the steady erosion of civil rights guaranteed to Eritreans by the UN-arranged federation, the annexation itself, and attacks on Eritrean villages that pushed thousands of refugees into Sudan. Unsuitable development programs that helped to lay the foundation for later famines are also overlooked. By employing a convenient rhetorical distinction between authoritarian and totalitarian regimes, Henze excuses the abuses of power that characterized the emperor's reign.

In a three-part essay for *Encounter* magazine, Henze juxtaposes Haile Selassie with the Derg, suggesting that traditional Ethiopians still bow to the palace in respect for the former emperor and that the general population eagerly awaits restoration of the U.S. presence. In this discursive construction, Haile Selassie, "the old Lion of Judah," symbol of Ethiopian essence, has been betrayed by the Derg, antithesis of Ethiopian history. Replacement of Mengistu will allow Ethiopia to resume its appropriate role as a U.S. ally.

Henze deploys various discursive tactics to delegitimize ideological enemies. For example, relying on the rhetorical technique of ventriloquism, he produces several Ethiopian students who state appropriate affection for the U.S. and aversion to Russians and Cubans. Similar expressions of ideologically suitable allegiance recur throughout his other works. Henze identifies Soviet influence as the key disruptive factor in the region and blames Soviet-style agricultural policies for famine. Such policies did have a negative impact, but famine has been endemic to the region for centuries and conditions for recent agricultural failures had deeper historical roots (Robinson and Yamazaki 1986).

Intent on discrediting ideologically opposed views, Henze resorts to falsification in his critique of Halliday and Molyneux's *Ethiopian Revolution*: "Contrary to pro-Soviet theorists who invent facts to justify the interpretation they would like to give the Ethiopian Revolution of 1974, the changes in government which occurred during that momentous year did not arise from a massive upswelling of peasant discontent. Nor was urban unrest more than an incidental factor in creating a revolutionary situation. Military restiveness was at least as important" (Henze 1986a, 1:8). Henze fails to show which facts Halliday and Molyneux invent but does appropriate their major theme (the role of the military in the revolution). Halliday and Molyneux (1981:91) describe interactions between the military and urban political groups but explicitly argue against "the commonly voiced thesis that the army entered the political arena at some stage subsequent to the revolution itself and either captured or pre-emptively stemmed this process." Henze ignores their assertion that the countryside was quiet in the first months of the revolution as well as their reference to "considerable disagreement about the extent of the rural response" (ibid.:n38). Distortion of opposing views is a typical device of propaganda. For example, David Korn (1986:5, 105), U.S. Charge d'Affaires in Addis Ababa from June 1982 to July 1985, ridicules "Western Marxists" who see the Ethiopian revolution as a "spontaneous uprising of the masses" but fails to identify any studies that suggest this and overlooks Marxist-oriented debates over the nature of the Ethiopian revolution or, indeed, whether what occurred actually was a revolution.

More falsification occurs in Henze's attack on the "favorite thesis of Leftist and emotional-liberal writing," which allegedly asserts that the

U.S. opposed the Derg's seizure of power. Similarly, Donald Peterson (1986), U.S. Ambassador to Somalia from 1978 to 1982, later Deputy Assistant Secretary of State for African Affairs and a member of the Policy Planning Staff for the Director of the Office of South African Affairs, bases an essay on a rejection of this thesis. As the thesis does not occur in any serious study, it appears that Henze, Korn, and Peterson have directed their efforts at disproving a theory they have invented and then attributed to ideological opponents. For example, Henze (1983a:182–183n25) has Halliday and Molyneux "maintain that the United States tried to prevent the Ethiopian revolution," but according to his reference they make no such claim.

In fact, relevant congressional records show that the U.S. was not firmly opposed to the Derg (U.S. Senate 1976; U.S. House of Representatives 1978). As it did later in the Philippines and Haiti, the U.S. readily embraced those who ousted a former ally. When the monarchy was overthrown in 1974 by military coup, the U.S. had no fundamental objections to the change of leadership or to the Derg's policies (Korn 1986). Anticipating Haile Selassie's downfall, it had already distanced itself from the monarchy. Acquisition of a communications base at Diego Garcia in the Indian Ocean reduced the importance of Kagnew station in Asmara and eliminated the need to support the emperor, and after the coup the U.S. quickly recognized the new government. David Korn (ibid.:12–13) suggests this was due to a new openness on the part of the U.S., which he claimed "had shed, albeit momentarily, its doctrinary aversion to socialism in the Third World." Donald Peterson makes an identical argument: "Washington had long since shed its once-doctrinaire aversion to Marxist socialism in the Third World and was unperturbed by the prospect of Ethiopian socialism" (Peterson 1986:31).

Despite the unanimity of former U.S. officials, their claims are unlikely. The Derg's Marxism was not apparent after the Emperor's deposition; according to Marina and David Ottaway (1978:7), there was no sign of socialism in its original policy. The Derg adopted the rhetoric of the civilian left, which it later exterminated, because it provided a means of retaining maximum control. Having deposed the Emperor, the military outlawed strikes and jailed labor leaders; in May 1975 the Derg abolished the Labor Confederation leadership and called for new elections. When the Labor Confederation attempted a general strike the Derg arrested its leaders, killed at least seven Ethiopian Airlines workers who opposed the arrests, wounded forty-three others, and arrested hundreds under martial law. The policy of Ethiopian socialism embodied in the slogan "Ethiopia First" was vague, and there was struggle within the Derg (causing the death of half its members) before it officially adopted Marxist-Leninist ideology. This did not prevent the Derg from killing students, workers, and children just before May Day in 1977 (estimates of the death toll range from 300 to 1,000). The slaughter of left-wing civilian groups such as the pro-Soviet MEISON and the EPRP may have indicated to Washington that the Derg could be a useful ally. Seeking to secure its remaining strategic interests and counter the Soviet presence in Somalia, the U.S. readily overlooked the Derg's domestic policies and human rights violations.

The U.S. was eager to continue good relations (Korn 1986:12). In 1978 the Committee on International Relations advised that Ethiopia was still a friend of the U.S. and that Soviet heavy-handedness would eventually ensure its loss of influence; Mengistu was seen as "thoughtful and determined but unstable" because of his dalliance with the Soviets (United States House of Representatives 1978:17, 48). In 1978 David Aaron, Deputy National Security Advisor, went to Addis Ababa, where, according to Korn (1986:50), he "assured Mengistu that Washington did not oppose the economic and social aims of the revolution, [held out the possibility of increased aid, reminded Mengistu of U.S. influence on neighboring areas, and] pointed out that the United States had never supported the insurgencies in Eritrea and had no reservation about endorsing, as it always had, Ethiopia's territorial integrity." Korn attributes shifts and inconstancies in Ethiopia's relations with the U.S. to the influence of the Soviet Union, which he suggests may have been controlling Mengistu through threat of assassination.

Some suggested that severance of U.S.-Ethiopian relations was forced by the Derg's savagery and U.S. determination to maintain humanitarian values. For example, in the *New York Times* (January 1, 1989), Jane Perlez states that this led the U.S. to stop military sales to Ethiopia in 1977. Although the regime's brutal character was evident, human rights violations in Ethiopia did not much concern the U.S. Peterson (1986:630) notes that the *Chicago Tribune* (December 1, 1974) had identified the Derg as "murderous beyond belief" and that "Ethiopians had bombed [Eritrean] villages indiscriminately and executed many suspected insurgents" but acknowledges that this did not create any "fundamental change in U.S. relations with Ethiopia. . . . The State Department advised patience, restraint and continued military aid to Ethiopia."

U.S. military support to brutal regimes is common, provided they exhibit the appropriate allegiances. For example, when the U.S.-backed Indonesian regime escalated atrocities in East Timor, arms supplies to the regime actually increased. Similarly, in 1974 and 1975 the U.S. approved new programs of cash and credit arms sales to Ethiopia, and military aid grew from $28.5 million in 1974 to $57.5 million in 1975 to a peak of over $100 million in cash sales during 1976. This was "a large increase over the previous level of $10 m. per year in the period immediately beforehand" (ibid.:631). In the three years after the Emperor's deposition in which the U.S. continued as Ethiopia's major arms supplier, the average military aid was 90 million dollars, "triple the average of 10 million dollars per year during the period immediately preceding the revolution" (Henze 1986b:27). From 1974 to 1977 the U.S. provided Ethiopia with $180 million in military aid and supplies. Again, U.S. aims were to ensure Ethiopia's territorial integrity, maintain influence, and block a Soviet presence.

As it had with Haile Selassie, the U.S. backed the Derg's war on Eritrea in the name of political stability, ignoring the obvious contradiction, and supported preservation of existing borders. Also important were fears that an independent Eritrea would join with Arab states to control the Red Sea. However, the Derg's anti-U.S. rhetoric, its growing ties with the Soviet Union, and its failure to provide compensation for expropriated U.S. property led to termination of military grant aid in 1977. Following Mengistu's victory in a power struggle within the Derg, President Jimmy Carter suspended arms supplies and reduced military assistance. Mengistu's response was to close the U.S. base, expel U.S. personnel, and expand ties with the Soviet Union. Despite these actions, a growing atmosphere of East-West confrontation and shifts in support to regional governments, U.S. military assistance to the Derg continued. In 1978, jeeps, spare parts for fighter planes, and cluster bombs were shipped to Ethiopia for eventual use in bombardment of Asmara and Massawa, in which many civilians were killed.

Despite duplicity elsewhere, Henze (1986a, 2:16) frankly notes that human rights do not determine foreign policy and that the U.S. was ready to embrace the Derg: "The United States made no effort to stem any phase of the revolutionary process in 1974, accepted the dethronement of Haile Selassie and the killing of 59 officials of his government in November 1974 (many of them had been closely associated with the USA for years) without threat of a break in relations. U.S. economic aid programs continued without interruption, and U.S. military support for Ethiopia was sharply *increased* after 1974."

In explaining the aberrant and transgressive relationship between Ethiopia and the Soviet Union, Henze ignores U.S. reluctance, immediately after Vietnam and Watergate, to provide weapons to Ethiopia in quantities demanded by Mengistu. Instead, he seeks more abstract explanations: Ethiopia "psychologically . . . found itself adrift" after deposition of the "energetic" emperor. Adopting the mythology of Ethiopia as a long-unified state, Henze suggests that without the (U.S.-allied) emperor, a decapitated Ethiopia veered toward (Soviet-engineered) disaster. Rather than analyzing Ethiopia's territorial integrity, as well as changing U.S. perceptions of the Horn's strategic importance and altered arrangements for arms supplies, Henze employs a near-metaphysical explanation that echoes Thomson's (1975:139, 152) idea that Ethiopia, addicted to centralized imperial authority by centuries of unbroken tradition, became "schizophrenic" after the 1974 coup and flopped about like "a headless chicken." In this scenario, national derangement results from transgression of the fundamental pattern of Ethiopian culture and psychology, including any deviation from ideologically appropriate alignment. Using this rhetoric of essentialism, Henze proposes that Ethiopians, having strayed from historical-racial destiny and after collectively cutting off their own heads, were performing an apocalyptic dance of death to a tune fiddled by their Soviet masters.

This discursive configuration rests upon an image rooted in medieval times when Ethiopia was regarded as the realm of Prester John and a mirror for Europe. In essence, the image of Prester John and the myth of the antiquity of the Ethiopian state are confirmations of state authority itself. Ethiopia's contemporary relationship with the West is mediated within a hierarchy structured by broader discourses of racialism, Christian mythology, and anticommunism. Henze (1985: 6) depicts Ethiopia as an "atypical African country" comparable not to Africa but to the older states of Europe, the Middle East, and Asia, and essentially allied with the West.

Henze presents alliance with the Soviet Union and deviation from the U.S. hegemonic order as so fundamental an aberration that it can only have been engineered by foreign agents. This rhetorical figure is common in hegemonic discourse and is not specific to the Horn. Henze suggests that infiltrators engineered Ethiopia's alliance with the Soviet Union. There is no evidence for this and Henze admits that "we simply do not know" if such infiltrators ever existed, but he nevertheless argues, "What we do know is that the Russians had never abandoned their long-standing goal of gaining much greater influence in Ethiopia and had worked steadily and patiently to advance their interests ever since Ethiopia's liberation in 1941" (Henze 1986a, 2:15). That this also had been the pattern of U.S. involvement goes unmentioned. The terms echo those used by imperialists such as Lord Lugard (1923:2): Africa is a "great blank space," and the inscription over the abyss is to be written by an alien hand and in the language of superpower rivalry.

Echoing the claims of Ethiopian leaders, Henze characterizes Eritrea as a recent, artificial entity, juxtaposing it with the image of Ethiopia as a historically integrated and legitimate state authenticated by antiquity, requiring him to ignore the foreign powers that strengthened Ethiopia's empire and allowed it to expand its territory. Dismissing Eritrean nationalism, Henze (1986a, 1:7) proposes that pride prevented Eritreans from employing the benefits of Italian colonialism that would have guaranteed them a bright future after federation,

> but other Eritreans resented their status, especially after the federation was dissolved in 1962 at the very time that all the other little bits-and-pieces of Africa were gaining independence—with their own ministers and flags, membership in the UN, and other trappings of statehood. Asmara, one of Africa's most appealing little cities, was condemned to provincial status while Ouagadougou, Bangui, and Nouakchott filled up with foreign embassies and sent Ambassadors to Paris, London, and Washington.

Like other colonized people, Eritreans aspired to independence. Henze caricatures this as resentment of "other little bits-and-pieces of Africa" that attained "trappings of statehood" and ignores the violation of international law represented by Ethiopia's annexation of Eritrea.

Reproducing the discourse of Ethiopian nationalism that charges Arab influence in the Eritrean independence movement, Henze consistently stresses the shallowness of Eritrean identity and emphasizes foreign, particularly Arab, influence in order to undermine the case for independence: "Dissidence in Eritrea amounted to very little until the late 1960s when radical Arabs and Communists began stoking the rebellion" (ibid.). He draws similar conclusions in his Rand Corporation report:

> Eritrea is not an ethnic problem. It is an issue of dissidence and frustration in a border region that gained certain advantages over the rest of the country as a result of 50 years of colonial experience. In Haile Selassie's final years, rebellion in Eritrea grew to serious proportions only because of external communist and radical Arab support. But Eritreans were always too factionalized to cooperate for long. . . . The Eritrean liberation movement consisted of an insignificant group of exiles, predominantly Muslim traditionalists, who had sympathy but no strength in their home territory. They were, despite efforts to represent themselves as a united front, always rent by tensions and rivalries reflecting those in Eritrean society itself. Life in Eritrea was little affected by

exile activities or insurgency until radical Arabs and various Soviet proxies began to support Eritrean dissidents. (Henze 1985:vi,135)

In contrast to the image of Ethiopia as an ancient unified state, Eritrea is dismissed as factionalized, internally divided and lacking identity. Henze reduces violations of international law to "frustration" in a "border region," obscuring verifiable facts and rendering them "insignificant." He selects aspects of Eritrean history to distort the character of nationalism there. External agents become the sole motivating force in an ephemeral and rootless Eritrean nationalism, in contrast to an Ethiopian territorial integrity authenticated by antiquity. Henze makes the Arab-inspired character of Eritrean nationalism into the sign of its illegitimacy. In the *Washington Quarterly*, Henze (1986b:23) again emphasizes the artificiality of Eritrean nationalism by employing the foreign agent image, noting "a sudden change in tempo [when] the insurgents began to receive arms and money from radical Arab governments and East Europeans, with the Soviets looking on approvingly in the background."

Henze also refers to Cuban and Chinese support in order to demonstrate the artificiality of Eritrean nationalism. He ignores the anomalous treatment of Eritrea in comparison with other ex-colonial states, annexation by Ethiopia, and violation of the UN federation. Rather than examining grievances that intensified existing calls for independence, Henze concentrates exclusively on "Communist and radical benefactors [who saw that] stoking rebellion in Eritrea jeopardized U.S. interests" (ibid.). Again, Henze neglects to mention that U.S. "interests" in Eritrea were premised upon jeopardizing those of the Soviet Union. Within this context Eritrea is simply a pawn to be used in global superpower strategies; U.S. "interests" are consistently regarded as legitimate whereas those of the Soviet Union are not, while Eritrean objectives go unmentioned. As John Foster Dulles frankly stated, U.S. policy demanded subordination of Eritrean "opinions" to U.S. "interests." By emphasizing Ethiopian antiquity, minimizing Eritrean nationalism, and stressing the influence of external agents, Henze pursues this goal.

History is thus reshaped according to these interests. Henze says Eritreans were "not strongly pro-separatist" (ibid.:24) and that "the end of the federation was not marked by public discontent in any serious form" (1986b:32). Similarly, Clapham (1990b:207) proposes that there was "no sign of violent opposition or the emergence of any composite Eritrean nationalism" during this period. Such interpretations overlook considerable Eritrean discontent and opposition. Britain found Eritrea split "from the top to the bottom" over federation (United Nations 1952:6). During the prefederation period, Ethiopian terrorists not only assassinated Eritrean leaders who opposed union but launched military attacks on villages supporting independence. Opposition to Ethiopian violations of the federation caused the 1958 general strike and growth of the underground organization Mahber Showate, both of which were violently suppressed. Although highly factionalized, an armed opposition movement had been organized by 1961 and political cells formed in several neighboring countries. Numerous cables of protest were sent to the Ethiopian Government and to the UN, and there were other forms of "public discontent" such as a demonstration at the Ethiopian Embassy in Cairo on November 17, 1962, in which two students and an Egyptian policeman were shot. Originally it was reported that the Ethiopian Ambassador himself had mowed down the demonstrators, but later he claimed that his staff beat him to the draw while he was trying to locate his revolver (*Africa Diary*, November 24–30, 1962).

Building on such assertions, Henze (1986b:33) claimed that in contemporary Eritrea "the population as a whole seems far from totally alienated from Ethiopia." Even among advocates of Greater Ethiopia, few supported such a claim. For example, Donald Levine and John Spencer, former adviser to Haile Selassie, testified before the U.S. Congress in 1976 that most Eritreans wanted independence; oddly, however, both stated that, irrespective of this, they should not obtain it. Explaining this paradox, Spencer warned that if Eritrea was "lost" the Soviet Union would rule the Horn, while Levine justified denial of Eritrean rights by suggesting that Ethiopia should continue to dominate Eritrea in order to avoid "civil war." Despite its fantastic aspect, this argument convinced Edward Korry, former U.S. Ambassador to Ethiopia, who agreed that the Derg's control of Eritrea was necessary to prevent a "bloodbath" (at this point, there had been fifteen years of warfare); Korry also offered the more usual justifications, including access to vital oil routes, the threat of a bad example to the rest of Africa and "the survival of Israel." The tone was broken by Senator Joseph Biden's observation that similar arguments had been used by the British "for 300 years to keep Ireland under suppression" (U.S. Senate 1976:43–49).

Henze notes the Derg's brutality but suggests this had little impact on the Eritrean people. Such a sanguine observation seems extremely unlikely in the context of more than a quarter-century of terrible warfare. Seen against a background of decades of village bombings, executions, disappearances, tortures, crop burnings, sieges in the cities, mass arrests, rapes, repression, extortion, theft, withholding of food aid to effect starvation, and mass exodus of the population from Eritrea or to EPLF camps for the displaced, Henze's speculation concerning Eritrean feelings towards Ethiopia seems dubious at best. Questionable interpretations typify Henze's work; for example, he offers tautology as analysis, for obscurantist ends: "If Menelik had ejected the Italians, there would be no Eritrean problem today, because Eritrea would merely be a forgotten imperialistic episode" (1986a, 3:30). This is a rhetorical technique noted by Zinn (1980) and identified by Barthes (1972:154) as the statement of fact: a historical incident of major significance is briefly mentioned but passed over with no discussion of its importance and thereby stripped of meaning. Menelik did not eject the Italians from Eritrea and in fact recognized the borders of the colony. The very purpose of Henze's text is to obscure such events and to transform Eritrea into a "forgotten imperialistic episode."

Henze further confuses the colonial past, saying Eritrean history begins in 1885 but giving no justification for this date. (Although Italy acquired Massawa in 1885, Assab had been declared a colony three years before and Italian commercial firms had purchased territory in 1869). He states that the Italians held Eritrea for fifty-one years, indicating that control over Eritrea ended in 1936. However, this is not the case. At that time, Italy invaded the neighboring country, Ethiopia, but even when Italian forces occupied Addis Ababa in May 1936 only about one-third of Ethiopia had been subdued, so that Henze's implication (i.e., Eritrea's separate existence was terminated by invasion of Ethiopia) cannot be sustained for this date. After 1936 Italian colonial expenditures were jointly calculated for Italian East Africa, including Somalia as well. Henze nowhere calls for the reunification of Somalia and Ethiopia.

In a Rand Corporation report, Henze indicates why the U.S. continued to support Ethiopia's territorial integrity rather than assisting any of the liberation fronts. He dismisses Afar and Oromo groups because of the small scale of their operations. The TPLF might have rated possible modest support insofar as it had no separatist aims and sought Mengistu's overthrow, but its "disquieting" Marxism and "unclear" connections with Eritrean fronts made it suspect; Henze's ultimate dismissal of the TPLF stems from the fact that "they cannot be equated with the Afghan freedom fighters" (1985:vi). As for Eritrea, Henze is more certain: "The West should not evaluate rebel or separatist movements in Eritrea without taking history into account. A Western effort to support Eritrean independence would be as frustrating an experience as intervention in Lebanon. There is no good case for it" (ibid.).

Henze frankly expresses the objectives underlying official U.S. discourse on Eritrea: "Can the West exploit it to its advantage? Is There an Eritrean Card to Play?" Absent is any suggestion that Eritrean independence might be supported on legal grounds or that Eritreans should be allowed to exercise their right to self-determination. The significance of the Horn is portrayed solely in terms of Cold War rivalry: "Trying to break up an old, long-recognized country because we dislike a distasteful government that has seized control of it makes no more sense in Ethiopia than it does in Iran. Why leave the Soviets to champion Ethiopia's territorial integrity when it is their meddling that has put it in jeopardy? None of our allies and no significant Third World states outside the Soviet bloc would join us to support Eritrean independence" (ibid.:34).

This is a contemporary restatement of Dulles's 1952 pronouncement on U.S. interests in the Horn. To compete with Soviet influence and to preserve other alliances, Eritrean interests are ignored and history is fictionalized. Local and global cycles of power and meaning mesh as the myth of Ethiopia as an ancient, unified state is incorporated into superpower rivalry. The "meddling" of the U.S., which achieved the disastrous federation in order to secure the Kagnew base and a dependable ally in a strategic location, is elided and the discourse of anticommunism supplies the rhetorical figure of the foreign agent, which is used to blame the Soviet Union for conflict in the Horn and to maintain Cold War polarities.

Participating in a 1990 symposium organized by Freedom House (an organization described by Herman and Chomsky [1988:28] as "a virtual propaganda arm of the government and the international right wing"), Henze offered more contradictory interpretations, arguing, in contrast to his earlier assertions that the Soviet Union was not firmly committed to Ethiopia, that holding onto Ethiopia was crucial for Soviet prestige. He also argued that the Soviet Union had followed a careful plan to obtain control over the entire Horn by ensuring that Ethiopia first became a victim of (Soviet-armed) Somali aggression and was then rescued by a massive injection of Soviet military supplies.

Henze (1985) imagines other conspiracies as well, claiming that the Soviet Union was supplying both the Eritreans and the Ethiopians in a strategy to keep the latter in a dependent relationship for arms supplies. As with many other dubious claims, Henze offers no proof regarding this assertion. The scenario appears extremely unlikely, although Henze perhaps found certain precedents for such double-dealing in CIA activities, such as its 1972 no-win policy toward Kurds fighting for autonomy in Iraq. In cooperation with the Shah of Iran, minimal support was given to them while negotiations and potentially successful offensives were discouraged; when the Shah made an agreement with Iraqi leaders in 1975 the Kurds were abandoned to a grim fate (Blum 1986; Pike Report 1977). Blaine Harden, in the *Manchester Guardian Weekly* (January 5, 1986), refers to Henze's suggestion, but neither offers any evidence to support this claim and it must be seen as Henze's invention.

Further contradictions occur in Henze's remarks at the Freedom House symposium. Ignoring the fact that the U.S. built up one of the largest armies in Africa to support Haile Selassie, Henze suggests that the U.S. had never sought hegemony in the Horn. Consistently, Henze has sought to undermine any potential acceptance of independent Eritrea. Locked into the Cold War framework, he has ignored indigenous aspirations and insisted that Eritrea remain linked with Ethiopia through a renewed federation. In part, economic factors are put forward as a rationale for maintaining this link. However, this is a spurious argument. The EPLF indicated that economic relations would continue between Ethiopia and an independent Eritrea. Henze's insistence on territorial integrity and renewed federation ignored the reality of the situation in the Horn.

Henze bases his analysis of the Eritrean case on the work of Haggai Erlich, which he consistently recommends. In turn, Erlich (1983:142), Chairman of the African Section of the Department of Middle Eastern and African History at Tel Aviv University, in his Hoover Institution study of the Eritrean independence struggle, cites Henze as "an authority on both Soviet and Ethiopian affairs" but refrains from noting Henze's CIA background. Mutual admiration has led to collaboration (Henze 1983a:183n29). Through mutual confirmation, Henze and Erlich construct the limits of acceptable discourse. For example, Clapham (1990b), whose ideological approach seems congruent with those of Henze and Erlich, recommends them both and distinguishes their work from what he disparages as polemical literature. Through the exercise of these authorities, certain identities and histories are cancelled.

However, like Henze's work, Erlich's study is flawed and contradictory in key aspects. For example, echoing arguments made by the Derg, he claims that "Italy's impact on Eritrean society was minimal," a remarkable conclusion, particularly as Erlich himself notes that the Italians:

> constructed an impressive road and railway network and developed urban centres . . . contributed to the maintenance of law and order, subsidized the economy, and promoted health care . . . [undermined the authority of] great [Christian] families and regional warlords . . . encouraged Islam and Arabic . . . [weakened the church through] land confiscations . . . [encouraged] the self-awareness of Tigrinya speakers and Tigrean sectarianism . . . [and cemented] the existence of Eritrea as a separate entity and the preservation and even promotion of its internal diversity. (1983:3–4)

It is difficult to see how this can be construed as "minimal" impact. In fact, Erlich's own text describes nothing less than a fundamental transformation of Eritrea by Italian colonialism. Nevertheless, Ethiopian, Israeli, and U.S. interests attempted to ignore such facts.

Dismissing Eritrea as an artificial creation, Erlich claims that colonialism's main effect was to strengthen Islam. Like Abir (1972), Erlich (1983:11) stresses the Muslim character of the ELF and Arab influence on Eritrean nationalism: in his view, Ethiopian inflexibility explains how "what was little more than a Muslim separatist movement developed into a full-fledged Eritrean nationalist movement." Erlich implies that Eritrean nationalism is religious in character. The same interpretation is offered by the former U.S. Ambassador to Ethiopia, Edward Korry, who described conflict in the Horn as "a Muslim-Christian issue" (U.S. Senate 1976:50). Wallerstein (in Balibar and Wallerstein 1991:191) also reduces the complexity of Eritrean nationalism to this religious division. Similarly, in the *Globe and Mail* (March 21–25, 1987), Carole Berger imputes to it a religious character. Erlich (1983:55) characterizes the Eritrean independence struggle as Muslim-dominated in its early phases and still "an integral part of Red Sea and Middle Eastern affairs rather than . . . an African conflict. All local actors in the Eritrean conflict (or on other major issues concerning the Horn of Africa) are directly connected, sometimes even closely allied, with Middle Eastern countries and organizations." A glance at a map indicates that Arab nations inevitably will influence Eritrea. Yet Arab involvement does not fully explain Eritrean nationalism. Exclusive emphasis on Arab support constructs Eritrea as essentially inert and manipulated by external forces. This same rhetorical device of the Arab as foreign agent was used by the Ethiopian Government: both Haile Selassie and the Derg emphasized the Arab character of Eritrean nationalism in attempts to delegitimize it (Markakis 1987:121). Until it could no longer ignore defeats inflicted by the EPLF, Ethiopian discourse portrayed conflict in Eritrea as bandit activity, frequently combining the rhetorical construct of the foreign agent with religious fanaticism by invoking images of Arab invaders. The disastrous Peasant March of June 1976, for example, was organized as a call to arms against Muslim encirclement (in addition to offers of land in conquered areas).

Israel also stresses Arab influence, perceiving Eritrean separatism as a threat to its strategic interests in the Red Sea; renewed shipments of Israeli weapons, including the napalm and cluster bombs dropped on the civilian population of Massawa in 1989, were deemed insurance against transformation of the Red Sea into an exclusively Arab sphere of influence. As noted, Ambassador Korry found this potential threat sufficient justification for denying Eritreans their legal rights.

Connections with Arab states and the Palestine Liberation Organization have existed, but Erlich and Henze exclude indigenous aspirations. Halliday and Molyneux (1981:44–45), discuss Arab support for Eritrean independence but find the Eritreans are "nobody's clients" and that external influence was not "an initiatory factor." Pateman (1990:93–110) provides many useful details on the changing relations between various Arab states and the Eritrean independence movement, as well as indicating Ethiopia's own efforts to win Arab support for its cause. The EPLF itself downplays connections with Arab powers. From the inception of the nationalist movement there were efforts to minimize differences between Christians and Muslims and to stress common identity. Nevertheless, early efforts to form a united Christian-Muslim movement were unsuccessful. Such divisions had a destructive impact on the course of Eritrean nationalism and, in the future, an independent Eritrea may face the problem of religious fundamentalism that has swept through the Middle East and North Africa. However, to reduce the entire course of Eritrean nationalism to this single factor is to seriously misinterpret it. Erlich attempts to obscure the history of Eritrean nationalism, claiming that it did not "emerge as a significant movement until the 1970s [and the] overwhelming majority of Christian Tigreans . . . wanted reunification with Ethiopia" (1983:5).

A vigorous movement for Eritrean independence was active from the 1940s and armed conflict, certainly a "significant" development, had erupted in the 1960s. Some support for union with Ethiopia did come from the Eritrean highlands, but Erlich offers no proof for the claim that an "overwhelming majority" wanted unification (here described as "reunification," a usage intended to endorse Ethiopian claims that project the contemporary state into the mysterious past). In contrast, a recently declassified secret cable from the U.S. Embassy refers to an estimate that 80 percent of Eritreans wanted independence at the time (*Journal of Eritrean Studies* 1987, 1988).

The U.S. supported Ethiopia's aims for complete incorporation of Eritrea but eventually both had to settle for federation. Using the rhetorical technique of inoculation, which Barthes (1972:150) describes as "admitting the accidental evil of a class-bound institution the better to conceal its principal evil," Erlich (1983:7–8) admits federation was "doomed" and "fictitious almost from the start," but says it was "a compromise based essentially on Ethiopia's historical rights and economic and strategic needs." He refrains from questioning these "rights" and "needs" and nowhere mentions the U.S. role in creating the federation, a significant omission. By constructing significant absences in the text, Erlich (ibid.:20) shifts argument from history to myth, contrasting Eritrean ephemera with Ethiopian antiquity and dismissing Eritrean nationalism as "a by-product of recent history . . . too shallow and rootless to help Eritreans overcome a historically rooted sectarianism and the temptations of destructive radicalism." Eritreans are portrayed as lacking political will and a sense of identity formed by common experience. Conforming to standard rhetorical explanations of African history, Erlich (ibid.:5) emphasizes external agency affecting essential African inertia. He also suggests the British administration in Eritrea created chaos by allowing political freedom and thus "unleashing uncontrollable forces."

Echoing Ethiopian nationalist claims, Henze approvingly cites Erlich's assertion that Eritrea is "an artificial creation of European imperialism" (1985:5). Levine also describes Eritrea as "an artifact of Italian colonialism" (quoted in U.S. Senate 1976:49). Both Haile Selassie and the Derg applied these terms to Eritrea. Once again, in the African context, where every state is an artificial creation in the sense that pre-existing forms of organization were disrupted and transformed by the colonial experience, such statements make little sense and are easily seen as distorting operations of ideological discourse. In contrast to the Amhara myth of a continuously existing unified Ethiopian state, Eritrean nationalists stress the impact of European colonialism in the formation of a unique Eritrean identity and, in this respect, the similarity between Eritrea and other former colonies that are now independent. Henze, Erlich, and Levine invert this and make it appear that Eritrean nationalism is illegitimate precisely because of the colonial impact. Such arguments are incoherent: the OAU decision to maintain boundaries inherited from the colonial period should also have been applied to Eritrea.

Erlich says lack of national identity and the diversity of Eritrean society led to disunity, internal struggle, and ultimately, the failure of nationalist aspirations. Although admitting that Eritrean victory was near in 1978, Erlich suggested that the opportunity had passed forever because of the rootless and fragmented nature of Eritrean society. Henze maintained a similar position throughout his writings. Korn (1986:161), too, dismissed Eritrean independence as a "chimera."

On the Eritrean issue, there has been a remarkable convergence of various discourses, a consensus accepted by those from all points on the political spectrum, including both superpowers, Marxists and conservatives, U.S.-supported emperors claiming biblical genealogies, and Soviet-supplied military dictatorships: the impossibility of Eritrean independence. Locked into the cycles of hegemonic discourse, these commentators all negate Eritrean identity, formed by common experience of colonialism and by three decades of terrible warfare. An analysis of the power of representation reveals that this discursive unity has been dedicated to producing what it ostensibly describes and to enforcing the legitimacy of Ethiopia's territorial integrity while delegitimizing Eritrean nationalism, seeking to prevent its recognition, and thereby its existence. Dissenting voices are banished as propaganda with no effort to engage with their claims. This discourse concentrates on external factors, dismissing Eritrean nationalism as artificial and a product of Arab and communist agitation rather than seeing it in the context of African history. Adherence to the myth of a centralized and historically united Ethiopian state overlooks both the recent development of that state and its essential instability, demonstrated by the proliferation of movements of various ideological orientations inside Ethiopia. Assertions that Eritreans lost their chance for victory in 1977 because of internal fragmentation overlook a major Ethiopian offensive assisted by the Soviet Union, Cuba, and South Yemen. Predictions of the failure of Eritrean nationalism have been refuted by decisive EPLF victories and the establishment of a provisional government, the collapse of Ethiopia's military machine, and the flight of its dictator. Many felt that Eritrean independence already had been achieved in 1991, although the EPLF made no formal declaration. Regardless of the nature of Eritrea's political future, serious negotiations remain to be undertaken to insure that the suffering of the entire region is not prolonged. Permanent resolution of conflicts in the Horn will not be aided by assessments that distort regional history.

The nature of conflict in the Horn encouraged the emergence of two narrative tendencies: the restoration motif that offers return to a lost paradise of hegemony over the Third World, and an apocalyptic narrative warning of dangers resulting from loss of control and the need to violently reassert it. These narratives are examined in the following chapter, but before proceeding to analysis of other texts it may be useful to recapitulate some of the major discursive elements noted. These include the assertion of expertise and authority over public naivete, explicit endorsement of a developmental paradigm with support for large-scale commercial agriculture, imposition of Cold War polarities on regional situations, celebration of charity by the Elect and emergence of a narrative of betrayal by the undeserving poor, the eclipse of "African" famine by "Ethiopian" famine, attribution of responsibility for famine to Africans, an indignation at atrocities committed by ideological enemies and a willingness to ignore those committed by allies, criticism of the Derg for using famine as a weapon accompanied by a willingness to use food aid for political advantage, and falsification for ideological purposes.

7

RESTORING ORDER IN ETHIOPIA

Lost Paradise

Africanist discourse is preoccupied with power and the fear of loss of control. At its core is an opposition between chaos and order, involving identity linked to racial essence. The power at issue is based on colonial rule over Africa and the West's continuing economic and political domination over the former colonies in general. Elaborated during the process of colonial expansion and incorporating many of the themes of racism, this discourse has deep roots in European consciousness, where the image of the Wild Man had a long history as an object of both fear and desire (Dudley and Novack 1972). Colonial identity, constituted through domination and control of the non-European Other, was a repository for these fears and desires and also a symbol of control over such ambivalently regarded impulses. Inscribed within the history of imperialism is a vast allegory of fear of the Savage and longing for the Other, played out in many different manifestations.

In the Horn, it is manifested in a peculiar racist vision involving both the image of savagery and the historical desire of the West to find in Ethiopia a supplementary reflection of itself, a desire expressed in an ensemble of discursive fragments: Ethiopia as ancient monarchy and Christian state, Prester John's mysterious realm, and Haile Selassie as dependable anticommunist ally. Just as Ethiopia had been the symbol of unconquered Africa that provided other Africans with a representation of past glory, it gave the West the image of a legitimate state. During the period of colonial expansion, this state served a useful role in the system of dependent colonialism (Holcomb and Sisai 1990). Various imperialist powers colluded in maintaining the Abyssinian rulers in order to ensure access to the Horn and avoid open conflict among themselves. Provided with their independence by the mutual agreement of the European Great Powers, the Abyssinian rulers expanded their territory through conquest of other peoples.

Ethiopia was presented as an atypical African country, linked with Israel and Europe rather than with the rest of the continent. Ascription of essential similarities with the West allowed later elaborations of political allegory: under the U.S.-allied emperor, mass starvation could be ignored and Ethiopia was portrayed as a modernizing nation, while under a Soviet-allied government, Ethiopia epitomized African disaster, degradation, and failure. Two narratives sprang from this mythic construction, and although each asserted that Ethiopia must be allied with the West, the first—that of restoration—predicted that Ethiopians would reject the Soviet Union and resume relations with the U.S. In other words, paradise would be reestablished. The apocalyptic narrative regarded famine as a revelation of disasters to come if this order was not restored. It is to these narratives that we now turn.

Winning Hearts and Minds

An example of the narrative of restoration is an article in *Harper's* magazine by Maria Thomas (1987), a former Peace Corps worker who describes her return to Addis Ababa after a thirteen-year absence. The garish title indicates the ideological orientation: "A State of Permanent Revolution: Ethiopia Bleeds Red." As in the *New Republic*, Ethiopia under the modernizing but tragic U.S.-allied emperor is contrasted with conditions under the Derg. Every Ethiopian who appears in the text expresses fervent love for the U.S. and passionate hatred of the Soviet Union. Essentially, the text is a compendium of Cold War clichés and jingoistic vignettes intended to hammer home an ideological message. As in *Newsweek*, the text operates through elision and occlusion of significant historical details to construct famine as a direct result of socialism.

Ideological character is also constructed through a process of counterpoint, combining anticommunism, antiquity, and modernization. Thomas (ibid.:53) finds that in Addis Ababa "time had stood still," a reference to her own past but an observation typical of Western visitors who encounter what they consider biblical or medieval scenes in the Horn or who, like Harris (1987:180), find the entire "continent unchanged since the first breath of creation." Allied discursive fields of early anthropological works, travel tales, and imperialist fiction share this tendency to transform other regions into the past, often the West's past, implying certain notions of evolutionary development. Antiquity has other uses. Employing a common rhetorical technique, Thomas presents Ethiopia's antiquity as an authenticating mark of identity, to which socialism is opposed as usurper. Contemporary politics mediate evolution and essentialism.

Haile Selassie is presented in the usual way, a dignified figure attempting to modernize Ethiopia in line with Western precepts. Thomas describes the final days of his reign as "classic tragedy, the aging monarch brought down by his own hand: he had been the one to educate his people, to invite in volunteers like me, Americans who told their Ethiopian students about democracy. He was the one who had started to modernize the country, making it impossible for it to remain his kingdom alone. This was what most of the Ethiopians I knew and talked with then had wanted. But somehow it went awry" (Thomas 1987:53).

This is a standard configuration: as in the *New Republic*, Haile Selassie appears as a modernizer, the West is portrayed as fundamentally charitable, and Ethiopian disaster is inexplicable ("somehow it went awry"), echoing *Newsweek*'s beleaguered reliance on "guesswork." The mysterious aberration within the narrative is that of the native who goes communist, straying from the path of modernization. Analysis could provide explanations but the ideological impact is intensified by presenting the process as inexplicable. This is indeed the "peculiar instability of meaning" that Miller (1985:39, 30) finds in Africanist discourse, but it is not, as he thinks, simply a result of that discourse's "involvement with the noncolors black and white" and an inability to retain these as meaningful opposites. It is a constructed absence, a deliberate omission of political and historical details, not an interior process of textuality; history is erased, but it is possible to fill the gaps and absences with existing information.

"Democracy" is a key term in the text signifying this proper order; it is loosely applied, however, and Thomas ignores the fact that there had been little of it under Haile Selassie. Within the discourse of hegemonic rule, the term actually signifies the appropriate superpower affiliation. The restoration narrative emphasizes the Soviet Union's superficial influence in Ethiopia; Thomas sees in Addis Ababa "a layer of revolutionary paraphernalia . . . thrown over the city, one could only think in haste, because it suggested the set of a low-budget right-wing film meant to show that it might be better to be dead than Red if you had to look at that same stencilled portrait of Marx-Lenin-Engels one more time, or read one more banner about the international proletariat" (1987:53). Thomas affects an ironic tone, referring to a "low-budget right-wing film" to distance herself from unsophisticated aspects of anticommunism, but her own text issues at precisely this level, perpetuating the same discourse it ostensibly ridicules. She consistently appeals to conventional notions of socialism that present it only as a repressive doctrinaire system. The description of "slapdash monuments" to Marxism-Leninism is intended to demonstrate that the Soviet presence is tenuous: "It felt as if the slightest breeze could make these structures roll and shudder like backstage thunder. . . . [Amid the many] props: blazing torches, hammers and sickles, clenched fists . . . [are] . . . glowering billboard portraits . . . Strangely, even in such a huge image, the face of Mengistu reveals no personality, leaves no impression" (ibid.:54). This recalls Christopher Miller's (1985:31) view of Africanist discourse as a "blank darkness," characterized by indeterminacy and plagued by the problem of "how to write about a nullity." While I believe that Miller's deconstructionist approach does not take us very far in the analysis of discourse on Ethiopia, here Thomas's text does provide an example of a different sort of "blank darkness": Mengistu is a cipher and the writing over a void is the inscription of superpower allegiance. The Derg's violent and repressive character was demonstrated immediately after it seized power, but its actions only became unacceptable as it shifted away from the West. However, the U.S. had consistently regarded Ethiopia's affiliation with the Soviet Union as temporary, and while the regime's Marxism was condemned there was still a belief that the former relationship with the West might be resumed. (This eventually proved to be an accurate assessment; the Derg readily switched allegiances to maintain its power, and as Soviet support dwindled Mengistu turned to the West.) The official position is mirrored in Thomas's text. Beneath the Marxist-Leninist veneer, she finds that Ethiopians are all enthusiastically pro-U.S.:

What I saw first on the streets of Addis was that Ethiopians, the revolution notwithstanding, were very busy celebrating America. Every other person seemed to be wearing a USA FOR AFRICA T-shirt, or a sweatshirt—made in Taiwan and smuggled in—with the name and insignia of an American university on it. And, of course, blue jeans. It was almost as though the Ethiopians were deliberately taking the government rhetoric and turning it on end, as though they were giving witness that nothing but the opposite of what they were told on the radio or at neighborhood meetings could be trusted. (1987:54)

Essentially, this is a self-congratulatory appeal to the domestic readership. The Derg's rhetoric is dismissed as simple indoctrination and empty sloganeering imposed on an unhappy population. This seems a fairly accurate assessment of the regime's approach but it should not obscure the ideological use to which it is put. The relentlessly emphasized desire of Ethiopians to dress, act, and speak like U.S. citizens constructs the reader as the inhabitant of the best of all possible worlds, occupying a position envied by others so that, regardless of events in Ethiopia, domestic order is legitimized and reconfirmed. Through the technique of ventriloquism, there is an appeal for intervention and restoration of U.S. influence; Thomas produces an Ethiopian to speak the lines required by the hegemonic text:

"Ethiopians love Americans. . . . Americans," he went on, "are polite and generous." Later I would find out that this compliment was meant specifically in contrast to Russians and Cubans, who are considered rude and greedy. . . . He was particularly interested that I had been a Peace Corps volunteer, because he had heard about the Peace Corps, about a time—legendary now, by the tone of his voice—when Ethiopians had Americans for teachers, known for how dedicated they were, how clever, how kind. . . . Walking with this kid, past the cheap monuments and what looked like bombed out ruins, listening to his expressions of faith in me, an American, I fancied being able to liberate the place, to toss candy bars among the blown-up buildings to hundreds of barefoot children. It was as if they expected it, wearing those T-shirts like pleas, as if T-shirts could make it happen. (ibid.)

Thomas consistently relies on ventriloquism, using Ethiopians to appeal for actions she advocates, playing on sentimental images to encourage intervention. "Somehow" things have gone awry and the U.S. must restore order: "There's an undercurrent of expectation in Addis. . . . [People hope that luck will come] in the form of Peace Corps volunteers or some other gentle foreign intervention" (ibid.: 55). The nature of "gentle foreign intervention" remains unspecified but it is invoked in "what looked like bombed out ruins," suggesting military confrontation, presumably effortless since the "cheap monuments" are unstable, to be followed by "toss[ing] candy bars among the blown-up buildings."

One Ethiopian, Teodros, acknowledges some negative aspects of the U.S. but "he did know, however, that it was the Americans who had sent food to Ethiopia" (ibid.:56); Thomas does not mention that the U.S. had ignored famine reports and delayed emergency food shipments for months, hoping that starvation would undermine Mengistu. Eventually, the U.S. did become the major supplier of food aid to Ethiopia; doubtless many Ethiopians saw through the Derg's attempts to disguise this and were sincerely grateful to the U.S. However, food aid is highly politicized and is not distributed solely for humanitarian purposes. Thomas asserts that "the work had succeeded," referring to relief operations; her insistence that Ethiopians "love Americans" and want to emulate them, indicates that it succeeded in other aims as well, winning hearts and minds of "little Commies": "And there were the recycled grain sacks that she used every day, which told her who had helped Ethiopia when there had been trouble" (ibid.). Similarly, the ideological impact of food aid was implicitly acknowledged in *Africa Emergency* (December 1985), issued by the UN Office for Emergency Operations in Africa; a photograph of a drought victim beside a sack of U.S. grain is captioned: "Reagan is the new Sudanese term for all relief grain."

Thomas continuously reassures *Harper's* readers that communism is only imposed superficially on Ethiopians, who are eager to welcome the U.S. back to the Horn:

> [Teodros complained] about the politics he was forced to study. This made him tired and nervous because it was only memorizing, and had no practical value. Imperialism, capitalism, socialism: the words were soft, spoken in English, sounds only, their meanings built with other words that had no meaning. "Imperialism," he answered when I asked him, "is the last stage of capitalism." But he wasn't sure what capitalism was. There were no words at all for these things in his own language. (1987:56)

Not only do Ethiopians "love Americans" and hope to emulate them, thus assuming their proper roles in hegemonic order, but they share a common-sense aversion to political thought and involvement. Lulled by continual outpourings of affection, gratitude, emulation, and desire that Ethiopians exhibit for the U.S., the reader is invited to sympathize with the confused Teodros. Thomas indicates that political thought causes exhaustion and nervousness; the intellectual effort required to understand imperialism and capitalism is presented as arduous and draining. Just as there are "no words . . . for these things" in Amharic, so they are purged from media discourse except as objects of scorn and derision.

Thomas characterizes inappropriate political thought as alien intrusion, externally imposed on those with no interest in or understanding of "imperialism, capitalism, socialism." Regardless of Soviet opportunism in Ethiopia and the Derg's undeniable ruthlessness, Thomas's statements manifest an ideology that portrays any modification to neocolonial world order as a foreign imposition engineered by an evil empire. She meets only simple folk befuddled by alien political concepts, eager for restoration of the lost paradise of U.S. hegemony: "None of these young women were revolutionaries or knew much about the politics of their country, except one thing: when the Russians came, that is when it got bad" (ibid.:57–58). "These young women" are presented as normal people (i.e., apolitical), again encouraging identification with quiescent acceptance of hegemonic order. Ignoring famine under Haile Selassie, the imprisonment and murder of trade unionists in 1975, bloody fighting between the EPRP and MEISON in 1976, and more than a decade of war against Eritrea, all of which preceded the Soviet alliance, Thomas employs ventriloquism to speak through "these young women" to blame the Soviet Union for Ethiopia's problems.

Anticommunism is supplemented with appeals to religious sentiment. Thomas uses images of Christianity to signify popular opposition: Ethiopians, "even nonbelievers, drew courage from the example of Poland and went to church" (ibid.:55). Given the extent of religious sentiment in the U.S., such references could serve as evocative signifiers in the ideological campaign against atheistic communism; Harris (1987) also employs this technique to contrast Ethiopia's Christian essence with a foreign, explicitly satanic political ideology. In reality, relations between the Derg and the Church were more complex. As its power crumbled, the Derg sought to present itself as allied with Christianity against what it portrayed as the Muslim-backed liberation fronts, and priests were enlisted to build support for its villagization policies.

Thomas combines rhetorical appeals to Christianity with another process of media discourse, the "constant reproduction of the same thing" (Horkheimer and Adorno 1972:359). Here, Ethiopia is equated with Poland resisting Soviet control. However, the more usual comparison, as in Kaplan's article for the *Wall Street Journal* (October 1, 1985), is to Cambodia (or, rather, to a Hollywood film about Cambodia, "Ethiopia: Africa's Killing Fields"). In the *American Spectator* (June 1986), Kaplan also compares Ethiopia's war in Eritrea to the situation in Afghanistan. Lack of explanation for such analogies encourages an interpretation whereby Ethiopia and Eritrea only acquire meaning through incorporation into a global system of signification operating through ideological oppositions.

Propaganda Texts

Although premised upon anticommunism, Thomas's text may be usefully compared with a Soviet media report to clarify techniques of inscription of political signification. A propaganda model of Soviet media is readily accepted, whereas North American media are portrayed as independent and critical (Herman and Chomsky 1988). In fact, U.S. and Soviet media reports may exhibit striking symmetry. While Soviet reports on the Horn typically concentrate on visits, official delegations, fraternal greetings, and the like, and rigid censorship ensures that material sympathetic to Eritrean nationalism is excluded, as in Poland (Hutchings 1987:12), occasional articles in English appear in *New Times*. Those mentioning Eritrea stress the theme of the foreign agent, reproducing the Derg's position that nationalists there were being aided by "imperialist circles and some Arab regimes" (Asoyan 1979). Yuri Bochkaryov (1986) claimed "there is no insurgency in Ethiopia" but only "gangs of separatists aided and abetted by hostile forces." Interviewed for *New Times*, Mengistu stated that the Eritreans were merely "bandits . . . mercenaries and assassins" who received "thick wads of dollars and sumptuous villas in Europe and the Middle East" in return for participating in "the criminal act against the national unity of Ethiopia [which] has become a booming multimillion-dollar business run by imperialism and reaction" (Usvatov 1985:10–11).

One report by Gennady Gabrielyan, a TASS correspondent, provides a mirror image of Thomas's text, allowing for some stylistic differences. Each boasts of popular support for the relevant superpower. Whereas Thomas finds Ethiopians praying for U.S. intervention and candy bars, Gabrielyan meets only intrepid revolutionaries in Eritrea. Appeals for democracy noted in *Harper's* are mirrored by equally universal enthusiasm for socialism. Workers are eager to labor "without days off or holidays . . . to repair the damage wrought by the separatists' sabotage" (Gabrielyan 1979:28), trade union leaders resolutely defend people's power, the confidently smiling chairman of a Peasants' Association asserts, "When we get our cooperative going properly, life will be better still," and the students at a reeducation camp are properly repentant about former involvement with the ELF and the EPLF, both portrayed as murderous bandits maintained by external powers, namely NATO, China, and "reactionary Arab regimes." Economic activity matches superpower affiliation: for Gabrielyan (ibid.:30) Soviet support means "Keren is about to recover. . . . before long its markets and shops will again buzz with activity," whereas Thomas (1987:54) claims "all commerce had stopped" in Addis Ababa under Russian influence and Hoben (1985:17) states that "trade flourished" under Haile Selassie.

Soviet and Western media promote the same image of Ethiopia as an ancient unified entity, including Eritrea. Gabrielyan approves an Ethiopian colonel's assertion that Eritrea is "a component part of Ethiopia in all respects—political, economic and cultural." Western media promote the same image of a unified state. Both the *Globe and Mail* (May 15, 1985) and the *Toronto Star* (December 1, 1984) find that "Ethiopia has been a society . . . for 3,000 years" (Murray 1986:12). Kaplan, in the *American Spectator* (June 1986), states, "Ethiopia has been independent for thousands of years." Both Soviet and Western media stress Ethiopian antiquity and territorial integrity. Gabrielyan says Asmara "stood firm [against] secessionists' attempts to capture it." Western media used the same terms to describe the Eritrean-Ethiopian war. Neither superpower supported Eritrean independence during the 1980s (although the U.S. was more consistent in denying Eritrean self-determination), and the media conformed to official policies.

Friends and Enemies in the Horn

Another example of antiquity as authentication appears in the *Globe and Mail* (March 16, 1987), where James Brooke juxtaposes authentic Ethiopia with the Derg's alien creed. Without explanation, Brooke adds a further five hundred years to Ethiopian unity: "Ethiopian nationalists proudly trace their history back to a legendary liaison between the Queen of Sheba and King Solomon 3,500 years ago."

Using ventriloquism, Brooke produces "an Ethiopian man . . . in a bar" to express suitable outrage at the Soviet flag atop the Parliament Building and concludes that the "Marxist Government [is] firmly entrenched but more widely resented than ever [and] private acts of rebellion [are masked by] public conformity."

Again, authentic Ethiopia's antiquity is stressed to show socialism as recent, foreign and illegitimate. However, a recurring problem was the fact that discontent had not created an ideologically acceptable protagonist: "Most of the rebel groups are composed of Marxist secessionists, and none poses a serious threat to the Government. The only major non-Marxist group, the Ethiopian People's Democratic Alliance [EPDA], reportedly received $500,000 (U.S.) a year from the U.S. Central Intelligence Agency from 1981 until last year."

Brooke does not explain why "Marxist secessionists" were fighting a Marxist government. In the absence of any ideologically suitable ally, the situation did not conform to the standard conflict model of media reports. Therefore, the rhetorical technique of neither-norism was employed (Barthes 1972). Through this technique, two equally unacceptable choices are juxtaposed in order that both may be rejected. Where no acceptable ally exists, both parties may be portrayed as brutal savages fighting to the death for inexplicable motives. The same obliteration of history and analysis occurs in *National Geographic* (September 1985:279), which describes Eritrea as a "Region in Rebellion[:] In northern Ethiopia, Marxists fight Marxists in a bloody war whose only winners are famine and disease."

Presenting conflict as an internecine Marxist squabble, Brooke says opposition groups pose no "serious threat" to the Derg. In fact, these opposition groups eventually toppled the regime. Yet at this point the war with Eritrea had already lasted over a quarter of a century, caused hundreds of thousands of deaths and worsened the drought and famine, which together killed a million people, created a massive refugee population, ravaged the regional economy, and locked Mengistu's regime (from which top officials were defecting in droves) into a multi-billion-dollar arms debt with the Soviet Union and a dependency on the West for food. To contend, even in 1987, that this war was something other than a "serious threat" demonstrates either a fundamental misunderstanding of the situation or an intentional decision to misrepresent it for ideological reasons.

Brooke states that "the only major non-Marxist group" is the EPDA; since other forces are summarily dismissed, the EPDA is presumably the only group worthy (by virtue of its non-Marxism) of attention. Considered "Ethiopia's Contras," the EPDA was "born of the rightwing feudal opposition that emerged following the downfall of Haile Selassie" (*MERIP Middle East Report* 1987:35). Although it received subsidies from the CIA and made speeches to various anticommunist groups, the EPDA was distinguished mainly by its lack of activity. In the *New York Times* (August 16, 1986), Jerry Tinker and John Wise, advisers to a Senate subcommittee on Ethiopia, provide some significant insights into the viability of the EPDA, as well as into

U.S. policy and the use of food aid. They do not name the EPDA but allude to a "democratic resistance" they find moribund ("if you hold a mirror to the lips of the democratic resistance in Ethiopia, it won't even fog"). Employing a standard rhetorical construction, they state, "The only freedom fighters in Ethiopia today are the separatist guerrillas fighting for the freedom of the northern provinces of Eritrea and Tigre. But they can hardly be defined as a 'democratic' resistance. In each case, they are Marxists struggling against a Marxist government; they may come in different Marxist hues, but they all toe the same basic line." Again, neither-norism is employed. Differences between the Derg and the liberation fronts, or among the fronts, are occluded by invocation of a Marxism presented as monolithic yet unstable and clearly untrustworthy: if "they all toe the same basic line," what is the cause of the war? The implied answer is either self-interest or bizarre fanaticism.

While U.S. policy makers consistently viewed the Derg's alliance with the Soviet Union as superficial, the absence of appropriate superpower affiliation on the part of the EPLF reduced the utility of Eritrean nationalism for the West and, therefore, its attraction for media. Statements acknowledging the legitimacy of Eritrean self-determination were rare. Media obscured the issues by innuendo or neither-norism; for example, the *Globe and Mail's* editorial of October 10, 1988, advocated peace but warned that the EPLF is "a Marxist-style military organization which has brutally eliminated all opposition."

There were a few suggestions that the EPLF could serve a useful role. For example, academicians Duignan and Gann (1988:148) suggest in a Hoover Institution essay that the U.S. should "help the Eritreans in their war with Ethiopia, thus placing additional strain on Ethiopia while helping to improve U.S.-Arab relations." Kaplan, in the *American Spectator* (June 1986), suggested that "for the United States, the EPLF and the TPLF are the best weapons against the regime of Lt. Col. Mengistu Haile Mariam, a Soviet puppet whose cruelty has been compared with that of Pol Pot." (Actually, it was Kaplan himself who had made the comparison, in the *Wall Street Journal*, October 1, 1985.) Humanitarian concerns or issues of international law are not primary, as Kaplan (1988a) explains in the *Atlantic Monthly* that "a separatist struggle in Ethiopia may be just as favorable to U.S. interests," but suggests that the situation may be "too complex to excite an American audience." This is a tacit admission of the fundamental role of the media. Rather than information, the media provide excitement and entertainment. Relying on a conflict model, complex issues are reduced to essential oppositions between good and evil, which is problematic in the Horn: "In addition, the fact that the rebels—like the government—are themselves Marxists, takes the sting out of the story. How can you tell the good guys from the bad?" (ibid.:25).

Intended ironically or not, Kaplan's remarks indicate the essential nature of media interest in the Horn. Implicit is the assumption that the political situation is too difficult for audiences to understand. All conflict must be reduced to basic oppositions of good and evil and, if this is impossible, the technique of neither-norism is employed. This is a key operation; critical thought is presented as boring and arduous, likely to produce nervousness and exhaustion for North Americans, just as for Thomas's Teodros. Analysis, other than that conforming to the hegemonic vision, is placed outside the boundaries of possible thought ("there were no words at all for these things in his own language"). This is both a conscious ideological decision and a result of the advertising-oriented nature of media corporations.

Thus, discourse on the Horn is not based on purely textual polarities; rather, channels of discourse maintain such polarities to fulfill essential commercial and ideological functions. The issue is not one of writing in a void, as Miller (1985) suggests, but rather that a certain kind of writing itself creates voids and textual absences, not because of linguistic terms employed but because of the interests served. The media are lucrative businesses, and they are business-oriented and business-dominated, providing reductionistic, easily assimilated, black and white (i.e., "balanced") constructions of reality that can be presented in the form of an on-going dramatic series ("the news") to attract viewers and advertisers alike. In promoting the ideology of the business elite, the media create certain polarities (the good guys and the bad guys) conforming to elite interests. In contrast to the Middle East or Central America, the polarities were not as easily found in the Horn. However, in the *American Spectator*, Kaplan suggests that "here the media and the public have been deceived. The Marxism of the EPLF and the TPLF is presented as largely irrelevant to U.S. interests, for both groups are fiercely anti-Soviet" (1986:25). While suggesting that the EPLF and TPLF are "the best weapons" the U.S. can manipulate in its battle against Mengistu, Kaplan dismisses the actual objectives of both organizations as irrelevant because of their anti-Soviet stance.

There is no evidence that such recommendations were put into practice. However, the Heritage Foundation urged Reagan to launch paramilitary attacks against Ethiopia and eight other countries perceived to be communist, socialist, nationalist, or pro-Soviet. Reagan condemned Ethiopia along with Afghanistan, Cambodia, Angola, and Nicaragua as "governments at war with their own people" and urged that Ethiopian freedom fighters be supported. In 1985 Reagan approved a $15 million covert CIA paramilitary operation in Angola and discussed support for covert operations in Mozambique. In the Horn, absence of an ally with substantial military force and ideological suitability encouraged efforts to win back Ethiopia from the Soviet Union. Despite its quarter-century war against Eritrea and domestic repression, Ethiopia was seen as a stabilizing element, in that it upheld the principle of maintaining established borders; the U.S., like African states, has opposed any modifications to these boundaries. Various suggestions were made to explain the Derg's alliance with the Soviet Union, including a national metaphysical crisis following deposition of the emperor, or that the alliance resulted from President Carter's failed attempt to win an easy victory in the Horn over the Soviet Union through support for Somalia (Korn 1986:35). The most decisive factor, however, was probably the Soviet Union's willingness to supply arms in the quantities required by the Derg.

In any event, the theme of restoration of appropriate relations was a consistent component of U.S. official policy since 1974. Korn, Peterson, and Henze maintained that former relationships could be reestablished and that order would be restored. Official policy was premised on the superficiality of Soviet influence; it was implemented by first withholding and then supplying food aid (in addition to small-scale and inconclusive covert actions) as a means to restore former political alignments.

When Reagan became president, conflict with Ethiopia focused on ties with the Soviet Union, compensation for expropriated property, and Ethiopian criticisms of U.S. foreign policy. However, the Derg's ties with the Soviet Union did not change the U.S. desire to maintain communication with Addis Ababa. Transition from Carter to Reagan did not alter belief in the superficial nature of Soviet influence in Ethiopia. Also, Soviet ties did not significantly affect Ethiopia's place in the world market. In 1978 the U.S. and the EEC accounted for 50 percent of Ethiopia's total trade compared with 2 percent with the Soviet Union and Eastern Europe. The U.S. remained the main buyer of Ethiopian coffee, accounting for 80 percent of Ethiopia's foreign exchange. In 1983 the Derg reopened the economy to private foreign investment, allowing transfer of shares and repatriation of capital. Settlement of some claims related to nationalization encouraged belief that improved relations were possible (Petras and Morley 1984:28–30).

Famine provided opportunities to improve relations. The U.S. strategy was to burn the candle at both ends by providing just enough food to enable Eritreans to survive and pressure the Derg, simultaneously giving most of its aid to the latter, and presenting itself as a charitable humanitarian. Western aid to Eritrea, provided through nongovernmental organizations and restricted to relief rather than development assistance, was kept at minimal levels. Most aid went through the Derg, which was unable and unwilling to feed Eritrea and Tigray. The Derg protested that Western donors were channelling large amounts of aid to those regions in an effort to undermine it, and while journalist Jonathan Power complained that "too much effort" had been made to avert starvation in those areas, the actual situation was rather different:

> U.S. assistance to the guerrilla-held areas increased only slightly, and not in sufficient quantities to stem the flow of migrants or to reduce the death rate significantly. . . . A Rand Corporation study commissioned by the White House and issued in December 1985 came out strongly against U.S. support to the movements. "Catering to separatist delusions," or tactical support of Marxist dissident movements on the argument that they are anti-Soviet . . . serves no purpose," wrote consultant Paul Henze. (Smith 1987:35–36)

Reporting to the U.S. Senate, Tinker and Wise noted that, despite frigid diplomatic relations, there had been "considerable progress in establishing constructive relations at every other level of Ethiopian society. Among the people an extraordinarily pro-American sentiment remains alive in Ethiopia" (United States Senate 1986:2). The report criticized those who advocated a confrontational strategy, such as Congressman Toby Roth of Wisconsin, who sought to halt relief aid to Ethiopia entirely. Tinker and Wise argued that to take such a course would "only damage whatever opportunity we have to influence events in Ethiopia [through the pro-U.S. sentiments built by] America's extraordinarily generous famine relief effort." Again, the U.S. appears as international humanitarian, essential to the ideological parable of charity and betrayal by the undeserving poor, but the text also reveals other motives behind relief, including the extension of U.S. hegemony.

Tinker and Wise advised the U.S. government not to be impatient for a major shift in relations. They note numerous changes, including a halt to public criticism of the U.S., replaced with expressions of thanks, Ethiopia's opening of its doors to international relief agencies, U.S. journalists and public officials, monitoring of resettlement programs, reestablishment of the U.S. Information Service's operations in Ethiopia, cultural exchanges, increased diplomatic relations, a new order with Boeing, and an agreement for compensation to U.S. firms affected by nationalization. Seeing "no likelihood that a covert operation could create a democratic resistance in Ethiopia," Tinker and Wise advised "hardliners" to abandon their "campaign to arm a nonexistent democratic resistance movement in Ethiopia" (Tinker and Wise 1986). Nowhere do they suggest that CIA covert operations are inappropriate, in Ethiopia or elsewhere; rather manipulation through food aid is considered more effective. In fact, suitable progress was made: on January 1, 1989, the *New York Times* announced that "Ethiopia is Leaning Westward Again." As Soviet support for the unwinnable war waned, the Derg frantically turned back to the West, abandoning socialist policies, inviting the return of Israeli military personnel, and hiring a New York public relations firm (which included the CIA among its clients) to improve its image.

The pliability of hegemonic discourse, its ability to incorporate strategic shifts and reversals of position, is demonstrated by a review of the frantic diplomatic efforts of the Derg during its last days. The Derg reiterated its intention to fight to the end but Soviet support was uncertain. An EPLF editorial in *Adulis* (January 1989) notes "conflicting signals" of the Soviet Union that had called for a "political solution" in *Pravda* (October 31, 1988), while escalating military aid. *Adulis* also stated that North Korea, Israel, and East Germany had renewed military support to the Derg. In a June 12, 1989, interview with Kuwait's *Al-Anba'*, EPLF representative Al-Amin Muhammad Sa'id stated that the EPLF had held meetings "at the leadership level" with the Soviet Union in previous months regarding peace initiatives. Issayas Afeworki, interviewed in *Adulis* (July-August 1989), stated that Soviet rhetoric concerning negotiations was contradicted by its new supply of weapons to the Derg and that Soviet references to a peaceful solution were merely "empty statements."

Concerned about "conflicting signals" from the Soviet Union and faced with a mutiny in the army in March 1989 at Keren, the Derg launched an intensive diplomatic campaign, visiting Egypt, Iraq, Syria, several European countries, and Japan. The anti-Arab rhetoric that had typified Ethiopian discourse was transformed as Mengistu welcomed Yassir Arafat at the state palace and upgraded the PLO's Addis Ababa office to embassy status. Addis Ababa's official radio announced on May 2 that both Syria and Iraq wanted "the northern issue [settled] within the framework of Ethiopian unity and sovereignty," while Mengistu attacked "secessionist and terrorist elements in the north [who are] distorting our real history . . . mercenaries . . . working against revolutionaries and exploiting narrow tribalism" (Daily Reports, May 4, 1989).

However, the EPLF pursued its own diplomatic initiatives. Issayas Afeworki met former President Carter in Khartoum (followed by meetings in May during Issayas's visit to the U.S.) and on April 24 signed a statement of cooperation toward peace with Sudan's Prime Minister Sadiq El-Mahdi. Carter visited Addis Ababa on April 20, and Mengistu, in a May 7 Rome radio interview, stressed a desire to improve relations with the U.S. and Israel, again attacking the Arab states' "racist attitude supported by their petrodollars" in allegedly backing Eritrea. Israeli support to Ethiopia had been consistent, although at times shadowy, with secret arms shipments reportedly transferred through an Amsterdam firm. Since 1980, Israeli arms sales to Ethiopia had been at the level of $5 million dollars a year (Patman 1990:369 n.131). In November 1989, full diplomatic relations were restored and Israeli military experts assisted Ethiopian attacks on Massawa in February 1990, in which cluster bombs and napalm were directed against the civilian population.

The failed May 16, 1989, coup attempt by senior Ethiopian military officers demanding an end to the war was followed by a wave of executions and arrests and further indicated the Derg's tottering position: thirty top officers were killed and two hundred and fifty were arrested. On June 5, the Derg offered "unconditional peace talks" with the EPLF and TPLF. Actually, the Derg's offer was not a significant departure from its previous position since territorial integrity was excluded from negotiations. The TPLF, with reservations, agreed to negotiate, but the EPLF (June 8, 1989) dismissed the offer, stating that the Derg's refusal to discuss Eritrean self-determination "is not only tantamount to setting pre-conditions but also betrays the lack of a genuine desire for negotiations and peaceful solution."

Extrapolating from the propaganda model, one would expect that Mengistu's expressed desire to open relations with the U.S. and Israel would be received approvingly in Western media. In fact, the *New York Times* (June 14, 1989) and the *Globe and Mail* (June 6, 1989) both repeated the Derg's characterization of the offer as "unconditional," and according to the *New York Times*, "western diplomats hailed it as the biggest concession the President had ever made to the insurgents." Although it was no "concession" at all but merely a restatement of its existing position, the Derg was congratulated on its efforts to secure peace while EPLF rejections were depicted as intransigence.

Africa Confidential (June 9, 1989), maintaining its position against Eritrean nationalism, dismissed the EPLF's proposal of an internationally supervised referendum on the options of independence, federation, or integration as "politically unviable" and concluded that "the growing belief among governments outside the Horn is that the EPLF should accept political realities and settle for a little less than full independence, and this by negotiation—if necessary, with Mengistu. But Mengistu will have to display an untypical generosity and unaccustomed statesmanship to keep the necessary external backing and aid for such a scenario." This "growing belief" was the same position that had been rigidly observed for three decades by "governments outside the Horn." Even at this late stage, it was only required that Mengistu simply display "generosity" and "statesmanship" to ensure "external backing and aid." Negotiations were initiated in Atlanta and London in 1989 but were rendered redundant by the EPLF and EPRDF victories and Mengistu's flight to Zimbabwe.

Apocalypse in Ethiopia

A second narrative tendency emphasizes the apocalyptic character of famine in the Horn. The texts that form this narrative read famine as a warning of the danger resulting from loss of control over the Third World, linking racism, anticommunism, and Christian mythology in a parable of betrayal; they resuscitate themes from the classic texts of imperialism, exemplified by Lugard's *The Dual Mandate* (1923) and Conrad's 1902 novella *Heart of Darkness*.

As well as spawning a new discourse within the mass media, famine inspired several books. In *Breakfast In Hell* (1987), Myles Harris recounts his experience as a Red Cross doctor in Ethiopia during the 1984 famine and presents Africa as chaos. While much of the continent has become a disaster zone gripped by war, famine, poverty, debt, drought, and political repression, in this discourse disaster is dehistoricized and appears as a manifestation of fundamental African qualities; Harris depicts chaos as an expression of Africa's essence, not the result of historical processes. Rather than seeing colonialism as fundamental disruption, he depicts it as marking Africa's entry into modernity, a path out of the darkness. Harris proposes that Africa's development was interrupted by decolonization, itself prompted by absurd and groundless Western guilt and encouraged by communists and liberals. In his text, disaster is created by deviation from racial essence and from the civilizing mission. After praising the benefits, such as roads and railways, imparted to Africa by colonial powers (overlooking the fact that such infrastructure was constructed not for the benefit of local populations but for resource extraction), Harris suggests that Africans threw all this away and plunged the continent into disaster through mismanagement and greed. Certain of African responsibility for famine, he ridicules the "general view [that] drought [is] due to a malign combination of Western bankers, the results of past colonial invasions, and a formless but pervasive Western greed" (Harris 1987:25).

Harris presents this "general view" as baseless and absurd. In fact, few studies directly link drought to such factors; Ball (1976) does note how these factors can intensify a drought's effects and several analyses correctly relate them to famine. Significantly, Harris claims that this is the "general view." A standard technique of propaganda is to present rare critical views as examples of a general "ultraliberal" or adversarial climate; Chomsky (1982:80–81; 1988:203–214) provides statistical evidence that refutes such claims regarding wars against Vietnam and Nicaragua. To claim, as Harris does, that emphasis on the role of imperialism and neocolonialism in African underdevelopment is the general view is a standard rhetorical technique intended to marginalize dissent. He provides no evidence that radical or liberal interpretation forms the "general view." It was not held by influential policy makers. For example, at the UN Special Session on Africa (May 27–31, 1986), where African representatives agreed that many of their policies had been misguided, U.S. spokesman Richard Hottelet demanded "realism": "If there's a lot of screaming and waving of arms about how you owe us recovery from the colonial era, it's going to fall on deaf ears" (*Globe and Mail*, May 28, 1986).

While realism should involve understanding historical roots of current problems, including colonial impact and neocolonial encouragement of inappropriate development, and address problems of Africa's foreign debt, donor countries only agreed to attend the session on condition that Africa's annual debt ($24.5 billion at the time) be reduced to a secondary issue.

Typically, hegemonic discourse banishes history or substitutes its own version. Harris replaces historical analysis with a vision of basic savagery: "True, Africa was a continent of colonially created states ripped apart by tribes that owed only loyalty to family and tribe. . . . But if the colonialist had never come, what difference would it have made?" (1987:25). For Harris, Africa is the abode of Absolute Evil and its essence is chaos. In this discourse, colonialism was a selfless mission seeking to create order; the noble endeavour was betrayed by communists, liberals, and "racial equality fanatics" who refused to take up the civilizing mission and allowed African venality to emerge. Harris ignores completely the violent transformation of African societies, operations of multinational corporations, fluctuations of an international economic order in which the Third World is assigned a position as a producer of primary resources, cheap labor, and captive markets, as well as the structure of neocolonialism that drains the Third World through institutions such as the International Monetary Fund and the World Bank, supported by a continuous propaganda assault through the mass media and backed up by military force. He claims that the West gave up its colonies because of neurotic liberal guilt and a wish to set a good example: "It was then that the West abolished the idea of evil, legislated away differences between people, and, to set an example, began to abolish their own colonial empires. In their place came aid, and the Aidgame. Its players were set to work in societies that, newly liberated from the straitjacket of colonialism, had returned not to a progressive Victorian optimism but to medievalism and feudalism dressed in modern military uniforms" (ibid.:18). This passage exhibits central discursive themes: important is the notion that the West abandoned its mission, allowing Africans to slip backwards on an evolutionary scale to the "medieval" level. Harris disparages misguided attempts to "legislate away" differences; it is clear that he means racial differences, which he thinks are objective and significant. He conceals previous experience in South Africa, fearing criticism from liberal colleagues whom he terms "racial equality fanatics." Although not openly advocating apartheid, he implicitly supports it by suggesting the destructive results of relaxing control over Africa.

Racism and class hatred are central components of Harris's text. For example, he ridicules the preparation of an African ruling class by departing colonial powers: "If you had stood . . . at Tilbury docks in London in the 1950s, you would have seen the seeds of this class arriving: young men clutching soggy cardboard suitcases, wearing cheap suits and sad stiff peasant shoes, on their faces fear mixed with a slight dab of arrogance, like a painter testing his palette with a smudge of violent color" (ibid.:26).

The tone protests usurpation of legitimate authority by African imposters. Rather than analyzing indigenous elites in the neocolonial context, Harris posits evil as an intrinsic African quality, the "smudge of violent color." The "cheap suits" reappear throughout the text, signifying inner corruption. Everything has a fixed, essential identity, and attempts by Africans to deviate from their essence, to imitate Europeans, can only create disaster. If order is disrupted things fall apart; these mimic men arriving on the docks are not simply laughable caricatures unprepared to assume control of their own destiny, but agents of disaster and chaos, rough beasts emerging from centuries of sleep. Indeed, it is uncertain if Africans are fully human: throughout Harris's text Ethiopian officials lose their names and are identified as animals—such as "Mr. Mole" and "Mr. Rat" (ibid.:72, 97). Fusing racist rhetoric with the imagery of the undeserving poor, Harris suggests an unfair exploitation of the Elect: "[Africans] discovered that the inhabitants of Leviathan all seemed to suffer some vast inexplicable guilt about their wealth. When words like colonialism, exploitation, mining interests and multinationals were mentioned, they would start like a murderer reminded of the corpse beneath the lawn, and offer machines or money to be left alone" (ibid.:28).

Similar visions of a naive, liberal West misled by sentimentality and betrayed by Third World treachery are promoted throughout this discourse. Aid is depicted as misplaced charity constituting a deviation from colonialism's civilizing mission and inspired by Marxists who betray their own race and create disaster for Africa and the West.

Harris suggests that charges of colonial exploitation are unfair and that the West provides unlimited charity to the Third World—both dubious claims. For example, the mining operations that Harris suggests are a major benefit to Africa clearly return huge profits to the West. In Liberia (the largest iron-ore exporter in Africa, third largest in the world), Western mining companies reap huge profits, only 25 percent of which remain in Liberia in any form. Because of the capital-intensive nature of the operations, there has been no development of a skilled labor force or manufacturing: "There is a serious danger that in a totally free-enterprise economy foreign companies will dig out Liberia's minerals and leave nothing behind but huge holes in the ground" (Mazrui and Tidy 1984:38).

Harris is partially correct in suggesting that aid has taken the place of colonial empires (see Carty and Smith 1981; Hayter and Watson 1985; Korner et al. 1986). However, he does not criticize aid because it is essentially a subsidy for Western corporations and benefits the West. Rather than acknowledging the considerable commercial advantages created by foreign aid, Harris portrays aid as misplaced charity and a sign of moral weakness, naive liberal guilt, "the West's overwhelming desire to be loved and forgiven by the poor for being so rich" (Harris 1987:17). This overwhelming desire was not much in evidence at the 1986 UN Special Session: although Africans, faced with continent-wide starvation and poverty, pleaded for $80 billion in aid and debt relief, there was no financial commitment made by donor nations. Similar scenes were replayed at the 1992 Earth Summit in Brazil, where initiatives to reduce the estimated $50 billion annual flow from poor to rich countries were shelved along with any mention of environmental responsibilities of multinational corporations.

A suggestion that the West offers "machines or money to be left alone" misrepresents the character of foreign aid. Western policy makers have described this frankly. For example, John Foster Dulles stated, "Our foreign loans primarily operate to provide payments in dollars here to our farmers and manufacturers for goods which they sell abroad, and to pay debts previously contracted for such purposes. . . . Actually the dollar proceeds of foreign loans stay in the United States and are used here either to pay principal or interest maturing on dollar loans previously contracted or to pay for American goods or services" (quoted in Kolko 1972:359–360).

Most aid money returns to the West in the form of goods and services. For example, in Latin America, "all AID loans were tied to U.S. products and, by 1969, 99 percent of AID-financed goods and services were being bought in the United States, often at prices 30 to 40 percent higher than the international rate. . . . During the Alliance [for Progress] years, according to U.S. Department of Commerce statistics, three dollars went back to the United States for every dollar invested" (Lernoux 1980:209–210).

Similarly, during the 1970s, 60 percent of Canada's total aid budget was actually spent in Canada, and Canadian foreign aid is presently tied at a level of 80 percent to the purchase of Canadian goods, services, and expertise regardless of whether these are either the most inexpensive or the most suitable for the country receiving such aid. Aid is typically used to develop new markets for Western products, often undercutting local production. This hardly fits Harris's view of guilt-stricken Western countries lavishly dispensing "machines or money" right and left in the Third World.

By constructing an absence around historical understanding of contemporary problems, Harris puts the blame on African governments alone. Many, such as Mengistu's regime, proved themselves extremely deserving of criticism; however, the issue here is not the Derg's obvious ruthlessness but incorporation of Ethiopia into a mythological structure, an ideological morality play. Harris, like *Newsweek*, focuses on "the mirage of socialist collective farming [that] had transformed the land into a desert" (1987:12). This ideological oversimplification ignores population pressure, overcultivation, overgrazing, lack of rainfall, soil depletion, and deforestation, all significant factors, although not in themselves the cause of famine. Harris also overlooks the fact that conditions for disaster were established before Mengistu seized power and that drought and famine occurred in countries that have not practiced collective farming. Causes of widespread poverty and effects of crippling debt are ignored. Most importantly, Harris (ibid.:196) dismisses three decades of devastating war because the EPLF and TPLF are names he has "only vaguely heard of." Despite the war's central importance in prolonging, if not creating, famine, it was not easily incorporated into an anticommunist parable. Therefore, it is ignored.

The Derg did have a negative effect on food production. However, the ideological abhorrence with which Harris and *Newsweek* view the regime's agricultural policies obscures several important factors. Most significant is the historical aspect that puts these policies in the long-term context of increasing population growth, environmental decline, and military conflict. The Derg increased agricultural expenditures, but these quickly exceeded revenues and led to debt and inflation. Forced and rapid collectivization created a declining agricultural growth rate, with a probable negative rate after 1980. However, this decline had been apparent throughout Haile Selassie's Five Year Plans from 1956 onward, and although it intensified under the Derg, "some collapse was probably inevitable" (Robinson and Yamazaki 1986: 336).

Harris dehistoricizes famine and makes it a function of essence. Dismissing history, Harris (1987:180) suggests that Africa ("a continent unchanged since the first breath of creation. . . . A place in which there is no room for the gray subtleties of Europe") has deviated from its fundamental spiritual/racial essence. Communists encouraged deviation: the Feast of Mescal (celebrating the finding of the True Cross) has been supplanted by a "rival religion, Marxism" (ibid.:173) bringing about "the whole continent's steady decline . . . a relentless and purposeful descent into chaos" (ibid.:159).

Harris's essentialism suggests that not just Marxism but also modern science, or perhaps any change at all, is bad for Africans. Dr. Abebe, an Ethiopian health worker, cannot prevent the death of his own son and finds himself "in the presence of something unutterably evil. Not evil in the sense of bad, or tragic, unjust or wrong, but an active intentional evil. . . . It was the evil of foreknowledge, hubris, the destruction of innocence" (ibid.:180).

Dr. Abebe, who has looked into the "Pandora's box" of Western medicine, finds himself cut off from his culture, believing in science like an "Abyssinian H. G. Wells" (Harris earlier noted that "Abyssinian" is used by Ethiopians as a term of contempt), no longer embedded in the feudal system but unable to accept the faith of Marxism-Leninism and thrust into the "massive regiment of puzzled, bewildered people stranded without culture among our machines" (ibid.:181). Like the Africans in *Newsweek*, Dr. Abebe brings this upon himself; Harris posits his sin as hubris, excessive pride, thinking himself capable of opening a "Pandora's box" of Western medical knowledge, presuming to decide his own fate and to depart from that greater scheme of things that has kept Africa "unchanged since the first breath of creation."

Here are the echoes of Lugard's (1923:80–90) contemptuous dismissal of "the intellectual negro" as a diseased, inbred freak and his dire warnings concerning establishment of "institutions which are not in some way a direct outcome of the negro character." It is not simply that the unfortunate Dr. Abebe has attempted to rise above his station or emerge from his primordial world by ineffective dabbling in Western science: all change in Africa is seen as evil. Furthermore, Harris's characterization of Dr. Abebe as "Abyssinian" rather than Ethiopian is not only an expression of contempt but also a deliberate use of anachronism, intended to place Ethiopia in the past and keep it there unchanged.

The only "authentic" Africans are peasants unchanged in five thousand years who inhabit a curious world somehow simultaneously biblical and medieval. Contrast between the authentic and modern Africa is symbolized at the airport where Harris sees Amharic script "sinisterly antique on the fuselage of something as modern as an aircraft, unrecognizable, meaningless and obscure." This "sinister" script is only "unrecognizable, meaningless and obscure" to foreigners who do not learn the language of the country in which they work, but the adjectives indicate what is to follow, just as the book's title is not simply lurid but part of what Harris constructs, literally, as a struggle between good and evil, light and darkness.

Christian imagery is central to the discourse. Michael Buerk's original BBC broadcast from Korem fixed the terms that characterized later descriptions: "Dawn, and as the sun breaks through the piercing chill of night on the plain outside Korem, it lights up a biblical famine, now, in the twentieth century. This place, say workers here, is the closest thing to hell on earth." Mohamed Amin, who had filmed the Korean camp in 1984, returned to Ethiopia to produce another film that also emphasized Christian imagery in its title, "African Calvary."

Matthews (1985:24) uses similar imagery to propose comparisons between Ethiopian famine and the fall of the U.S. Embassy in Saigon. He sees in a group of famine victims waiting for registration a reflection "of the New Testament story of the nativity, when thousands of people—including Mary and Joseph—were called by the Roman governor to return for registration at the place of their birth."

These images are rooted in earlier Africanist discourses, which had both promoted the West's civilizing mission and warned of the savagery of the natives, exhibiting the contradictory impulses to either uplift or exterminate the brutes. Discourse of famine in Ethiopia, however, elaborates a peculiar transformation that incorporates the terminology of biblical famine into an ideological parable of ontological betrayal. Within this discourse, the terms are reversed: it is not Africans who suffer but the West. The "African Calvary" is transformed into a crucifixion of the Elect who are despised by the undeserving poor. The merging of Ethiopian famine and the U.S. defeat in Vietnam is part of a narrative construction of history that depicts the West as the agent of modernity and progress, constantly threatened by primitive forces of darkness in the Third World.

In Harris's text the modern, civilized West confronts primal, evil Africa. These are the literal terms of his opposition. He expands upon this confrontation of fundamentally opposed metaphysical principles through a subtext of literary references that construct a spiritual odyssey from a hotel named "The Dante" through continuous biblical allusions straight into *Heart of Darkness*, embodying preoccupations of the Africanist discourse proposed by Miller (1985): instability, fundamental obscurity, loss of the self, and erosion of authority. However, what deconstructionism would construe as a process interior to the text, a displacement of the author due to instability of tropes employed in Africanist discourse, is more properly viewed in its external context, as loss of political hegemony and racial distinctions, a threat to identity based on domination.

Aidgamers, in Harris's view, go to the Third World tempted "by the Gorgon-headed horror that lurks in all such places, the Conradian *Heart of Darkness*" (1987:22). Confrontation occurs in the Rift, "a stepped entrance to Hades" (34), a "biblical desert" (33), where people carry "biblical" staffs and "speak English in a curious fluent biblical style," now stalked by "the god Lenin" (32), where Harris, himself "too far from God" (140), experiences a crisis of faith created by the crumbling of tradition: "Vatican Three had drawn a veil over evil and stripped its marvelous liturgy of the old comforting magic. All they could do was offer . . . a few kind words in English and that is no good when you have seen the devil himself" (22–23).

Like Africa, which has deviated from its preordained racial-spiritual trajectory, the West has strayed from its racial mission of guiding the "child races" (Lugard 1923:72). Betrayed by socialists and communists who "turned against their own kind" (Borgin and Corbett 1982:22), it has "abased itself" before the Third World (Bauer 1976: 31). Harris proposes that, like Kurtz in *Heart of Darkness*, the West has deviated from its colonial civilizing mission of developing the Third World and has succumbed to the lure of savagery, although rather than engaging in bloody primitive rituals it has turned this violence inward upon itself. Disaster for all follows from abdication of authority and racial mission. Harris inverts Kurtz's (ambiguous) self-condemnation, seeing redemption in reassertion of power and domination. The same appeal for reassertion of traditional hegemony was made by Kaplan (1988b), who called for an application of the Reagan Doctrine to the Horn, an apocalyptic vision "luminous and terrifying, like a flash of lightning in a serene sky: 'Exterminate all the brutes!'" (Conrad 1973:87).

Within this discourse Africans are to blame for famine. Whereas the media portrayed Africans as starving children, Harris suggests Africans starve because they are children, incapable of surviving without the guiding hand of white supremacy. However, he adds an extra twist. The foreign agent in his racist morality play is Martin Luther King, Jr., "a man who said he had a dream, a dream of justice, equality and freedom for the black people of the world. Now the son is seeing the dream" (1987:265).

The logic is incoherent but in Harris's text the struggle for civil rights for blacks in the U.S. causes famine in Ethiopia. The dream of equality becomes a nightmare because Africans are fundamentally incapable of managing the continent; it is a clear warning against equal rights for blacks whether in South Africa or in North America. Clearly, the nightmare is one for the West, not just for Africans. The modern civilized West meets "biblical . . . medieval" Africa and fails because it is too liberal, too eager to abase itself before "racial equality fanatics" (ibid.:23). Loss of political-racial control leads to famine in Ethiopia, a portent of apocalyptic disaster for the West: In Ethiopia, "biblical families faced total extinction. It might, I thought, be the world of the future for all of us, a semi-extinct planet over which hovered a capsule with a few survivors, specimens of a lost world. It was what was so frightening about Ethiopia—given more factories, a couple of million more miles of road, a few more years of 'scientific' farming, it could happen in Europe" (ibid.:262).

Whereas medieval Europe projected the desire for its own perfected self-image onto Ethiopia in the figure of Prester John, Harris uses Ethiopia to warn of disastrous consequences of loss of racial identity, and any change to established order and authority. He is not alone in seeing famine in the Horn as a sign of imminent apocalypse. In a chapter of his book entitled "A Journey in Hell," Hancock (1985:95) sees the Korem camp as "a vision of the end of the world." Following inevitable nuclear war "the lights will go out across Europe and, in a hundred thousand Korems, a new dark age will be born." The image was an evocative one. For example, Canada's Ambassador to the UN, Stephen Lewis, found this passage sufficiently striking to read aloud during a lecture at the University of Toronto in the spring of 1985.

Thus, just as Foucault (1977) described the semiotic, instructional character of public torture, it is possible to see that the spectacle of mass starvation also provided moral lessons. The media both emphasized the scale of suffering through the staggering images of the camps and distilled this horror in personalized images, especially the persistent focus on emaciated mothers and children and the breakdown of the body with minute examinations of the details of starvation. Discourse transformed this disintegration into concerns for the decay of the body politic, with the medieval and biblical imagery warning of regression and social breakdown not just in Ethiopia but, more crucially, in the West. Images of starvation were transformed into a warning that if socialism were not stopped, "it could happen in Europe."

Breakfast in Hell ends on Christmas Eve, with Harris tuned to the BBC from a hotel in the heart of darkness, listening to the Archbishop of Canterbury call for a return to traditional values, apparently including a tighter grip on the "benighted nations" if Western civilization is to survive. This militant message is at the core of the "African Nightmare." Buerk's narration for the original BBC report on famine in Ethiopia placed the victims in a place outside time, consigning them not to history but to myth, and the discourse that layered itself upon the original broadcast kept them there. Commentators on famine in the Horn consistently employ biblical references, although there is nothing particularly biblical about starvation. These associations stem partially from mythic resonances contained in the Solomon and Sheba legend, Prester John, and the divine kingship of Haile Selassie, the ancient Christian dream-emperor symbolizing the Western-allied Third World (Kaplan 1988b:10–11). Juxtaposition of these signifiers with other potent images constructed a powerful mythological narrative warning of betrayal, danger, and treachery.

For example, when Matthews combines Ethiopian famine, biblical references, and the fall of the U.S. Embassy in Saigon to create an image of the betrayal of the West, the terms are inverted. The discourse warns of danger to the West, although it is Africans who starve, just as it was Vietnamese associates who were left to their fate in Saigon. It is not Africa's nightmare that is of concern in discourse but the West's.

The texts not only construct Mengistu as the Anti-Christ but suggest an imminent Second Coming. Ideas of confrontation between good and evil and racial and spiritual betrayal as prelude to apocalypse are not Harris's preoccupations alone. Fear of loss of control, both of the self and of political hegemony, forms a central theme of a discourse rooted in the classic texts of imperialism and spreads throughout a network of contemporary texts and institutions.

A Western Nightmare

Breakfast in Hell exemplifies the apocalyptic tendency within discourse on the Horn. In contrast to works that promise restoration of a lost paradise where happy natives will assume their subordinate place after the deposition of aberrant communist leaders, apocalyptic texts warn of the threat and the danger posed by the Third World, populated by rebellious, demonic savages who fail to appreciate benefits brought by the civilizing mission and who wish to seize the wealth of the Elect. Rather than predicting an eventual and natural restoration of order, these texts argue for its forcible reimposition.

Major themes of *Breakfast in Hell* include colonialism as civilizing mission, racial essentialism and betrayal, Western guilt, socialist treachery, and threats of world destruction. Comparing Harris's ideas to other texts about Africa reveals how works on Ethiopia constitute part of a broader discourse. The core ideas of this discursive formation are shared by Karl Borgin and Kathleen Corbett in their book, *The Destruction of a Continent*. Claiming that colonialism benefited Africa, they praise "the people who really built up the continent and founded everything upon which modern Africa is based: Lord Delamere . . . Frederick Lugard . . . George Whitehouse" (1982:9). Here, Africa is constructed as inert and passive, developed only by European activity. The apotheosis of Lugard is significant, although not in the manner intended. Lugard's *The Dual Mandate* (1923) is a colonial handbook for ruling the "subject races," concerned with division and classification in the interests of power, containing all the paternalistic cliches of the civilizing mission and the White Man's Burden. In praising the racial imperative to imperial rule (618–619), defense of colonial plunder (348), the natural laws of the market (404), and a genetic disposition to capitalism (238), as well as championing apartheid (149, 327) and insisting that Africans are incapable of governing themselves (198), Lugard employs an array of condescending images: from mockery of the hubris of the "intellectual negro" prone to socialism (82) to attacks on "Bolshevist theorists" conspiring to drag Western civilization to a level lower than "the cannibal savage—nay, the anthropoid apes" (75). Lugard's text, seminal for contemporary Africanist discourse, thus combines racist and anticommunist rhetoric to warn of ontological regression.

Like Harris, Borgin and Corbett dismiss Africans' role in liberating themselves from colonialism. This dismissal is shaped by racist notions and shares Lugard's (1923:197) assumptions that "the subject races of Africa are not yet able to stand alone" and that political agitation must come from foreign agents:

> The African colonies were demolished not by the Africans themselves, as many believe, but by the colonial powers themselves when they were still building a new world in Africa. The African colonists were destroyed at the peak of their development by a new breed of men and women, different from anyone the world had ever seen before. They were the crusaders for a new world free of imperialism and exploitation. They did what no one did before: they turned against their own kind. (Borgin and Corbett 1982:22)

While Harris implicates Martin Luther King, Jr., in Ethiopian famine, Borgin and Corbett detect another culprit. Elaborating on the theme of racial betrayal, they do not simply accuse Marxists of indoctrinating Africans to hate whites but identify the key foreign agent "flirting with any pro-Marxist organization in Africa . . . always recognizing any terrorist organizations fighting against colonial rule. . . . Kurt Waldheim is unique in the history of Western civilization as the only man with high position and power . . . who . . . supported any struggle . . . against his own kind" (ibid.:23).

Although "unique," Waldheim is not alone. Borgin and Corbett warn that guilt-driven advocates of foreign aid undermine imperial progress:

> All are obsessed with the idea of transferring resources from the industrialized countries to Africa, and they are fanatical adherents to the concept of a New International Economic Order. (ibid.:30) [These] aid fanatics . . . and the greedy countries of the Third World [have conspired to blackmail the

West, forcing] millions of people in the industrialized West . . . [to] forever work in order to transfer huge sums of money, large amounts of goods, and other forms of resources without any form of compensation or repayment to the developing countries. (ibid.:50)

Inverting the character of foreign aid, which is of substantial benefit to Western business, Borgin and Corbett (ibid.:133–135) argue that "socialist politicians and intellectuals" ruined Africa through irrational hatred of colonialism and misled Africans into abandoning sensible development. Like Harris, they deploy anticommunist and racist themes and shape African history to their own argument. The foreign agents here are "aid fanatics," who play the same role as Harris's "racial equality fanatics," all Marxist-led and committed to a perverse and inexplicable disruption of hegemonic order.

An extensive discourse promotes such ideas. For example, John H. Spencer (1984:216), former adviser to Haile Selassie, laments the passing of an ordered system into a situation in which "the developed world trembles before the demands of the Third World." Similar themes recur in Rangel's *Third World Ideology and Western Reality* (1986). In his foreword, Jean-François Revel claims that the objective of this perverse and pervasive Third World ideology is "to accuse and . . . destroy the developed societies, not to develop the backward societies" (Rangel 1986:ix). Revel charges that proponents of this ideology are motivated by a "thirst for guilt" that explains their attempt to blame the West for the backwardness of the Third World. Rangel also praises Western imperialism, claiming that it improved those it contacted, particularly in terms of "their spiritual tone, the condition of being awake, alert and demanding. There is a vast difference for the better between present-day Arabs and those [of] . . . a hundred years ago, sleeping like lizards among the ruins of Petra and Palmyra" (ibid.:77).

Significantly, Rangel claims that imperialism's mission was a spiritual one, waking primitives from idle dreams. The Third World is presented as inert, passive, unconscious, in contrast to the West, which is portrayed as vital and active—an opposition consistent in discourse on the Horn. Rangel also links development and racial essence: "Imagine the transplantation of 50 million Indonesians to Germany (or, for that matter, to France) and of 50 million Germans (or French) to Indonesia. Which would be the rich country and which would be the poor country in a period of ten years?" (ibid.:153).

Similarly, in *The Causes of World Hunger*, the Christian aid agency Bread for the World claims that Western colonialism was the main agent of Third World progress and that many imperialists "were inspired by the noblest concern for the poor" (Byron 1982a:66). Richard Neuhaus praises the civilizing mission in which imperialism brought progress to backward peoples. He conflates technology with racial essence, and while conceding that the West is not necessarily superior notes that "Jewish Scriptures, the Christian faith, the intellectual heritage of Greece and the legal achievements of Rome . . . constitute the motor force of modernity . . . coveted by the rest of the world" (1982:70–71). His reference to *Heart of Darkness* as the "most classic indictment" of European imperialism is not a casual aside, as Conrad's novella provides the central metaphor for Africanist discourse; Philip Caputo virtually paraphrases Conrad's text in his novel *Horn of Africa*, which features a "Bronze Age army" roaming a primeval battlefield modeled on Eritrea (Caputo 1980:114). Caputo had reported on Eritrea for the *Chicago Tribune*; as a novelist, he employs the clichés of Africanist discourse: the journey backwards in time and into an earlier existential state, barbaric ceremonies, human sacrifice, Africa's corroding influence on Western morality and civilized behavior. Eritreans, fictionalized as "Bejayans," are portrayed as primitive warriors, religious fanatics and Marxist ideologues. Dealing in such stereotypes, Caputo reinvents the fantastic geography and the most lurid imaginings of imperialist mythology, but the themes drawn so crudely in his novel also provide the underlying structure for more serious discourse on the Horn.

As for Conrad's text as an "indictment" of colonialism, it is surely an equivocal one, preserving the redeeming idea behind imperialism as "something you can set up, and bow down before and offer a sacrifice to" (Conrad 1973:31–32). Neuhaus places imperialism in the Christian tradition of the West, the "motor force of modernity," and contrasts this with Conrad's Africa, not just technologically undeveloped but representing ontological regression, a journey backwards in time. Neuhaus sees anticommunism as part of the West's spiritual mission. Again, the danger is from treacherous elements in the West who have deviated from their racial mission by allying themselves with the savage rather than guiding the decent native into modernity. Like the Ethiopians in *Harper's* magazine, the decent natives "love Americans": "Wherever people have been free to express a choice, they have made clear their desire to emulate 'the American way of life,' on which many Americans have soured" (Neuhaus 1982:68). Rejection of "the American way of life" can only be irrational fanaticism, as no rational or moral foundation for dissent is acknowledged. Betrayal of the Elect surfaces in Neuhaus's description of multinational corporations as agents of progress, whose charitable activities are subverted by Third World nations.

The threat is plain: the West is under siege by the greedy Third World and drastic action is required. Borgin and Corbett suggest that the best solution would be to cut off aid and leave Africans to their own devices. A Heritage Foundation report adopts their argument that aid stems from unwarranted Western guilt and comes to similar conclusions (Bandow 1985). The Heritage Foundation questions the moral basis for providing foreign aid, holds Third World leaders responsible for poverty, promotes multinationals as agents of progress, and concludes that criteria for aid should be political rather than humanitarian: "A country of strategic significance to Washington should be considered for a broader range of assistance, including that of humanitarian nature, than a country of less strategic significance" (in Bandow 1985:9).

Former President Richard Nixon (1988:296) makes similar recommendations, arguing "there should be no aid without strings." This is already the case but, like others, Nixon distorts the nature of foreign aid and suggests that it is given away for sentimental reasons and without political motives. He attacks "Western liberals [for their] guilty hand-wringing over the Third World . . . [as well as] college students and professors and newspaper editors [and others who] become apoplectic over racial injustice in South Africa" (ibid.:282–283). Nixon also argues that the U.S. should drop what he characterizes as its obsession with human rights and support authoritarian regimes to prevent their populace from going communist, following seduction by the UN, "a propaganda mouthpiece for state socialism" (ibid.:298).

These works exemplify the broader scope of the discursive formation that includes texts on war and famine in the Horn. This formation emphasizes the legitimacy of domination in the service of racial-religious mission and anticommunism. The attribution of any critique of inequality to unwarranted guilt was not a new rhetorical tactic. For example, in the *New York Times Magazine* (November 7, 1976), Max Singer and Paul Bracken of the Hudson Institute argued that calls for a new international economic order were a "guilt-mongering attack" on the U.S. launched by poor countries and Western neurotics; they note the benefits brought by colonialism, reject the notion of exploitation, and claim that the U.S. "is entitled to its wealth because it was earned by hard and creative work. It was not taken from anyone."

Similar arguments are made by Lord Bauer, an economist at the London School of Economics. Bauer believes that colonialism benefited Africa and that decolonization unleashed a destructive African essence. This idea of disaster caused by loss of control over the Third World is central to the discourse and is at the core of the apocalyptic narrative of famine in Ethiopia. Bauer (1984:39) challenges the idea of Third World poverty, maintaining that the line between rich and poor is arbitrary and that one can easily categorize the world as two-thirds rich and one-third poor; Bandow (1985:vii) repeats the argument. Both appeal to common-sense notions through the rhetorical tactic identified by Barthes (1972) as the statement of fact. By emphasizing the arbitrary nature of categorization Bauer attempts to invalidate it, a tactic which, presumably, could be extended to exclude the poor entirely. In Bauer's view there is no sense in speaking of developed and developing countries and the only criterion typifying the Third World is receipt of foreign aid. He says the West has created the Third World as an entity hostile to itself, one that plays upon Western guilt in order to extract more money from Western taxpayers. The rhetorical construction is typical of the discourse; appeals to essentialism replace historical analysis: "External donations have never been necessary for the development of any society anywhere. Economic achievement depends on personal, cultural, social and political factors, that is people's own" (Bauer 1984:43). The assertion that "external donations" played no part in .Western development overlooks centuries of colonial plunder and continuing relationships of neocolonial domination and dependency, in which massive resources are transferred from the former colonies to the industrial nations. Bauer's assumption that virtue creates prosperity parallels Christian mythology and cannot be sustained in view of a world-system model which demonstrates that societies are not discrete units but part of "a totality of interconnected processes" (Wolf 1982:5).

Bauer's seminal argument appears in his article, "Western Guilt and Third World Poverty," which embodies the anxieties of threatened hegemony that characterize discourse on the Horn. He argues that the West has been too generous and liberal in its selfless attempt to modernize the world and has allowed morally deficient nations to make unwarranted accusations about colonial exploitation. Bauer (1976:31) claims that the West has "abased itself before groups of countries which have negligible resources and no real power." He believes this abasement has been forced by allegations from the Third World and from communists that the West is responsible for world poverty, allegations "expressed vaguely [and] virulently . . . in the universities, in the churches, and in the media." The rhetorical pattern is standard: the West is the agent of modernity, communists and liberals have betrayed the civilizing mission and forced this abasement. The apocalyptic message warns of the need to reassert domination over the avarice of idle but dangerous primitives.

Bauer lists benefits imparted to Africa by colonialism, concentrating on infrastructural development. Colonialism did bring beneficial innovations but Bauer overlooks the fact that much of this infrastructural development was intended to serve Western interests by effecting resource extraction and maintaining a manageable labor force. Bauer adds to this list the establishment of economies based on cotton, peanuts, and cocoa, noting that there were "no exports" of these crops prior to colonialism but that they are "now staples of world commerce, all produced by Africans" (ibid.:32). This is true: at the time Bauer's article appeared, groundnuts accounted for three-quarters of all export earnings in Senegal and covered half the country's total cultivable area; in Ivory Coast, cocoa and coffee produced over half the national export earnings; in Ghana, three-fifths came from cocoa; in Chad, fourth-fifths from raw cotton; in Uganda, three-quarters from coffee and cotton; in Malawi, three-fifths from tobacco and tea; in Kenya, half from coffee and tea (Lofchie 1975:555). However, Bauer ignores issues of foreign ownership, class, and relations of production and simply equates producers with beneficiaries. Furthermore, this monocrop dependency, so dangerously subject to fluctuations of the international market and responsible for many of Africa's current economic and environmental problems, is a dubious benefit.

To justify the civilizing mission, Bauer argues that Third World peoples with little contact with the West remain the poorest and most backward, using Australian aborigines as an example. Through the construction of significant absence, Bauer disregards three centuries of contact with Europeans that included attempts at genocide. At least twenty thousand aborigines were massacred by settlers and thousands more died from disease, malnutrition, alcoholism, and despair. Bauer claims that the most "backward" groups "(aborigines, desert peoples, nomads and other tribesfolk) were quite unaffected by ethnic discrimination on the part of Europeans," whereas areas that did experience discrimination made great advances (1976:36). His claims are false: most of these "tribesfolk" were exterminated in military campaigns or died from infectious diseases brought by colonialism. The surviving "tribesfolk" have been pushed into peripheral areas, deprived of their resource base, excluded from adequate education and health care, legally prevented from practicing their cultural traditions, poisoned by industrial wastes, and are widely subjected to racist violence. Bauer's revision of the historical record constructs the primitive world as a backward zone led into modernity by the West; as with discourse on African famine, historical events are inverted or erased.

Bauer's argument is unsupportable, yet it had great appeal to some. Harris and Neuhaus take it up. Emphasizing Africa's essential backwardness and inertia, they ask what would have happened to Africa without colonialism and claim that former colonies are now prosperous, while uncolonized areas like Ethiopia have become the poorest. Charles Krauthammer (1981) reproduces the argument in the *New Republic*; without acknowledging Bauer, Krauthammer repeats his claim that nations which had the least contact with Western colonialism are now the most backward. He, too, misrepresents the historical record by ignoring centuries of slaughter and the extermination of entire cultures. Taking the case selected by Bauer and Krauthammer, one readily finds expressions of genocidal sentiment, as in an Australian newspaper of 1846: "The perpetuation of the race of Aborigines is not to be desired. That they are an inferior race of human beings it is in vain to deny . . . and it is no more desirable that any inferior race should be perpetuated, than that the transmission of an hereditary disease, such as scrofula or insanity, should be encouraged" (in Barta 1987:243).

While Bauer does not refer to South Africa to demonstrate the supposed progress brought by racial discrimination, Borgin and Corbett warn of communists who threaten to undo advances brought there by white "settlers"; Harris also attacks "racial equality fanatics" of a socialist bent who are eroding colonial progress. Bauer (1976:33) does object to Marxists who promote "the spurious belief that the capacities and motivations of people are the same the world over."

Similarly suggesting that race is destiny, Borgin and Corbett indicate unjustified demands on the Elect: "Those who demand most are those who have accomplished the least. . . . Countries with large national resources, like the U.S., Germany, France, England, and the Scandinavian countries, are in possession of their resources due to hard work, intelligent planning, and a sound political and economic system. There is therefore no justification for the transfer of resources to countries where hard work is unknown" (Borgin and Corbett 1982:52–54). What is overlooked is the nature of these demands, which may be for basic necessities. George (1988:108) quotes a Belgian doctor's observations in Zaire: "Yesterday I saw a little girl eating grass and another one who was eating waste from the brewery. She was scooping it up to take some home. She told me she hadn't eaten for three days." The same demands are made in Brazil: "The parents have gone out foraging in the garbage heaps. Noticing how poorly the children look, the social worker asks them whether they have eaten recently. 'Yes, miss, yesterday Mummy made little cakes from wet newspapers. . . . Mummy takes a sheet of newspaper . . . soaks it in water . . . kneads it into little cakes. We eat them, drink some water and feel nice and full inside'" (ibid.:137).

It is hardly the case that "hard work is unknown" in the Third World, where many of the poor live in virtual slavery, performing grim tasks in dangerous conditions. Nevertheless, such claims bolstered anticommunist discourse, which often served to defend privilege against any perceived threat regardless of its ideological character.

Institutional Links

Discourse on the Third World exhibits a convergence of anticommunism, Christian mythology, and racism. Eulogizing colonialism, Borgin and Corbett (1982:22) conflate racial and political betrayal, perpetrated by socialists who have "turned against their own kind," as does Bauer (1976:33), who berates socialists for failing to see that not all people have the same "capacities." Neuhaus (1982) characterizes colonialism as the preordained spiritual mission of the West. Rangel (1986:30) writes of the Khmer Rouge's "satanic genocide" in Cambodia, ignoring U.S. saturation bombing, and proclaims that Marxism demands human sacrifice. Standing before them is Lugard (1923:82), who places communists below cannibals on his scale of morality and ridicules those Africans who presume to "institutions which are not in some way a direct outcome of the negro character."

Identification of communism with satanic forces, images of biblical famines, and ideas of racial betrayal and confrontation with absolute evil, suggesting imminent Armageddon, were not limited to these texts. Such ideas motivated a network of institutions. Among them was the Christian fundamentalist organization Opus Dei, part of an international militant Catholic network devoted to the destruction of communism and establishment of a perfect society integrating church and state (Lernoux 1989a; 1989b). Opus Dei is connected to other fundamentalist groups such as Legatus, the Knights of Malta, Word of God, and Sword of the Spirit, as well as the CIA. The network included Joseph Coors, adviser to Ronald Reagan and a founder of the Heritage Foundation, plus *La Prensa* editor Humberto Belli and Cardinal Miguel Obando y Bravo, important anti-Sandinista figures in Nicaragua.

The fundamentalist Christian network actively supported the right-wing agenda on a broad scale. For example, Gospel Outreach supported Rios Montt's genocidal campaigns against the Indians of Guatemala; Bob Weiner, president of Marantha Campus Ministries ("God's Green Berets"), claimed "that God chose 'English-speaking Teutonic peoples' to come to America and 'administer government among savage and senile peoples' and to 'establish a system where no chaos reigned'" (in Diamond 1987:27–28). In Mozambique, the Mozambique National Resistance, responsible for what the U.S. State Department estimated as 100,000 civilian murders, was supported by the Pentecostal Shekinah Ministries, as well as Freedom, Inc., Free The Eagle, Freedom Research Foundation, and various U.S. businessmen. Other Christian groups supported apartheid; the Reverend Sun Myung Moon's *Washington Times* received over four million dollars from the South African government for favorable coverage. Moon's organization belonged to the World Anti-Communist League (WACL), "an international coalition of fascist and conservative groups and political parties founded in 1966 by agents of the governments of Taiwan and South Korea" (Clarkson 1987:36–38). Headed by retired U.S. Major General John Singlaub, WACL included Nazi collaborators, such as the Yugoslavian Ustasha and the Croatian Iron Guard, neo-Nazis, European terrorist organizations such as Fuerza Nueva and the Italian Social Movement, death squad leaders like Roberto D'Aubuisson from El Salvador and Mario Sandoval Alarcon from Guatemala, Paraguayan dictator General Alfredo Stroessner, CIA agents, and Republican senators in the U.S. (Anderson and Anderson 1986). Under Singlaub's direction, WACL supported anticommunist soldiers in Ethiopia, Angola, Mozambique, Laos, South Vietnam, Cambodia, and Nicaragua.

Fundamentalist groups such as the National Religious Broadcasters, whose Board of Directors included Jerry Falwell, Billy Graham, Pat Robertson, and Jimmy Swaggart, cooperated with WACL, the Moonies, and organizations such as Friends of the Americas and Gospel Crusade, which supplied the contras in Central America, assisted by Lt. Col. Oliver North. Many of the violent fantasies of these groups appealed to state officials. For example, in 1971 at a lobbyists' banquet in Sacramento, Ronald Reagan referred to biblical prophecies (Chapters 38 and 39 of Ezekiel) to explain Libya's "communism" as a portent of Armageddon; he stated that it was "inevitable" that Ethiopia would become a communist state in order to fulfill biblical prophecy and predicted that Ethiopia would turn against Israel to join the Soviet Union's final battle against God. On June 9, 1982, television evangelist Pat Robertson, later a Republican presidential candidate, used these prophecies to explain Israel's invasion of Lebanon as a sign of imminent Armageddon: Gog (the Soviet Union) would be assisted by Rush (Ethiopia), Put (Libya), Gomer (South Yemen), Persia (Iran), and Beth Tugarma (Armenia) in this final battle (Halsell 1986:40–50, 16). Although his dispensationalist views (a belief in the Second Coming after Armageddon) may have been supplanted by astrological interests, Reagan appeared fascinated with eschatological prophecy, possibly explaining his reluctance to discuss arms control in favor of building a first-strike nuclear arsenal to be used in a Middle East apocalyptic battle (Kickham 1987). *Awake!* magazine (March 8, 1987) identified Ethiopian famine with the Third Horseman of the Apocalypse and pointed out biblical prophecies that "the earth will be cleansed of all who oppose Christ's rule. Selfish man-made governments will be removed (Daniel 2:44)."

Famine in Ethiopia provided useful imagery to support these fundamentalist theories about Armageddon. It also was incorporated into racist parables about African incompetency and betrayal and into a broader discourse of anticommunism. Racism, Christian fundamentalism, and anticommunism merged as Ethiopia became an important element of Western political discourse during the 1980s. Through inversion of its earlier image as a paradise on earth, beloved of the gods, Ethiopia became a symbol of hellish chaos, and entered into popular culture as a signifier of absolute degradation, disaster, and despair.

CONCLUSION

The old idea of Ethiopia, which once signified stability and continuity rooted in antiquity, has exploded. In its place lie the ruins of that image; in the popular culture of the West, the former dream kingdom became one of nightmares, and Ethiopia now serves as a synonym for disaster. This book has sought to describe some of the lines of fissure in this now-shattered image and the manner in which new significations have been constructed.

Throughout history Ethiopia seems to have invited the projection of images and external obsessions. During the 1980s, Ethiopia was incorporated into a network of signification bounded by discourses of racism, Christian fundamentalism, and anticommunism. These discourses were integral aspects of the post–World War II plan intended to structure the world according to U.S. interests (Augelli and Murphy 1988; Chomsky 1991; Kolko 1988). Following the war against Vietnam and a series of revolutions in former Western colonies, the Third World took on a particular significance as a zone of betrayals and ontological dangers. In the heightened Cold War atmosphere of the Reagan years, the reassertion of U.S. power was expressed in terms of a spiritual mission (Kirkpatrick 1983). Ethiopia, a former ally that had gone over to the enemy camp, was conceived as part of an evil empire and was portrayed accordingly. The famine that struck in the 1980s was incorporated into this narrative of betrayal, and disaster was linked to the ideological orientation of the Mengistu regime. Famine in Ethiopia was merged into a narrative of global confrontation between good and evil forces, embodied by the U.S. and the Soviet Union. Attempts made by the Derg to use famine as a weapon against its opponents were rightly condemned, but these condemnations were immediately incorporated into an anticommunist discourse that overlooked the willingness of the U.S. to use famine against its own enemies. Similarly, due to its alliance with the Soviet Union, human rights abuses by the Derg were condemned while those of ideologically acceptable regimes were overlooked. However, because the Derg's opponents were also considered unacceptable, discourse on the Horn of Africa took on a particular configuration that distinguished it from other situations where anticommunists could be valorized as freedom fighters.

Discourse on famine in Ethiopia contained a moral parable concerning charity and betrayal. In general, this parable rejected any historical understanding of famine and, interpreting the colonial impact as beneficial rather than disruptive, argued that African corruption and savagery were responsible for the deterioration of the continent. This discourse not only distorted the nature of foreign aid as charity but argued that this was driven by irrational guilt and encouraged by treacherous socialists. Famine in Ethiopia served an apocalyptic function as well, being interpreted as a warning sign for impending disaster in the West, brought about by "aid fanatics," "racial equality fanatics," and "socialists," and requiring a return to more conservative values.

Media discourse on the Horn concentrated on sensational images of starvation. Famine was portrayed as an event rather than a process. Overlooked by the mass media until it had reached a point of crisis, the famine provided an opportunity to deliver truly shocking images and appropriate ideological messages. Chief among these were the depiction of Africans as either passive victims, incompetents, or barbaric savages, and the presentation of famine as a result of socialist agricultural practices. Famine became a commodity, packaged for easy consumption. The multifaceted causes of famine were oversimplified and reduced, and the historical dimensions were ignored or distorted. The effect of relief aid itself was typically celebrated as an unprecedented act of Western charity, although some have argued that the manner in which such aid was provided contributed to further suffering and death by allowing the Mengistu regime to carry out its resettlement programs. Through this incomplete depiction of famine, which concentrated only on the dramatic image of starvation victims, decontextualization became falsification. While the media coverage of famine did have some beneficial effects in terms of short-term fund-raising, it also undermined the necessary long-term commitment for recovery and rehabilitation. Emphasis on the immediate provision of relief also overlooked the need to provide assistance for recovery and rehabilitation. Although famine conditions have persisted, with intermittent but temporary improvements, media have long since abandoned Ethiopia. In 1992 there was some renewed interest in the Horn as Somalia crumbled, thousands starved, and Western troops were sent to the area, but other matters of regional negotiation and reconstruction were largely ignored. The perceived need for novelty, sensational images, human interest, and the avoidance of complexity combined to ensure that they would continue to be overlooked as the media sought out other crises.

While famine provided an opportunity to attack the Mengistu regime by overlooking starvation under previous regimes, as well as in other parts of Africa, it also allowed critique of the nationalist movement in Eritrea and opposition forces in Tigray. Not only were basic political objectives of Western aid overlooked in order to present the strategic use of famine as a tactic unique to the opposing forces in the region, but some journalists argued that inordinate efforts had been made to assist Eritrea and Tigray. Virtually ignored in such reporting on famine was the striking imbalance in the provision of relief aid. The fact that famine victims in Eritrea and Tigray received only small amounts of aid was justified by reference to the territorial integrity of Ethiopia and arguments that working openly with ERA and REST would be a violation of diplomatic protocol. Left unquestioned was the legitimacy of Ethiopia's control over Eritrea as well as the legitimacy of a state that used starvation against segments of the population it claimed to represent.

It would be incorrect to assert that such imagery completely dominates contemporary discourse on famine. The very horror of the images of starvation in the Horn has intensified research since 1984 concerning the causes of famine, including economic and ecological approaches, the nature of foreign aid, gender and development, agrarian reform, subsistence strategies, social impact of famine, and general studies in international political economy. Much of this is of enormous value. Particularly important is the interrogation of the notion of development itself and the recognition that development institutions such as the World Bank and the IMF are agents in a specific system of global ordering. Nevertheless, the same problems still persist and many of these scholarly insights have yet to be incorporated into practice.

Western discourse on Eritrea and Ethiopia was not simply a hegemonic vision imposed over the Horn. Rather, it incorporated a number of pre-existing discursive fragments, such as the images of Solomon and Sheba, Prester John, Ethiopia as a long-unified state, and Haile Selassie as a modernizing Western ally, as well as the primitivist stereotypes of Africa in general. Western discourse adopted the mythologies of local ruling elites in order to attain joint objectives, and in this process other subaltern discourses of history and identity were ignored or suppressed.

The notion of Ethiopia as a long-unified state rooted in the remote past was a projection of the modern into antiquity, a device intended to consolidate the power of local ruling elites. Once viewed as an atypical African country that somewhat paradoxically came to symbolize those glories of the African past that had been banished from Western histories, Ethiopia must now be seen as subject to the same forces that have shaped the rest of the continent. The personalized histories of the past that focused on the emperors are being rethought, and the notion of Greater Ethiopia has been challenged. The character of the more recent Ethiopian state created by the centralizing emperors Teodros, Yohannes, Menelik, and Haile Selassie remains contested among claims of restoration of unity, regional autonomy under recognized authority, and portraits of a tormented and splintering empire ruled only by force. Similarly, conflicting versions of national identity have been conceived in radically different ways, as a primordial essence, a historical construction, a colonial artifice, a creation of foreign agents, an open framework, or an imposition of raw power. Whereas Eritrean nationalist discourse typically relied on appeals to standards of international law and emphasized the contemporary character of national identity, Ethiopian nationalists mainly have employed mythological arguments and appeals to primordial unity; Tigrayan nationalism has shifted from an emphasis on regional identity, exemplified in the image of *Weyane*, to a more inclusive form, while Oromo nationalists have employed the imagery of reawakening and recovery of a lost heritage. All of these struggles were viewed in terms of opposing images, as repression or unity, liberation or separatism, resurgence or tribalism. Differences in the form of nationalist mythologies reflect the fact that nationalism is a consequence of conflict rather than its primary cause, and these variations, shifts, and reversals of narratives are indications of the ebb and flow of power (Markakis 1987:xvi).

These contested classifications must be recognized as struggles over the power to "to impose the legitimate definition of the divisions of the social world and thereby, to make and unmake groups" (Bourdieu 1991:221). They are conducted through the manipulation of images of the past and of symbols of identity that are intended to mobilize support for the narratives they construct. The production of subaltern histories is a challenge to established social control. All texts, including this one, which comment on the nature of history and identity in the region, are drawn into contemporary struggles over representation, sometimes serving contradictory ends at different times (Thomas 1989:15). Involvement in these struggles does not require polemical motives, nor is it simply a matter of truth, since knowledge invariably has its effect, often unintended, and the most factually accurate accounts may be couched in an overtly or covertly ideological framework.

Hegemonic discourse resisted challenges to entrenched history and identity. While successive Ethiopian governments dismissed the Eritrean independence movement as bandits, Ethiopian intellectuals at home and in exile have condemned not only Eritrean and Oromo nationalism but have also sought to discredit foreign commentators and scholars who have interpreted history in ways that do not support the mythologies of Greater Ethiopia. Similarly, efforts to cancel out oppositional versions of the past have been made by Western academics and government officials who have remained committed to the idea of Greater Ethiopia despite their aversion to the Derg. Through rhetorical processes such as the construction of significant absence, falsification, insistence on the influence of foreign agents, and insinuation, as well the assertion of their own authority through mutual expressions of appreciation and cross-referencing, a number of so-called experts on Ethiopian history have sought to relegate subaltern and oppositional discourses to the status of propaganda. As Thomas (1989:24) demonstrates in regard to anthropological discourse, such experts, by asserting their own professional identity and their authoritative versions of history, attempt to establish their own monopoly over representation, seeking the colonization and control of discursive space.

Other Africans have also resisted reconceptualization of Ethiopia's history and territorial integrity. In some cases, this can be seen as the result of strategic alliances. For example, the insistence by many southern Sudanese that Eritrea remain linked with Ethiopia must be seen in terms of Ethiopia's support to the Sudanese People's Liberation Army against the government in Khartoum. Others, fearing secessionist movements within their own borders, have proclaimed that Eritreans do not exist. This is plainly false given that, regardless of its precise origins, a strong sense of national identity does exist among many Eritreans, and the victory of the EPLF now seems to have made that identity more concrete. Furthermore, apart from the instrumental character of African resistance to this identity, it is clear that the particular circumstances of Eritrean history do not provide a model for separatist arguments elsewhere.

However, it also seems clear that it is not only these explicitly political and instrumental concerns that have fostered African opposition to Eritrean independence. Ethiopia still retains its symbolic significance for Africa, despite the fact that Ethiopian elites have rejected their own African identity and insisted upon their Semitic heritage. For some, therefore, any division of Ethiopia represents a transgression of African history as well as a threat to a greater unified identity and to the concept of an African self. The question remains, however, as to the stability of any forced unity.

An understanding of national identity in the Horn is complicated by the recognition that subaltern discourses also may be internally divided. Afar, Eritrean, and Oromo nationalisms all contain their own oppositions and contradictions. Whereas some have read these contradictions as a sign of the illegitimacy of any national identity among these groups, such oppositions do not negate the existence of a national consciousness but rather indicate the more complex nature of this consciousness and its historical formation. Oppositions and contradictions do not signify the aberrant character of these nationalist movements but instead may be typical of postcolonial nationalism in general (Geertz 1973:234–254). The future significance of these ethnic identities within an independent Eritrean state will be a matter of some interest.

Debates over the nature of the Ethiopian revolution, the Mengistu regime, and its various opponents have portrayed them variously as socialist, fascist, state-capitalist, neo-imperialist, or as competing military dictatorships. These conflicting interpretations have contained debates over the nature of socialism itself. The fact that the Derg and its opponents employed Marxist rhetoric has been taken as a sign of the incomprehensible nature of the conflict, and thus the primitive character of the opposing protagonists, as well as an indication of a fundamental flaw in socialist philosophies. While some have seen the image of the Derg mirrored in its opponents, others have found, particularly in the EPLF, an alternative version of socialism, depicted as more humane, participatory, and emancipatory. For its part, the TPLF is still haunted by the widely reported comment in 1989 by one of its representatives that it viewed Albania as a model. The debates were rendered more quixotic by the fact that by 1991 both the Derg and the EPLF had distanced themselves from Marxist rhetoric and proclaimed commitment to either a mixed economy or to capitalist development. The old image of the Oromo has also been challenged; formerly depicted as a chaotic, primitive force threatening the ancient princely order of Amhara culture, some now see the Oromo as the exemplars of indigenous and superior democratic traditions.

The destruction of the old image of Ethiopia has opened up rich new fields for scholarly research, and previously denigrated cultures are now seen as valid and significant in their own right. However, as Asmarom (1973) points out, Western scholarship has been characterized by violent identifications with particular African cultures, allowing researchers to indulge certain shared biases and to dismiss other cultures. That observation remains salutary even in the present context, for it may be tempting to substitute new stereotypes in the place of the old images. Unless one questions one's own point of view, one risks exercising only a partial objectivity and becoming an accomplice with one's adversaries in "the very game that constitutes them as competitors" (Bourdieu 1990:184).

It is not only imagery that has been transformed; Ethiopia itself has undergone enormous changes. After the downfall of the Derg in 1991, a reordering of Ethiopia is inevitable. Following the April 1993 referendum Eritrea has now emerged as the newest independent country in Africa. Seen in the context of events such as the disintegration of the Soviet Union, the even more violent fragmentation of Yugoslavia and Somalia, continuing debates over self-determination for native people and Quebec's role in Canada, as well as new economic relationships in Europe and North America, the reorganization of the state and the questioning of national boundaries cannot be considered processes unique to Ethiopia in the 1990s.

Nevertheless, such a reorganization of Ethiopia will not be easy for any of those involved. For many, the idea is traumatic. Those who have subscribed to an Ethiopian nationality have reacted in anger, bitterness, and confusion at what they see as a violation of their history and identity. Some refused to accept any reordering. For example, Ethiopia's former Foreign Minister, Goshu Wolde, in an address to the National Press Club in Washington (July 11, 1991), protested that the EPRDF was "engaged in a systematic dismantling of the Ethiopian state and damaging its fundamental interest." Even at this late date, Goshu insisted on the unified nature of Ethiopian identity and rejected any idea of independence for Eritrea: "But for a short interval of 50 years, when it was under Italian colonial administration, Eritrea has always been an integral part of the Ethiopian state. Eritrea was for centuries the cultural, political and economic center of Ethiopia. . . . Eritrea stands for Ethiopia as a symbol of determined defense of national unity and territorial integrity.

Similarly, some Ethiopian expatriates reacted to the EPLF's victory with outrage and with calls to return to fight for the motherland. Others feel that the country they fled no longer exists and they are now adrift, facing the dissolution of identity.

For Eritreans, however, this reordering promises an end to exile and a reassertion of the national identity they have long been denied. Although the EPLF announced that a referendum would be held in 1993, it was generally acknowledged that independence had already been achieved in 1991. But with the emergence of Eritrea as an independent nation also come revelations of the costs of the war. At least 50,000 Eritreans were killed in the war. In addition, the economy and infrastructure of Eritrea have been ravaged in the course of the conflict and Eritreans must start from less than zero. Huge numbers of refugees have fled the prolonged war in Eritrea and the return of these people poses major logistical problems for the new government in Asmara, both in immediate needs for food, shelter, and health care but also in long-term requirements for reintegration, education, and employment. Environmental conditions continue to create problems. In 1991, erratic rainfall was followed by a poor harvest, leaving approximately two million people dependent on food aid. In 1992 food stocks remained low and starvation was reported. While the EPLF and the Eritrean Relief Association did make remarkable social achievements in areas such as education and health care in the past, there are other formidable problems to be faced in the future.

Regarding the Oromo, the future of the struggle for national identity and for self-determination is unclear. Among the refugee and immigrant population in North America there is a growing sense of this identity, a strong interest in reviving and recreating Oromo culture, and considerable support for the notion of independent Oromia. However, the extent of the appeal of this distinct Oromo identity within Ethiopia continues to be debated. While Holcomb (1991) and Sisai (1990) suggest that a distinct Oromo identity is also strong in Ethiopia, Gebru (1990, 1991) and Clapham (1990b) dismiss Oromo nationalism and the OLF's ability to mobilize the peasants to its cause. Clapham in particular seems to reject almost the existence of any Oromo identity, but the significance of Oromo nationalism should not be underestimated. The Transitional Government of Ethiopia put forward its program for what it promises will be a democratic reorganization of the country, and if such a reorganization were implemented it could meet Oromo demands, as expressed by some Oromo informants. However, it is clear that the proposed reorganization has not satisfied those who call for an independent Oromia. Indeed, many OLF supporters have rejected the program and charged that the Transitional Government is simply continuing the Derg's policies under a different name and with modified rhetoric. Human rights abuses have been reported; sporadic violence would not be surprising in the context of the Derg's collapse and the militarization of Ethiopia, but even more disturbingly, Oromo publications charge that there is a systematic intent to the incidents, designed to weaken the OLF and maintain Oromo subordination. Whether or not continued violence can be averted remains to be seen. If the experience of other groups can be taken as a precedent, Oromo national identity may be strengthened to the same extent that it is denied and oppressed, and its appeal is likely to increase if the new government is not able to improve material conditions. Furthermore, the issue may become even more complex than the Eritrean case, where identity has been expressed in terms of territorial rather than ethnic nationalism, because the matter of an independent Oromia raises questions not only of its boundaries but also of the status of non-Oromos included within them.

These remarks have been confined to Eritrea and Ethiopia, but events there occur in a broader context that includes Somalia and Sudan, where ideas of identity, history, and nation have been challenged on the basis of religious, cultural, ethnic, and clan divisions and which have both now become transformed into regions of scarcely believeable suffering. With conditions in the Horn changing daily, any conclusions about the future of the region as a whole seem inappropriate. The struggle of many for sheer survival, as well as for control over representation, for national identity, for the creation of new regional affiliations, is ongoing. There are clearly enormous difficulties but there are also opportunities, particularly for Eritrea. While the old images have been shattered, then, the process of imagining continues.

BIBLIOGRAPHY

Note: In the Horn of Africa most people identify themselves by their first names. The bibliography has been prepared to reflect this.

Abir, Mordechai. 1972. "The Contentious Horn of Africa." *Conflict Studies* 24.

Addis Hiwet. 1984. "Analysing the Ethiopian Revolution." *Review of African Political Economy* 30:32–47.

Africa Confidential. 1987. "Ethiopia: Eritrea Takes Stock." 28 (9): 2–5.

———. 1989. "Ethiopia: The Politics of Power and the Politics of Peace." 30 (12): 6–7.

Agriculture and Rural Development Unit. 1988. "Eritrea Food and Agricultural production Assessment Study Final Report." Leeds: University of Leeds Centre of Development Studies.

Ake, Claude. 1981. *A Political Economy of Africa*. Harlow: Longman.

Alem Habtu. 1986. "Books on the Ethiopian Revolution: A Review Essay." *Socialism and Democracy* 3:27–60.

Amare Tekle. 1989. "The Determinants of the Foreign Policy of Revolutionary Ethiopia." *Journal of Modern African Studies* 27 (3): 479–502.

Anderson, Benedict. 1983. *Imagined Communities*. London: Verso.

Anderson, Harry, Jerry Buckley, Theodore Stanger, and Shawn Doherty. 1984. "A Flood of Generosity." *Newsweek*, November 26, 56–57.

Anderson, Scott, and John L. Anderson. 1986. *Inside the League*. New York: Dodd, Mead.

Andreas Eshete. 1986. "Beyond National Self-Determination: A Comment." In *Conflict and Conflict Resolution in the Horn of Africa*. Proceedings of the First International Conference on the Horn of Africa, 23–28. New York: Center for the Study of the Horn of Africa.

Asante, S.K.B. 1977. *Pan-African Protest: West Africa and the Italo-Ethiopian Crisis, 1934–1941*. London: Longman.

Asmarom Legesse. 1973. *Gada*. New York: Free Press.

Asoyan, Boris. 1979. "The Revolution's Arduous Path." *New Times* 37:26–28.

Assefa Abreha, 1989. "Perspectives on and Prospects for Peace in the Horn of Africa." In *Conditions for the Possibility of Peace in the Horn of Africa*. Proceedings of the Fourth International Conference on the Horn of Africa, 100–116. New York: Center for the Study of the Horn of Africa.

———, 1989/1990. "Remarks by an Ethiopian on Paul Henze's Paper, 'Eritrean Options and Ethiopia's Future,' Presented at the United States Institute of Peace in Washington, D.C., August 11, 1989." *Journal of Eritrean Studies* 4 (1/2): 48–53.

Augelli, Enrico, and Craig Murphy. 1988. *America's Quest for Supremacy and the Third World*. London: Pinter.
Aykroyd, W. R. 1974. *The Conquest of Famine*. London: Chatto and Windus.
Azad, A. 1983. "Ethiopia—Trailblazer for the African Revolution." *The African Communist* 94:79–90.

Babile Tola. 1989. *To Kill a Generation*. Washington: Free Ethiopia Press.
Babu, Abdulrahman Mohamed. 1986. "Eritrea: Its Present Is the Remote Future of Others." In *Eritrea: The Way Forward*, 16–22. London: United Nations Association.
Bagdikian, Ben. 1983. *The Media Monopoly*. Boston: Beacon Press.
Balibar, Etienne, and Immanuel Wallerstein, eds. 1991. *Race, Nation, Class*. London: Verso.
Ball, N. 1976. "Understanding the Causes of African Famine." *Journal of Modern African Studies* 14 (3): 517–522.
Bandow, Doug, ed. 1985. *U.S. Aid to the Developing World*. Washington: The Heritage Foundation.
Barraclough, Geoffrey. 1979. *Main Trends in History*. New York: Holmes and Meier.
Barta, Tony. 1987. "Relations of Genocide: Land and Lives in the Colonization of Australia." In *Genocide and the Modern Age*, ed. Isidor Walliman and Michael N. Dobkowski, 237–251. New York: Greenwood Press.
Barthes, Roland. 1972. *Mythologies*. New York: Hill and Wang.
Bauer, P. T. 1976. "Western Guilt and Third World Poverty." *Commentary 61* (1): 31–38.
———. 1984. *Reality and Rhetoric*. London: Weidenfeld and Nicolson.
Baxter, Paul. 1983. "The Problem of the Oromo or the Problem for the Oromo?" In *Nationalism and Self-Determination in the Horn of Africa*, ed. I. M. Lewis, 133–149. London: Ithaca Press.
Bereket Habte Selassie. 1980. *Conflict and Intervention in the Horn of Africa*. New York: Monthly Review Press.
———. 1983. "The Eritrean Question in International Law." *Horn of Africa* 6 (2): 25–30.
———. 1989. *Eritrea and the United Nations*. Trenton, N.J.: Red Sea Press.
Berkhofer, Robert F., Jr. 1978. *The White Man's Indian*. New York: Alfred A. Knopf.
Black, Laraine. 1986. "CBC Reporting of the Ethiopian Famine." Unpublished manuscript, York University.
Blum, William. 1986. *The CIA*. London: Zed.
Bochkaryov, Yuri. 1986. "What A Hope!" *New Times* 20:16–17.
———. 1987. "A Pack of Lies." *New Times* 11:16–17.
Bondestam, Lars. 1974. "People and Capitalism in the North-Eastern Lowlands of Ethiopia." *Journal of Modern African Studies* 12 (3): 423–439.
Borgin, Karl, and Kathleen Corbett. 1982. *The Destruction of a Continent*. New York: Harcourt Brace Jovanovich.
Bourdieu, Pierre. 1990. *In Other Words*. Stanford, Calif.: Stanford University Press.
———. 1991. *Language and Social Power*. Cambridge: Harvard University Press.

Bourne, Randolph. 1977. "War is the Health of the State." In *The Anarchist Reader*, ed. George Woodcock, 98–103. Glasgow: Fontana.
Brodhead, Tim. 1986. "If Africa is the Question, Is NGO the Answer?" *International Journal* 41 (4): 869–881.
Brooke, James. 1987. "Ethiopian Leaders Firmly Entrenched, But Widely Resented." *Toronto Globe and Mail*, March 16, A8.
Bush, Rod. 1985. "A Report from Ethiopia: Famine and Revolution in Africa." *Contemporary Marxism* 11:113–125.
Byron, William, ed. 1982a. *The Causes of World Hunger*. New York: Paulist Press.
———. 1982b. "Whose Right to Food?" In *Famine*, ed. Kevin M. Cahill, 63–71. Maryknoll, N.Y.: Orbis.

Caputo, Phillip. 1980. *Horn of Africa*. New York: Holt, Rinehart and Winston.
Carty, Robert, and Virginia Smith. 1981. *Perpetuating Poverty*. Toronto: Between The Lines.
Chege, Michael. 1979. "The Revolution Betrayed: Ethiopia 1974–1979." *Journal of Modern African Studies* 17 (3): 359–380.
Chomsky, Noam. 1982. *Towards a New Cold War*. New York: Pantheon.
———. 1986. *Turning the Tide*. Montreal: Black Rose Books.
———. 1987. *On Power and Ideology*. Boston: South End Press.
———. 1988. *The Culture of Terrorism*. Boston: South End Press.
———. 1989a. *Necessary Illusions*. Toronto: CBC Enterprises.
———. 1989b. "The Fifth Freedom." *The Listener* 121 (3106): 6–9.
———. 1991. *Deterring Democracy*. London: Verso.
Chomsky, Noam, and Edward S. Herman. 1979. *The Washington Connection and Third World Fascism*. Boston: South End Press.
Clapham, Christopher. 1990a. "Conclusion: Revolution, Nationality and the Ethiopian State." In *The Political Economy of Ethiopia*, ed. Marina Ottaway, 221–231. New York: Praeger.
———. 1990b. *Transformation and Continuity in Revolutionary Ethiopia*. Cambridge: Cambridge University Press.
———. 1991. "The Structure of Regional Conflict in Northern Ethiopia." *Disasters* 15 (3): 244–253.
Clarkson, Fred. 1987. "God is Phasing Out Democracy." *Covert Action Information Bulletin* 27:36–46.
Clay, Jason W. 1989. "Ethiopian Famine and the Relief Agencies." In *The Moral Nation*, ed. Bruce Nichols and Gil Loescher, 232–277. Notre Dame, Ind.: University of Notre Dame Press.
Clifford, James. 1988. *The Predicament of Culture*. Cambridge: Harvard University Press.
Cohen, William B. 1980. *The French Encounter with Africans*. Bloomington: Indiana University Press.
Connell, Dan. 1987. "Alignments in the Horn: Famine Reshuffles the Deck." *MERIP Middle East Report* 17 (2): 29–30.
Conrad, Joseph. 1973. *Heart of Darkness*. Harmondsworth: Penguin.
Curtin, Philip D. 1964. *The Image of Africa*. Madison: University of Wisconsin Press.

Dando, William. 1980. *The Geography of Famine*. London: E. Arnold.

Daniel, N. 1958. *Islam and the West*. Edinburgh: Edinburgh University Press.
———. 1966. *Islam, Europe and Empire*. Edinburgh: Edinburgh University Press.
———. 1975. *The Arabs and Medieval Europe*. London: Longman.
Dasylva, Claire. 1984. "Ethiopia: Breaking the Chains of Slavery." *Communist Viewpoint* 16 (4): 27–30.
Davidson, Basil, Lionel Cliffe, and Bereket Habte Selassie, eds. 1980. *Behind the War in Eritrea*. Nottingham: Spokesman.
Davis, Charles C. 1988. "Operation Bootstrap: Impressions of Ethiopia." *Canadian Dimension* 22 (15): 33–37.
Dawit Wolde Giorgis. 1989. *Red Tears*. Trenton, N.J.: Red Sea Press.
———. 1990. "The Power of Decision-Making in Post-Revolutionary Ethiopia." In *The Political Economy of Ethiopia*, ed. Marina Ottaway, 53–72. New York: Praeger.
Diamond, Sara. 1987. "Shepherding." *Covert Action Information Bulletin* 27: 18–31.
———. 1990. *Spiritual Warfare*. Montreal: Black Rose Books.
Dimbleby, Jonathan. 1988. "At the Front in Ethiopia." *The Spectator* 260 (8330): 13–14.
Donham, Donald. 1986. "Old Abyssinia and the New Ethiopian Empire: Themes in Social History." In *The Southern Marches of Ethiopia*, ed. Donald Donham and Wendy James, 3–48. Cambridge: Cambridge University Press.
Dougherty, James E. 1982. *The Horn of Africa: A Map of Political-Strategic Conflict*. Cambridge, Mass.: Institute for Foreign Policy Analysis.
Dower, John. 1986. *War without Mercy*. New York: Pantheon.
Drinnon, Richard. 1980. *Facing West*. Minneapolis: University of Minnesota Press.
Dudley, Edward, and Maximillian E. Novak. 1972. *The Wild Man Within*. Pittsburgh: University of Pittsburgh Press.
Duignan, Peter, and L. H. Gann. 1988. "Hope for Africa." In *Thinking about America*, ed. Annelise Anderson and Dennis L. Bark, 139–151. Stanford, Calif.: Hoover Institution Press.

Ehrlich, Paul. 1968. *The Population Bomb*. New York: Ballantine Books.
Ellingson, Lloyd. 1977. "The Emergence of Political Parties in Eritrea, 1941–1950." *Journal of African History* 18 (2): 261–281.
Epstein, Edward Jay. 1973. *News from Nowhere*. New York: Random House.
Eritrean People's Liberation Front. 1985. "The EPLF and Its Relations with Democratic Movements in Ethiopia." *Adulis* 1 (11): 3–8.
———. 1989. "Statement Concerning the 'New' Declaration of the Dergue." Washington, D.C.: Unpublished manuscript.
Erlich, Haggai. 1983. *The Struggle over Eritrea, 1962–1978*. Stanford, Calif: Hoover Institution Press.
Ethiopia: The Politics of Famine. 1990. New York: Freedom House.

Falmattuu Biyyaa. 1992. "To the Oromo in the Diaspora." *Qunnamtii Oromia* 2 (4): 4–6.
Farago, Ladislas. 1935. *Abyssinia on the Eve*. London: Putnam.

Fenet, Alain. 1988. "The Right of the Eritrean People to Self-Determination." In *The Long Struggle of Eritrea*, ed. Lionel Cliffe and Basil Davidson, 33–45. Nottingham: Spokesman.

Fenton, James. 1985. "Ethiopia: Victors and Victims." *New York Review of Books* 32 (17): 18–22.

Firebrace, James, with Stuart Holland. 1985. *Never Kneel Down*. Trenton, N.J.: Red Sea Press.

Foucault, Michel. 1977. *Discipline and Punish*. New York: Pantheon.

Franke, Richard W., and Barbara H. Chasin. 1980. *Seeds of Famine*. Montclair, N.J.: Allanheld, Osmun.

Gabrielyan, Gennady. 1979. "In the Liberated Areas of Eritrea." *New Times* 16:28–30.

Gadaa Melbaa. 1988. *Oromia*. Khartoum: n.p.

Gakou, Mohamed Lamine. 1987. *The Crisis in African Agriculture*. London: Zed Press.

Galaanaa Abbaa Gadaa. 1992. "The Tigrean Adventure in Oromia." *Qunnamtii Oromia* 2 (4): 28–32.

Galperin, G. 1985. "Aid: Facts and Fictions." *New Times* 2:12–13.

Galtung, J., and M. H. Ruge. 1965. "The Structure of Foreign News." *Journal of Peace Research* 1:64–91.

Gamst, Frederick C. 1986. "Conflict in the Horn of Africa." In *Peace and War*, ed. Mary Le Cron Foster and Robert A. Rubenstein, 133–151. New Brunswick, N.J.: Transaction Books.

Gartrell, Beverly. 1985. "Searching for 'the Roots of Famine': The Case of Karamoja." *Review of African Political Economy* 33:102–110.

Gebru Tareke. 1983/84. "Resistance in Tigray (Ethiopia)." *Horn of Africa* 4:15–27.

———. 1990. "Continuity and Discontinuity in Peasant Mobilization: The Cases of Bale and Tigray." In *The Political Economy of Ethiopia*, ed. Marina Ottaway, 137–155. New York: Praeger.

———. 1991. *Ethiopia: Power and Protest*. Cambridge: Cambridge University Press.

Geertz, Clifford. 1973. *The Interpretation of Cultures*. New York: Basic Books.

George, Susan. 1977. *How the Other Half Dies*. Harmondsworth: Penguin.

———. 1988. *A Fate Worse than Debt*. Harmondsworth: Penguin.

Getachew Haile. 1986. "The Unity and Territorial Integrity of Ethiopia." *Journal of Modern African Studies* 24 (3): 465–487.

Gibbon, Edward. 1929. *The History of the Decline and Fall of the Roman Empire*. London: Methuen.

Gilkes, Patrick. 1975. *The Dying Lion*. New York: St. Martin's Press.

Gill, Peter. 1986. *A Year in the Death of Africa*. London: Paladin.

Gitlin, Todd. 1982. "Prime Time Ideology: The Hegemonic Process in Television Entertainment." In *Television: The Critical Eye*, ed. Horace Newcomb, 426–454. New York: Oxford University Press.

Glantz, Michael H. ed., 1987. *Drought and Hunger in Africa*. Cambridge: Cambridge University Press.

Golkin, Arline T. 1987. *Famine: A Heritage of Hunger*. Claremont, Calif.: Regina Books.

Greenfield, Richard. 1965. *Ethiopia: A New Political History*. London: Pall Mall Press.

Griffin, Keith B. 1987. *World Hunger and the World Economy*. Houndmills: Macmillan.

Halliday, Fred. 1983. *The Making of the Second Cold War*. London: Verso.

Halliday, Fred, and Maxine Molyneux. 1981. *The Ethiopian Revolution*. London: Verso.

Halsell, Grace. 1986. *Prophecy and Politics*. Westport, Conn.: Lawrence Hill.

Hancock, Graham. 1985. *Ethiopia: The Challenge of Hunger*. London: Victor Gollancz.

Handler, Richard. 1988. *Nationalism and the Politics of Culture in Quebec*. Madison: University of Wisconsin Press.

Hansberry, William Leo. 1974. In *Pillars in Ethiopian History*, ed. Joseph E. Harris. Washington, D.C.: Howard University Press.

Harbeson, John W. 1988. *The Ethiopian Transformation*. Boulder: Westview.

———. 1990. "State and Social Transformation in Modern Ethiopia." In *The Political Economy of Ethiopia*, ed. Marina Ottaway, 73–91. New York: Praeger.

Harris, Myles F. 1987. *Breakfast in Hell*. New York: Poseidon Press.

Harrison, Paul, and Robin Palmer. 1986. *News out of Africa*. London: Hilary Shipman.

Hayter, Teresa, and Catharine Watson. 1985. *Aid Rhetoric and Reality*. London: Pluto Press.

Healy, Sally. 1983. "The Changing Idiom of Self-Determination in the Horn of Africa." In *Nationalism and Self-Determination in the Horn of Africa*, ed. I. M. Lewis, 93–109. London: Ithaca Press.

Henze, Paul. 1982. "Arming the Horn, 1960–1980." International Security Studies Program Working Paper Number 43. Washington, D.C.: The Wilson Center.

———. 1983a. "Getting a Grip on the Horn: The Emergence of the Soviet Presence and Future Prospects." In *The Pattern of Soviet Conduct in the Third World*, ed. Walter Laqueur, 150–186. New York: Praeger.

———. 1983b. "History and the Horn." *Problems of Communism* 32 (1): 66–75.

———. 1985. *Rebels and Separatists in Ethiopia: Regional Resistance to a Marxist Regime*. Santa Monica, Calif.: Rand Corporation.

———. 1986a. "Behind the Ethiopian Famine." *Encounter* 67 (1): 5–17 (Part 1); 67 (2): 15–27 (Part 2); 67 (3): 20–31 (Part 3).

———. 1986b. "Eritrea: The Endless War." *The Washington Quarterly*, Spring, 23–36.

Herman, Edward S., and Frank Brodhead. 1986. *The Rise and Fall of the Bulgarian Connection*. New York: Sheridan Square Publications.

Herman, Edward S., and Noam Chomsky. 1988. *Manufacturing Consent*. New York: Pantheon.

Herman, Edward S., and Gerry O'Sullivan. 1989. *The Terrorism Industry*. New York: Pantheon.

Hoben, Allan. 1985. "The Origins of Famine." *The New Republic* 192 (3): 17–19.

Hobsbawm, Eric. 1990. *Nations and Nationalism since 1780*. Cambridge: Cambridge University Press.

Hobsbaum, Eric, and Terence Ranger. 1983. *The Invention of Tradition*. Cambridge: Cambridge University Press.

Holcomb, Bonnie. 1991. "Interview with Qabbanee Waaqayyoo (Bonnie K. Holcomb) by A. T. Qana'aa." *Qunnamtii Oromia* 2 (3): 12–18.

Holcomb, Bonnie, and Sisai Ibssa. 1990. *The Invention of Ethiopia*. Trenton, N.J.: Red Sea Press.

Holden, David. 1973. "Ethiopia—Forty Years On." *Encounter* 40 (2): 76–87.

Horkheimer, Max, and Theodor Adorno. 1972. *Dialectic of Enlightenment*. Translated by John Cumming. New York: Herder and Herder.

Horowitz, Donald L. 1985. *Ethnic Groups in Conflict*. Berkeley and Los Angeles: University of California Press.

Horsman, Reginald. 1981. *Race and Manifest Destiny*. Cambridge: Harvard University Press.

Hutchings, Raymond. 1987. *Soviet Secrecy and Non-Secrecy*. London: Macmillan.

International Commission of Jurists. 1981. "Eritrea's Claim to Self-Determination." *Review* 26:8–14.

Jackson, Robert H., and Carl G. Rosberg. 1982. *Personal Rule in Black Africa*. Berkeley and Los Angeles: University of California Press.

Jansson, Kurt, Michael Harris, and Angela Penrose. 1987. *The Ethiopian Famine*. London: Zed Press.

Jones, A.H.M., and Elizabeth Monroe. 1969. *A History of Ethiopia*. New York: Negro Universities Press.

Jordan Gebre-Medhin. 1989. *Peasants and Nationalism in Eritrea*. Trenton, N.J.: Red Sea Press.

Journal of Eritrean Studies. 1987, 1988. "Behind the U.N. Sponsored Federal Act: Secret Deals Amongst the Interested Parties." Part 1, 2 (1): 37–52; Part 2, 2 (2): 25–40.

Kaplan, Robert D. 1985. "Ethiopian Exodus." *The New Republic* 192 (3): 20–22.

———. 1986. "Behind Ethiopia's Hunger." *American Spectator*, June, 25–27.

———. 1988a. "The Loneliest War." *The Atlantic Monthly* 262 (1): 58–65.

———. 1988b. *Surrender or Starve*. Boulder: Westview.

Kapuscinski, Ryszard. 1983. *The Emperor*. San Diego: Harcourt Brace Jovanovich.

Keen, Benjamin. 1971. *The Aztec Image in Western Thought*. New Brunswick, N.J.: Rutgers University Press.

Keller, Edmond J. 1981. "The Revolutionary Transformation of Ethiopia's Twentieth Century Bureaucratic Empire." *Journal of Modern African Studies* 19 (2): 307–335.

———. 1984. "The Ethiopian Revolution: How Socialist Is It?" *Journal of African Studies* 11 (2): 52–65.

———. 1985. "United States Foreign Policy on the Horn of Africa: Policymaking with Blinders On." In *African Crisis Areas and U.S. Foreign Policy*, ed. Gerald J. Bender, James S. Coleman, and Richard L. Sklar, 178–193. Berkeley and Los Angeles: University of California Press.

———. 1988. *Revolutionary Ethiopia*. Bloomington: Indiana University Press.

———. 1990. "Constitutionalism and the National Question in Africa: The Case of Eritrea." In *The Political Economy of Ethiopia*, Marina Ottaway, ed., 95–113. New York: Praeger.

Keneally, Thomas. 1989. *To Asmara*. Toronto: Lester and Orpen Denys.

Kickham, Larry. 1987. "The Theology of Nuclear War." *Covert Action Information Bulletin* 27:9–14.

Kiernan, V. G. 1969. *The Lords of Human Kind*. Harmondsworth: Penguin.

Kifle Wodajo. 1986. "Redefining the Problems of the Horn of Africa." In *Conflict and Conflict Resolution in the Horn of Africa*. Proceedings of the First International Conference on the Horn of Africa, 38–48. New York: Center for the Study of the Horn of Africa.

Kirkpatrick, Jeane J. 1983. *The Reagan Phenomenon*. Washington, D.C.: American Enterprise Institute for Public Policy Research.

Kolko, Gabriel. 1972. *The Limits of Power*. New York: Harper and Row.

———. 1988. *Confronting the Third World*. New York: Pantheon.

Korn, David A. 1986. *Ethiopia, the United States and the Soviet Union*. London: Croom Helm.

Korner, Peter, Gero Maass, Thomas Siebold, and Rainer Tetzlaff. 1986. *The IMF and the Debt Crisis*. London: Zed Press.

Korten, David C. 1971. "The Life Game: Survival Strategies in Ethiopian Folktales." *Journal of Cross-Cultural Psychology* 2 (3): 209–224.

Krauthammer, Charles. 1981. "Rich Nations, Poor Nations." *The New Republic* 184 (15): 20–23.

Lawrence, T. E. 1962. *Seven Pillars of Wisdom*. Harmondsworth: Penguin.

Lefebvre, Jeffrey A. 1987. "Donor Dependency and American Arms Transfers to the Horn of Africa: The F-5 Legacy." *Journal of Modern African Studies* 25 (3): 465–488.

Lefort, Rene. 1983. *Ethiopia: An Heretical Revolution?* London: Zed Press.

Legum, Colin, and Bill Lee. 1977. *Conflict in the Horn of Africa*. London: Rex Collings.

Leonard, Richard. 1984. "European Colonization and the Socio-Economic Integration of Eritrea." In *The Eritrean Case*, Permanent Peoples' Tribunal of the International League for the Rights and Liberation of Peoples, 55–114. Rome: Research and Information Center on Eritrea.

———. 1988. "Popular Participation in Liberation and Revolution." In *The Long Struggle of Eritrea*, ed. Lionel Cliffe and Basil Davidson, 105–135. Nottingham: Spokesman.

Lernoux, Penny. 1980. *Cry of the People*. Harmondsworth: Penguin.

———. 1989a. "The Papal Spiderweb I: Opus Dei and the Perfect Society." *The Nation* 248 (14): 471–487.

———. 1989b. "The Papal Spiderweb II: A Reverence for Fundamentalism." *The Nation* 248 (15): 513–516.

Levine, Donald N. 1965. *Wax and Gold*. Chicago: University of Chicago Press.

———. 1974. *Greater Ethiopia*. Chicago: University of Chicago Press.

———. 1975. "Menelik and Oedipus: Further Observations on the Ethiopian National Epic." In *Proceedings of the First United States Conference on Ethiopian Studies*, ed. Harold G. Marcus, 11–23. East Lansing: African Studies Center, Michigan State University.

Liebenow, Gus J. 1986. *African Politics*. Bloomington: Indiana University Press.

Liebenstein, Harvey. 1982. "Famine and Economic Development." In *Famine,* ed. Kevin Cahill, 108–119. Maryknoll, N.Y.: Orbis.
Lofchie, M. 1975. "Political and Economic Origins of African Hunger." *Journal of Modern African Studies* 13 (4): 551–567.
Luckham, Robin, and Dawit Bekele. 1984. "Foreign Powers and Militarism in the Horn of Africa." *Review of African Political Economy* 30:8–20; 31:7–28.
Lugard, Sir Frederick D. 1923. *The Dual Mandate in British Tropical Africa.* London: William Blackwood and Sons.

McCann, James. 1987. *From Poverty to Famine.* Philadelphia: University of Pennsylvania Press.
———. 1990. "The Myth and Reality of Agricultural Crises in Ethiopia: Empirical Lessons from History, 1900–1987." In *The Political Economy of Ethiopia,* ed. Marina Ottaway, 177–196. New York: Praeger.
Magubane, Bernard Makhosezwe. 1987. *The Ties that Bind.* Trenton, N.J.: Africa World Press.
Makonnen Makonnen. n.d. "Declaration." Ethiopian National Alliance to Advance Democracy (ENATAD). Unpublished manuscript.
Mani, Lata, and Ruth Frankenberg. 1985. "The Challenge of Orientalism." *Economy and Society* 14 (2): 174–192.
Marcus, George E., and Michael M. J. Fischer. 1986. *Anthropology as Cultural Critique.* Chicago: University of Chicago Press.
Marcus, Harold G. 1975. *The Life and Times of Menelik II.* Oxford: Clarendon Press.
———. 1987. *Haile Selassie I: The Formative Years, 1892–1936.* Berkeley and Los Angeles: University of California Press.
Mari, T./Italian Community of Toronto. 1935. "What Do You Know about Ethiopia?" Toronto: Italian Publishing Co.
Markakis, John. 1987. *National and Class Conflict in the Horn of Africa.* Cambridge: Cambridge University Press.
Markakis, John, and Nega Ayele. 1986. *Class and Revolution in Ethiopia.* Trenton, N.J.: Red Sea Press.
Matthews, Christopher J. 1985. "The Road to Korem." *The New Republic* 192 (3): 23–25.
Maugham-Brown, David. 1985. *Land, Freedom, Fiction.* London: Zed Books.
Mayer, Jean. 1984. "A Five-Point Plan for Action." *Newsweek,* November 26, 58.
Mazrui, Ali A., and Michael Tidy. 1984. *Nationalism and New States in Africa.* London: Heinemann.
Meillassoux, Claude. 1974. "Development or Exploitation: Is the Sahel Famine Good Business?" *Review of African Political Economy* 1:27–33.
Melaku Tegegn. 1989. "Eritrea: Problems of the National Movement." In *Conditions for the Possibility of Peace in the Horn of Africa.* Proceedings of the Fourth International Conference on the Horn of Africa, 134–156. New York: Center for the Study of the Horn of Africa.
MERIP Middle East Report. 1987. "Ethiopia's Contras." 17 (2): 35.
Mesfin Araya. 1986. "Reflections on Eritrean Nationalism." In *Conflict and Conflict Resolution in the Horn of Africa.* Proceedings of the First International Conference on the Horn of Africa, 11–17. New York: Center for the Study of the Horn of Africa.

———. 1990. "The Eritrean Question: An Alternative Explanation." *Journal of Modern African Studies* 28 (1): 79–100.
Miliband, Ralph, and Marcel Liebman. 1984. "Reflections on Anti-Communism." In *The Socialist Register*, ed. Ralph Miliband, John Saville, and Marcel Liebman, 1–22. London: Merlin.
Miller, Christopher L. 1985 *Blank Darkness*. Chicago: University of Chicago Press.
Mkhatshwa, Jabulani. 1989. "Ethiopia: A Coup Attempt That Misfired." *The African Communist* 199:64–75.
———. 1990. "Ethiopia Peace Talks to Resolve the Problem of Eritrea." *The African Communist* 120:88–89.
Mohammed Hassen. 1990. *The Oromo of Ethiopia*. Cambridge: Cambridge University Press.
Murray, Lou. 1986. "North American Perceptions of Conflict in the Horn of Africa." Waterloo, Ont.: Conrad Grebel College.

Negussay Ayele. 1988. "On the Determinants of Prospects for Peace and Development on the Horn of Africa: The Other Side of the Coin." In *Contemporary Economics, Politics and Culture in the Horn of Africa*. Proceedings of the Third International Conference on the Horn of Africa, 111–120. New York: Center for the Study of the Horn of Africa.
Neuhaus, Richard John. 1982. "The Colonial Legacy: From Guilt to Responsibility." In *The Causes of World Hunger*, ed. William Byron, 64–80. New York: Paulist Press.
Ng'Weno, Hilary. 1984. "Placing the Blame." *Newsweek*, November 26, 55.
Nimmo, Dan, and James E. Combs. 1985. *Nightly Horrors*. Knoxville: University of Tennessee Press.
Nixon, Richard. 1988. *1999: Victory without War*. New York: Simon and Schuster.
Nzongola-Ntalaja. 1987. "The National Question and the Crisis of Instability in Africa." In *Africa: Perspectives on Peace and Development*, ed. Emmanuel Hansen, 56–86. London: Zed Press.

O'Brien, Jay, and William Roseberry. 1991. *Golden Ages, Dark Ages*. Berkeley and Los Angeles: University of California Press.
Okbazghi Yohannes. 1991. *Eritrea: A Pawn in World Politics*. Gainesville: University Presses of Florida.
Oromo Liberation Front. 1990. "OLF Statement about the TPLF Sponsored OPDO." *Waldhaansso* 15 (2): 19–23.
Ottaway, Marina. 1982. *Soviet and American Influence in the Horn of Africa*. New York: Praeger.
Ottaway, Marina, and David Ottaway. 1978. *Ethiopia: Empire in Revolution*. New York: Africana Publishing.

Palmieri, Victor H. 1982. "Famine, Media and Geo-Politics: The Khmer Relief Effort of 1980." In *Famine*, ed. Kevin M. Cahill, 19–27. Maryknoll, N.Y.: Orbis.
Pankhurst, Richard. 1961. *An Introduction to the Economic History of Ethiopia from Early Times to 1800*. London: Lalibela House.

———. 1968. *Economic History of Ethiopia*. Addis Ababa: Haile Selassie I University Press.
Parenti, Michael. 1986. *Inventing Reality*. New York: St. Martin's Press.
Pateman, Roy. 1986. "Revolution and Agrarian Reform in Ethiopia." *Peasant Studies* 13 (4): 271–275.
———. 1987. "Eritrea Under the Dergue." *Journal of Eritrean Studies* 1 (2): 1–9.
———. 1988. "Drought, Famine and Development." In *The Long Struggle of Eritrea*, ed. Lionel Cliffe and Basil Davidson, 163–186. Nottingham: Spokesman.
———. 1989. "Peasants and State Farms: Problems in the Transition to Socialism in Africa and Latin America." *Peasant Studies* 16 (2): 69–86.
———. 1990. *Even the Stones Are Burning*. Trenton, N.J.: Red Sea Press.
Patman, Robert G. 1990. *The Soviet Union in the Horn of Africa*. Cambridge: Cambridge University Press.
Pearce, R. H. 1953. *The Savages of America*. Baltimore: Johns Hopkins University Press.
Perham, Margery. 1969. *The Government of Ethiopia*. London: Faber and Faber.
Permanent Peoples' Tribunal of the International League for the Rights and Liberation of Peoples. 1984. *The Eritrean Case*. Rome: Research and Information Center on Eritrea.
Peterson, Donald. 1986. "Ethiopia Abandoned? An American Perspective." *International Affairs* 62 (4): 627–645.
Petras, James. 1987. "Speculators, Lumpen-Intellecturals, and End of Hegemony." *Economics and Political Weekly* 221 (6): 223–225.
Petras, James, and Morris H. Morley. 1984. "The Ethiopian Military State and Soviet-U.S. Involvement in the Horn of Africa." *Review of African Political Economy* 30:21–31.
Pike Report. 1977. Nottingham: Spokesman.
Pool, David. 1980. "Revolutionary Crisis and Revolutionary Vanguard: The Emergence of the Eritrean People's Liberation Front." *Review of African Political Economy* 19:33–47.
———. 1982. *Eritrea: Africa's Longest War*. London: Anti-Slavery Society.
———. 1983. "Eritrean Nationalism." In *Nationalism and Self-Determination in the Horn of Africa*, ed. I. M. Lewis, 175–193. London: Ithaca Press.
———. 1984. "Ethiopia and Eritrea: The Pre-Colonial Period." In *The Eritrean Case*, Permanent Peoples' Tribunal of the Interntional League for the Rights and Liberation of Peoples, 32–54. Rome: Research and Information Center on Eritrea.
Power, Jonathan. 1987. "West Should Not Meddle: Intervention in Ethiopian Civil War Would be Out of Order, Expert Says." *Winnipeg Free Press*, December 22, 7.
Puddington, Arch. 1986. "Ethiopia: The Communist Uses of Famine." *Commentary* 81 (4): 30–38.

Ramadan Mohamed Nur. 1983. "Address by Comrade Ramadan Mohamed Nur, Secretary-General of EPLF to the Second Congresses of the NUEWn and NUEW." *Voice of the Eritrean Women*. N.P.: National Union of Eritrean Women.

Rangel, Carlos. 1986. *Third World Ideology and Western Reality.* New Brunswick, N.J.: Transaction Books.
Ranger, Terence. 1983. "The Invention of Tradition in Colonial Africa." In *The Invention of Tradition,* ed. Eric Hobsbawn and Terence Ranger, 211–262. Cambridge: Cambridge University Press.
Reagan, Ronald. 1988. "The United States and the World in the 1990s." In *Thinking about America,* ed. Annelise Anderson and Dennis L. Bark, 555–564. Stanford, Calif.: Hoover Institution Press.
Robinson, Cedric J. 1985. "The African Diaspora and the Italo-Ethiopian Crisis." *Race and Class* 2:51–65.
Robinson, Warren C., and Fumiko Yamazaki. 1986. "Agriculture, Population and Economic Planning in Ethiopia, 1953–1980." *Journal of Developing Areas* 20:327–338.
Rostow, Walt. 1960. *The Stages of Economic Growth.* Cambridge: Cambridge University Press.
Roundy, Robert W. 1973. "The Cultural Geography of Communicable Disease in Ethiopia." In *Proceedings of the First United States Conference on Ethiopian Studies,* ed. Harold G. Marcus, 427–441. East Lansing: African Studies Center, Michigan State University.
Rubenson, Sven. 1976. *The Survival of Ethiopian Independence.* London: Heinemann.

Said, Edward. 1979. *Orientalism.* New York: Vintage Books.
———. 1988. "Orientialism Revisited." *MERIP Middle East Report* 18 (1): 32–36.
Sbacchi, Alberto. 1985. *Ethiopia under Mussolini.* London: Zed Books.
Schneider, William H. 1982. *An Empire for the Masses.* Westport, Conn.: Greenwood Press.
Schwab, Peter. 1976. "Human Rights in Ethiopia." *Journal of Modern African Studies* 14 (1): 155–160.
———. 1979. *Haile Selassie I: Ethiopia's Lion of Judah.* Chicago: Nelson-Hall.
———. 1980/81. "Rethinking of Human Rights." *Horn of Africa* 3 (4): 3–40.
———. 1985. *Ethiopia: Politics, Economics and Society.* London: Francis Pinter.
Scott, William R. 1978. "Black Nationalism and the Italo-Ethiopian Conflict, 1934–1936." *Journal of Negro History* 62 (2): 118–134.
Semere Haile. 1987. "The Origins and Demise of the Ethiopia-Eritrea Federation." *Issue* 15:9–17.
Sen, Amartya. 1981. *Poverty and Famines.* Oxford: Clarendon Press.
Sen, Sudhir. 1982. "Spreading the Green Revolution." In *Famine,* ed. Kevin M. Cahill, 82–95. Maryknoll, N.Y.: Orbis.
Serapiao, Luis B. 1987. "International Law and Self-Determination: The Case of Eritrea." *Issue* 15:3–8.
Shack, William A. 1974. "Ethiopia and Afro-Americans: Some Historical Notes, 1920–1970." *Phylon* 35 (2): 142–155.
Shepherd, George W., Jr. 1987. *The Trampled Grass.* New York: Praeger.
Shepherd, Jack. 1984. "Africa: Drought of the Century." *The Atlantic Monthly* 253 (4): 36–40.
———. 1985a. "Ethiopia: The Use of Food as an Instrument of U.S. Foreign Policy." *Issue* 14:4–9.
———. 1985b. "When Foreign Aid Fails." *The Atlantic Monthly* 255 (4): 41–46.

Shepperson, George. 1953. "Ethiopianism and African Nationalism." *Phylon* 14 (1): 9–18.
Sherman, Richard. 1980. *Eritrea: The Unfinished Revolution*. New York: Praeger.
Sisai Ibssa. 1990. "The Place of Gada in Independent Oromia." *Waldhaansso* 15 (2): 3–8.
Smith, Anthony D. 1983. *Theories of Nationalism*. New York: Holmes and Meier.
Smith, Gayle. 1987. "Ethiopia and the Politics of Famine Relief." *MERIP Middle East Report* 17 (2): 31–37.
Snowdon, Frank, Jr. 1970. *Blacks in Antiquity*. Cambridge: Harvard University Press, Belknap Press.
Solomon Inquai. 1983/84. "Revolution in Tigray." *Horn of Africa* 4:4–14.
Spencer, John H. 1984. *Ethiopia at Bay*. Algonac, Mich.: Reference Publications.
Suau, Anthony. 1985. "Eritrea: Region in Rebellion." *National Geographic* 168 (3): 384–405.
Suret-Canale, Jean. 1971. *French Colonialism in Tropical Africa, 1900–1945*. London: C. Hurst.

Tanov, G. 1979a. "At Odds with Logic." *New Times* 8:14.
———. 1979b. "Embarrassing." *New Times* 18:16.
Tekie Fissehatzion. 1983. "The International Dimensions of the Eritrean Question." *Horn of Africa* 6 (2): 7–24.
Tesfatsion Medhanie. 1986. *Eritrea: The Dynamics of a National Question*. Amsterdam: B. R. Gruner.
Thomas, Maria. 1987. "A State of Permanent Revolution." *Harper's* 274 (1640): 53–60.
Thomas, Nicholas. 1989. *Out of Time*. Cambridge: Cambridge University Press.
Thomson, Blair. 1975. *Ethiopia: The Country that Cut Off Its Head*. London: Robson Books.
Timberlake, Lloyd. 1985. *Africa in Crisis*. London and Washington, D.C.: International Institute for Environment and Development.
Tinker, Jerry, and John Wise. 1986. "A Misguided Policy on Ethiopia." *New York Times*, August 16, I, 23.
Tonkin, Elizabeth, Maryon McDonald, and Malcolm Chapman. 1989. *History and Ethnicity*. London: Routledge.
Torry, W. 1984. "Social Science Research on Famine." *Human Ecology* 12 (3): 227–252.
Trevaskis, G.K.N. 1960. *Eritrea: A Colony in Transition*. London: Oxford University Press.
Triulzi, Alessandro. 1983. "Competing Views of National Identity in Ethiopia." In *Nationalism and Self-Determination in the Horn of Africa*, ed. I. M. Lewis, 111–127. London: Ithaca Press.

Ullendorf, Edward. 1973. *The Ethiopians*. London: Oxford University Press.
Union of Oromo in North America. 1990. "Editorial Note." *Waldhaansso* 15 (2): 1–2.
United Nations, General Assembly, Ad Hoc Political Committee. 1950a. "For-

mer Italian Colonies (Eritrea); Iraq: Draft Resolution, Revised." New York: UN Publications. A/Ac.38/L.32/Rev.1.

———. 1950b. "Former Italian Colonies (Eritrea); Joint Draft Resolution." New York: UN Publications. A/Ac.38/L.37.

———. 1950c. "Former Italian Colonies (Eritrea); Statement by the Chairman of the Delegation of the Moslem League of Eritrea Made at the Fifty-Fifth Meeting of the Ad Hoc Political Committee in Reply to Questions which He Had Been Asked by Members of the Committee." New York: UN Publications. A/Ac.38/L.51.

———. 1952. "Eritrea: Report of the Government of the United Kingdom of Great Britain and Northern Ireland to the General Assembly Concerning the Administration of Eritrea." New York: UN Publications. A/2233.

United States House of Representatives. 1978. "War in the Horn of Africa: A Firsthand Report on the Challenges for United States Policy: Report of a Factfinding Mission to Egypt, Sudan, Ethiopia, Somalia, and Kenya, December 12 to 22, 1977." Committee on International Relations, United States House of Representatives, 95th Cong., 2d sess. Washington, D.C.: Government Printing Office.

United States Senate. 1970. "United States Security Agreements and Commitments Abroad, Ethiopia." Committee on Foreign Relations, Hearings before Subcommittee on Security Agreements and Commitments Abroad. 91st Cong., 2d sess. Washington, D.C.: Government Printing Office.

———. 1976. "Ethiopia and the Horn of Africa." Committee on Foreign Relations, Subcommittee on African Affairs. 94th Cong., 2d sess. Washington, D.C.: Government Printing Office.

———. 1986. "Ethiopia and Sudan One Year Later: Refugee and Famine Recovery Needs." Minority Staff Report prepared for the use of the Subcommittee on Immigration and Refugee Policy to the Committee on the Judiciary. 99th Cong., 2d sess. Washington, D.C.: Government Printing Office.

Usvatov, Alexander. 1985. "Mengistu Haile Mariam: Considerable Progress Already." *New Times* 48:10–11.

Valdes Vivo, Raul. 1977. *Ethiopia: The Unknown Revolution*. Havana: Social Science Publishers.

Vaughan, Meagan. 1987. *The Story of an African Famine*. Cambridge: Cambridge University Press.

Watson, Russell, Ray Wilkinson, Charles Harrison, John A. Callcott and Jane Whitmore. 1984. "An African Nightmare." *Newsweek*, November 26, 50–55.

Watts, Michael. 1983. *Silent Violence*. Berkeley and Los Angeles: University of California Press.

Wolf, Eric. 1982. *Europe and the People without History*. Berkeley and Los Angeles: University of California Press.

Wolfe, Alan. 1984. "The Irony of Anti-Communism: Ideology and Interest in Post-War American Foreign Policy." In *The Socialist Register*, ed. Ralph Miliband, John Saville, and Marcel Liebman, 214–229. London: Merlin.

Worthington, Peter. 1988. "Eritrea: Thorn in a Tyrant's Flesh." *Reader's Digest* 133 (800): 105–110.

Wubneh, Mulatu, and Yohannis Abate. 1988. *Ethiopia: Transition and Development in the Horn of Africa.* Boulder: Westview.

Young, Robert. 1990. *White Mythologies.* London: Routledge.

Zamora, Luis P. 1982. *The Apocalyptic Vision in America.* Bowling Green, Ohio: Bowling Green University Popular Press.

Zink, Lubor J. 1988. "Ethiopia Shows Its True Colours." *Toronto Sun,* April 15, 11.

Zinn, Howard. 1970. *The Politics of History.* Boston: Beacon.

———. 1980. *A People's History of the United States.* New York: Harper and Row.

Zinsmeister, Karl. 1988. "All the Hungry People." *Reason* 20 (2): 22–30.

INDEX